# Retirement Saving, Investment, and Spending

# Retirement Saving, Investment, and Spending

## New Lessons from Behavioral Research

Edited by

Olivia S. Mitchell
and
Nikolai Roussanov

OXFORD
UNIVERSITY PRESS

OXFORD
UNIVERSITY PRESS

Oxford University Press is a department of the University of Oxford.
It furthers the University's objective of excellence in research, scholarship,
and education by publishing worldwide. Oxford is a registered trade mark of
Oxford University Press in the UK and in certain other countries.

Published in the United States of America by Oxford University Press
198 Madison Avenue, New York, NY 10016, United States of America.



Library of Congress Cataloging-in-Publication Data
Names: Mitchell, Olivia S. editor | Roussanov, Nikolai editor
Title: Retirement saving, investment, and spending : new lessons from
behavioral research / edited by Olivia S. Mitchell and Nikolai Roussanov.
Description: New York, NY : Oxford University Press, [2026] |
Series: Pension research council series |
Includes bibliographical references and index.
Identifiers: LCCN 2026008359 (print) | LCCN 2026008360 (ebook) |
ISBN 9780197845752 hardback | ISBN 9780197845769 epub | ISBN 9780197845783
Subjects: LCSH: Retirement—Planning | Retirement income—Planning | Retirement
Classification: LCC HG179 .R39527 2026 (print) | LCC HG179 (ebook)
LC record available at https://lccn.loc.gov/2026008359
LC ebook record available at https://lccn.loc.gov/2026008360

DOI: 10.1093/oso/9780197845752.001.0001

Printed by Marquis Book Printing, Canada

The manufacturer's authorized representative in the EU for product safety is
Oxford University Press España S.A. of El Parque Empresarial San Fernando de Henares,
Avenida de Castilla, 2 – 28830 Madrid (www.oup.es/en or product.safety@oup.com).
OUP España S.A. also acts as importer into Spain of products made by the manufacturer.

MIX
Paper | Supporting
responsible forestry
FSC
www.fsc.org
FSC® C103567

# Preface

Behavioral research on financial decision making has exploded over the last decade, spurred by social scientists working at the interface of economics, finance, psychology, and sociology. Our goal in this volume is to bridge the gap between theory and practice, ensuring that retirement plans are not only financially sound but also take into account plan participants' behavioral tendencies. Contributors collect insights and offer new perspectives on this research, with a focus on ways to design and sustain more effective and successful retirement plans. In examining key studies and practical examples, the volume will inform researchers, plan sponsors, policymakers, and investment experts seeking to enhance retirement plan offerings.

In preparing this book, many people and institutions played key roles. Co-editor Nikolai Roussanov was instrumental in identifying topics requiring examination, along with numerous experts who contributed to this endeavor by exploring novel datasets and testing diverse hypotheses. We are deeply grateful to our advisory board and members of the Pension Research Council for their continuing intellectual and research support. Additional funding was provided by the Boettner Center for Pensions and Retirement Research, the Pension Research Council, and the Ralph H. Blanchard Memorial Endowment at the Wharton School of the University of Pennsylvania. We also are delighted to continue our long-term association with Oxford University Press, which publishes our series on global retirement security. The manuscript was expertly prepared by Sandra Scutt and Hanna Bettner.

Our work at the Pension Research Council and the Boettner Center for Pensions and Retirement Security of the Wharton School of the University of Pennsylvania has focused on aspects of pensions and retirement well-being for over 70 years. This volume confirms our ongoing commitment to generate cutting-edge research on and engage debate around retirement security and retirement policy.

# Contents

# List of Figures

# List of Tables

# Notes on Contributors

**Vickie Bajtelsmit** is a professor emerita of finance and real estate at Colorado State University. She has taught a wide variety of undergraduate and graduate finance courses, including financial planning, investments, corporate finance, insurance, risk management, and entrepreneurial finance. She holds a PhD in insurance and risk management from the University of Pennsylvania's Wharton School of Business, a JD from Rutgers University School of Law, and a BA from the University of Virginia.

**John Beshears** is a professor of business administration in the Negotiation, Organization & Markets Unit at Harvard Business School. He is also a research associate at the National Bureau of Economic Research. Previously, he was an assistant professor of finance at the Stanford Graduate School of Business.

**Patricia Boyle** is a professor of behavioral sciences and neuropsychology at the Rush Alzheimer's Disease Center in Chicago. Her research focuses on the prevention of cognitive and functional decline in old age, including age-related changes in cognition, financial and health decision making, and psychological well-being. Boyle received her PhD from the University of Massachusetts at Amherst and completed her internship and postdoctoral fellowship at Brown University in Providence.

**R. Anton Braun** is a research economist and senior adviser on the macroeconomics and monetary policy team of the research department at the Federal Reserve Bank of Atlanta; he is also a director of the Atlanta Census Research Data Center. His major interests are macroeconomic risks and the effects of monetary policy. Previously he taught at the University of Tokyo. He received a BS degree in economics from Indiana University at South Bend and earned his master's degree and doctorate in economics from Carnegie-Mellon University.

**Alycia Chin** is a senior financial economist with the Office of the Investor Advocate at the US Securities and Exchange Commission. Her research focuses on the psychological and economic factors that influence consumers' and investors' financial behavior, including the efficacy of financial product disclosure, consumer stock market expectations, and characteristics of individuals who seek out financial education. Previously she worked at the Federal Reserve Board and the Consumer Financial Protection Bureau.

She holds a BA in economics and politics from Scripps College and a PhD in behavioral decision research from Carnegie Mellon University.

**James J. Choi** is a professor of finance at the Yale School of Management. His primary research is in household finance and behavioral finance; his work on automatic enrollment has led to changes in pension plan design around the world. He is also a scientific advisor to the Retirement and Disability Research Center at the National Bureau of Economic Research. He holds a PhD in economics and an AB in applied mathematics from Harvard University.

**Joel M. Dickson** is global head of investment research and development and a principal at the Vanguard Investment Strategy Group, where he analyzes trends and developments in the exchange-traded fund market and related issues. Previously he headed the Active Quantitative Equity Group within Vanguard, and he was staff economist at the Federal Reserve Board. His AB is from Washington University in St. Louis and his PhD in economics from Stanford University.

**Aaron Goodman** is an economist on the investor behavior and retirement teams, Investment Strategy Group, at Vanguard. He holds an undergraduate degree from Dartmouth College and a PhD in economics from Massachusetts Institute of Technology.

**Fiona Greig** is the global head of investor research and policy at Vanguard. She previously was managing director and co-president at the JPMorgan Chase Institute, and a consultant for McKinsey & Company. Her research interests include household finance, health care, labor markets and the online platform economy, gender, and behavioral decision making. She has also held adjunct professor appointments at the University of Pennsylvania and Georgetown University. She received her BA from Stanford University and PhD in public policy from Harvard University.

**Michael Haliassos** holds the chair of macroeconomics and finance at Goethe University Frankfurt. He is research fellow of the Centre for Economic Policy Research, founding director of the CEPR Network on Household Finance, and research professor and executive board member of the IMFS. He also advises the European Central Bank on the Eurozone Survey of Household Finances and Consumption, and he serves as an international research fellow of NETSPAR. Haliassos received a BA from Cambridge University and a PhD from Yale University.

**Rawley Z. Heimer** is an associate professor in the Department of Finance at Arizona State University. Previously, he taught at Boston College and worked as a research economist at the Federal Reserve Bank of Cleveland. His research interests include financial decisions in risky asset markets and conventional debt markets, and the effect of legal institutions on consumer financial services. He holds a PhD from Brandeis University.

**Michael D. Hurd** is a senior principal researcher at the RAND Corporation, where he directs the RAND Center for the Study of Aging. His research interests in the economics of aging include private pensions and Social Security and their effects on retirement decisions, the economic status of the elderly, the determinants of consumption and saving, the use of health care services, and most recently, the monetary costs of dementia and long-term care. Hurd has a PhD in economics and an MS in statistics from the University of California, Berkeley.

**Heidi Johnson** is the director of behavioral economics at the Financial Health Network, where she leads the application of behavioral insights to design and deliver effective financial health solutions. Previously she served as a program lead for the Consumer Financial Protection Bureau, where she led a behavioral research program on innovative financial products; she also was a research associate at the Urban Institute. She holds a master's in public policy from Harvard University and a bachelor's degree in sociology from Colgate University.

**Karen A. Kopecky** is a research economist and adviser on the macroeconomics team in the research department at the Federal Reserve Bank of Atlanta. Her interests include macroeconomics, public finance, insurance markets, retirement, health, and computational methods for macroeconomic modeling. She is also a visiting scholar at Emory University. Previously, she taught at the University of Western Ontario and was a visitor to the Federal Reserve Bank of Minneapolis. She received her doctorate and master's degrees from the University of Rochester, and her BA in economics and her BS in mathematics from the State University of New York at Buffalo.

**David Laibson** is the Robert I. Goldman Professor of Economics at Harvard University, where he leads Harvard University's Foundations of Human Behavior Initiative. His research focuses on behavioral economics. He is also a member of the NBER, and a fellow of the Econometric Society and the American Academy of Arts and Sciences. He also sits on the board of the Health and Retirement Study (for the National Institutes of Health) and Harvard's Pension Investment Committee, the Academic Research Council of the Consumer Financial Protection Bureau, and the Advisory Board of Wharton's Pension Research Council. He earned his AB from Harvard University, his MS from the London School of Economics, and his PhD from the Massachusetts Institute of Technology.

**Féidhlim McGowan** is a lecturer above the bar (equivalent to assistant professor) at the University of Galway's J. E. Cairnes School of Business and

Economics. He is also a research affiliate with ESRI's Behavioural Research Unit. His interests include psychology, behavioral economics, and consumer policy. Féidhlim holds a PhD in economics from Trinity College Dublin, a MSc in behavioral economics from the University of Nottingham, a LLM in international and European business law from Trinity College Dublin (TCD), and a BA in economics and psychology, also from TCD.

**Brianna L. Middlewood** is a behavioral research scientist at Fidelity Investments. Her interests include social psychology and applied statistics, with expertise in emotion and decision making. She previously worked as a research psychologist in the decision-making and behavioral studies section of the Consumer Financial Protection Bureau's Office of Research. She earned her PhD in social psychology from Penn State University.

**Olivia S. Mitchell** is the International Foundation of Employee Benefit Plans Professor and professor of insurance/risk management and business economics/policy, executive director of the Pension Research Council, and director of the Boettner Center on Pensions and Retirement Research, all at The Wharton School of the University of Pennsylvania. Concurrently she serves as a research associate at the NBER, independent director on the Allspring Mutual Funds Boards, and executive board member for the Michigan Retirement Research Center. She earned her BA in economics from Harvard University, and her MS and PhD degrees in economics from the University of Wisconsin-Madison.

**Gary R. Mottola** is the research director of the FINRA Investor Education Foundation, where he conducts research aimed at better understanding financial capability in America, protecting investors from financial fraud, and improving financial disclosure statements. He received his BA from the University at Albany, his MA from Brooklyn College, and his PhD from the University of Delaware.

**Arna Olafsson** is an assistant professor of finance at Copenhagen Business School, a research fellow at the Danish Finance Institute, a Research Affiliate at CEPR, a CEPR Household Finance Network Member, a member of the Center for Big Data in Finance (BIGFI) at Copenhagen Business School, and a research fellow at the Pension Research Centre (PeRCent) at Copenhagen Business School. Her main areas of research are household finance, behavioral finance, consumer credit, and labor and finance. She received her PhD from the Stockholm School of Economics in 2014.

**Michaela Pagel** is associate professor of finance at Olin Business School at Washington University in St. Louis. She works on topics in behavioral economics, household finance, and macroeconomics, analyzing transaction-level data on income, spending, balances, credit limits, and logins stemming from a financial aggregation app. She received her PhD from the Economics Department at UC Berkeley.

**Gianpaolo Parise** teaches finance at Tilburg University. His research interests are in asset management and household finance. He previously taught at EDHEC Business School. He obtained his PhD from the Swiss Finance Institute at the University of Lugano, and he graduated from Bocconi University in Italy.

**Kim Peijnenburg** teaches finance at Tilburg University, the Netherlands, and a research fellow at CEPR. Previously she was on the faculty at EDHEC Business School, HEC Paris, and Bocconi University. Her research areas focus on household finance. She received her PhD in finance from Tilburg University.

**Jonathan Reuter** is an associate professor of finance at Boston College's Carroll School of Management. His research focuses on individual investors and financial institutions, including mutual funds, investment banks, and the financial media; the behavior of retirement plan participants; the value of financial advice; and the strategic behavior of target-date retirement funds. Previously he taught at the University of Oregon. He received his PhD in economics from the Massachusetts Institute of Technology.

**Susann Rohwedder** is a senior economist at RAND, associate director of the RAND Center for the Study of Aging, and professor at the Pardee RAND Graduate School. Her research focuses on the economics of aging in the areas of household consumption and saving behavior, retirement, long-term care and the prevalence of dementia, expectation formation, and subjective well-being. She is also a research fellow of the Network for Studies on Pensions, Aging, and Retirement in the Netherlands, and she serves on the board of directors of the Western Economics Association International. She holds a PhD and MA in economics from University College London, and master's degrees from the University of Warwick and the Sorbonne in Paris.

**Nikolai Roussanov** is Moise Y. Safra Professor of Finance at the Wharton School of the University of Pennsylvania, and research associate at the National Bureau of Economic Research. He also serves on the advisory board of Wharton's Pension Research Council. His research focuses on interactions between asset pricing and macroeconomics, including equity, fixed income, currency, and commodity markets; he also explores entrepreneurship and individual financial behavior. He received his undergraduate degree in mathematics from Harvard College and his PhD in finance from the University of Chicago.

**Shane Timmons** is a senior research officer at the Economic and Social Research Institute in Dublin, Ireland, and an adjunct associate professor of psychology at Trinity College Dublin. His research focuses on policy-relevant projects spanning financial, environmental, and health behaviors. Previously he taught modules in statistics and research skills at TCD, DCU, and American College Dublin. He holds a BA and PhD in psychology and a PG Dip in statistics from Trinity College Dublin.

**Lei Yu** is associate professor of neurological sciences and statistician with Rush Alzheimer's Disease Center. His research activities focus on providing statistical advice on study design and data analysis, and developing methods and applications tailored to the projects on aging and Alzheimer's disease and related dementia. Previously he was a visiting scientist at the Broad institute of Harvard and MIT. Yu received his PhD in statistics from the University of Kentucky.

Chapter 1

# Lessons from Behavioral Research for Retirement Saving, Investment, and Spending

## An Overview

*Olivia S. Mitchell and Nikolai Roussanov*

Behavioral research on financial decision making has exploded over the last decade, spurred by social scientists working at the interface of economics, finance, psychology, and sociology. This volume collects insights and offers new perspectives on this research, with a particular focus on ways to design and sustain more effective and successful retirement plans.

Our perspective aligns with the fundamental economic principle that individuals strive to maximize their self-interest, while also acknowledging that these decisions often result in less-than-perfect outcomes. Contributors to this volume explore how consumers save, invest, and spend while being confronted with mental or emotional constraints that can hamper their ability to devote the necessary attention and effort to making good financial decisions. Relatedly, we discuss the implications of this research for plan sponsors and policymakers responsible for designing, regulating, and evaluating institutions that ensure economic security in old age. By examining key studies and practical examples, the volume provides a guide for policymakers, employers, and financial planners seeking to enhance retirement outcomes. The book aims to bridge the gap between theory and practice, to ensure that retirement plans are not only financially sound but also account for plan participants' behavioral tendencies.

In what follows, we provide an overview of the various lessons and perspectives on the impact of behavioral factors on retirement financial well-being.

Olivia S. Mitchell and Nikolai Roussanov, *Lessons from Behavioral Research for Retirement Saving, Investment, and Spending.* In: *Retirement Saving, Investment, and Spending.* Edited by: Olivia S. Mitchell and Nikolai Roussanov, Oxford University Press. 
DOI: 10.1093/oso/9780197845752.003.0001

## How Noncognitive Factors Affect Retirement Saving

Why is it that some people are better prepared financially for retirement than others? Several chapters in this volume explore the role of personality traits such as conscientiousness and emotional stability, biased beliefs, as well as basic financial and numerical literacy.

The chapter by Gianpaolo Parise and Kim Peijnenburg (Chapter 2) explores noncognitive determinants of retirement saving behavior, including 'soft' personality traits like conscientiousness, stress resistance, grit, and locus of control (an individual's belief about the extent to which they can control events in their lives). These are distinct from cognitive abilities gained through education such as knowledge, financial literacy, and numeracy. The authors are particularly interested in conscientiousness, or rather the tendency to be organized, practical, persistent, self-disciplined, and achievement-oriented. Using household survey data from the Netherlands, they find that respondents with high conscientiousness are more likely to plan for retirement systematically and have higher savings and financial wealth buffers than those at the other end of the spectrum. This trait translates into specific positive or negative outcomes: for instance, those in the highest quintile of conscientiousness and emotional stability have a 1% probability of being in financial distress, such as not paying their mortgage or utility bills on time. In contrast, those in the lowest quintile of emotional stability have 10 times the chance of being in financial distress.

The authors also document that people with high conscientiousness are also more likely to periodically take stock of their savings and adjust financial choices. Typically, they hold more of their financial wealth in equity and have less unsecured debt, whereas those exhibiting low conscientiousness end up with more debt over time, both of which contribute to greater retirement readiness. While recent research has revealed the importance of certain personality traits such as 'openness' and 'neuroticism' for investment choices through the channel of risk aversion (Jiang et al. 2024), the emphasis of this chapter on the role of conscientiousness is novel and important for furthering our understanding of life-cycle financial wellness. Indeed, this chapter's authors also trace such noncognitive ability to the influence of early life experiences and genetic endowments. Fostering noncognitive abilities in adulthood appears to be difficult, but improving them in children can have a positive influence on late life outcomes.

In his chapter, Rawley Z. Heimer (Chapter 3) explores subjective factors such as people's perceptions of their own longevity and the implications of this for retirement planning. He finds that younger people tend to underestimate how long they will live, so they overspend and save too little.

Later in life, many overestimate their lifespans, rein in spending, and draw down their retirement income slowly. Somewhere along the way, they realize they have not saved enough for retirement and begin to invest more in equity.

Individuals might save more for retirement early on if they better understood actuarial probabilities; however, imparting 'correct' beliefs is difficult, and it is not obvious that simple interventions that provide them with objective information are sufficient. Biased mortality beliefs persist even when people confront life-threatening conditions, suggesting that their beliefs are not easy to shift. Heimer's analysis suggests that financial products that adjust for such mortality miscalibrations could help enhance retirement saving.

Another hurdle for workers seeking to build retirement savings is the so-called undersum bias, discussed in the chapter by Shane Timmons and Féidhlim McGowan (Chapter 4). This bias occurs when people underestimate how quickly savings will accumulate, particularly when they do not understand financial concepts like compound interest. According to experimental evidence, even when presented with situations where the growth rate is linear rather than exponential, people tend to underestimate the eventual outcome—for example, when presented with a bill composed of a large number of relatively inexpensive items, the customer is surprised by the surprisingly large total cost. As a result, individuals affected by this bias not only underestimate the cumulative impact of saving but also how much small expenses accumulate.

In their experiments, the authors show that this phenomenon could also lead to underestimation of risk forecasts, especially the accumulated impact of financial shocks that might arrive over a person's lifetime. Combined, the undersum bias leads consumers to underestimate their expenses later in life, overestimate their ability to accumulate the necessary resources, and underestimate the impact of saving small amounts over their lifetimes. As a result, individuals prone to this bias are likely to fail to save sufficiently for retirement.

The authors' experiments also reveal that interventions can help, including a 'nudge and boost' communications tactic to encourage people to open savings accounts. One such experiment produced a larger-than-expected increase in saving account uptake (over 25%), and the effort was particularly helpful for those with lower incomes. It also showed that simple infographics explaining the cumulative probability of financial shocks can help motivate a saving habit.

Behavioral research has also highlighted the central importance of automatically enrolling workers into retirement saving plans, which has proven to be a strong inducement to save. In Chapter 5, Alycia Chin,

Heidi Johnson, and Brianna L. Middlewood discuss the chief benefits of automatic enrollment, one of which is the reduced time and effort that people need to commit to get started saving. The recent passage of the SECURE 2.0 Act requiring automatic enrollment of employees in new 401(k) and 403(b) plans, as well as auto-enrollment into state-based IRAs for workers lacking access to employer-based retirement plans, builds on this research evidence. These coauthors also document that automatic enrollment can help people build nonretirement savings.

On the flip side, auto enrollment may lead people to have little or no direct involvement in managing their retirement savings, forget about their saving amounts, or abandon their accounts. Automatic enrollment might also lead some people to save too much, leading them to take early withdrawals or loans from their retirement accounts. In some circumstances, they might also take on more debt, especially in home mortgages and auto loans. The authors conclude that more research is needed to learn how auto enrollment in both retirement and nonretirement accounts interact, as well as drive diverging outcomes between workers that have access to employer-sponsored plans and those who do not.

## Investment Behavior of Retirement Savers

In addition to removing obstacles to retirement wealth creation for women, older Americans, and people with cognitive impairments, robust frameworks are needed to help people save—and save wisely. In his chapter, Jonathan Reuter (Chapter 6) traces the evolution of defined contribution (DC) plans over the last five decades. While he agrees that automatic enrollment has significantly increased participation rates, Reuter highlights newer research that finds that the long-run effects on savings are smaller than the short-run effects, with some savings effectively financed via accruing additional debt, implying much smaller impact on net wealth. He also reviews efforts to expand access to employer-based retirement savings and liquid savings, the pros and cons of target date funds as default investment options, potential conflicts of interest in plan design, and potential benefits of customized defaults.

Reuter concludes by outlining several open research questions, including the need for additional study about asset decumulation—a critical topic for retirees. He also discusses the automatic state-run retirement accounts, led by Oregon's OregonSaves program launched in 2017 and adopted by more than half of the US states. Such plans offer customized savings choices, flexibility in contribution rates, and portability, among other attractive features. Nevertheless, the evidence suggests that few workers contribute very much, or for very long, and those that do often withdraw funds from their accounts before retirement.

Gender differences can also account for some of the observed differences in retirement investment patterns of women versus men, as explained in the chapter by Vickie Bajtelsmit (Chapter 7). The evidence is that women are less likely than men to have access to employer plans, participate less in offered plans, and receive less generous employer matches. Additionally, some research finds women select lower-risk investments than men, resulting in lower investment returns. Yet Bejtelsmit also argues that earlier research finding that women invest more cautiously has relied on self-assessments of risk preferences, but women tend to not answer questions when they are not confident about their answers. For this reason, the gender-retirement gap cannot be attributed solely to asset choices. Instead, many women have lower retirement wealth due to labor market differences and bearing more caregiving and household responsibilities. As a result, she argues that bridging the gender wealth gap must focus on equalizing labor market opportunities and enhancing financial literacy.

People often blame others for their financial woes, yet when it comes to retirement saving, the research by Michael Haliassos (Chapter 8) shows that others can also have a potent influence on retirement saving and investment behavior. These others can include neighbors, peers, family members, co-workers, and financial advisors. His chapter describes findings from several projects exploring how shared financial literacy and financial advice, peer group wealth, and external stresses can shape consumption and saving behavior.

One aspect of his research examines peer effects from neighbors, using data from a Swedish refugee allocation program between 1987 and 1991 that covered about 280 municipalities. Most critically, it tracked participants over 10–20 years and demonstrated that having many neighbors with college-level economics and business education promoted retirement saving. He also documents that immigrants placed in neighborhoods having more college-educated neighbors were more likely to have private retirement accounts and hold stock decades later. This is due to what he calls a 'social multiplier' in financial literacy, where educated people pass on their knowledge to others. He also shows that being exposed to greater wealth inequality at the beginning of one's economic life leads some households to take on more investment risk in later life, perhaps a result of individual wealth aspirations.

In other analysis, he studies the impact of having professional financial advisors, versus lay advisors such as family and peers. Consistent with prior work, he documents that professional advisors' recommendations are influenced by their own income, age, risk aversion, and risk exposure. A more surprising finding is that professional advisors recommend smaller allocations to risky assets for retirement when compared to lay advisors. Haliassos additionally examines how financial stress caused by shocks like the COVID-19 pandemic, a financial crisis, or a war can alter consumption and saving decisions. He concludes that such cognitive loads preoccupy and drain people's ability to concentrate and perform important tasks. Interestingly, while some might conclude that stress-induced cognitive loads would lead people to overspend and save less, his research finds the opposite: his subjects who faced cognitive loads became more cautious—consuming less and saving more.

One reason older Americans' investment behavior may leave them disappointed is that many suffer cognitive impairments affecting their ability to make financial and health decisions in later life. Chapter 9 by Gary R. Mottola, Lei Yu, and Patricia Boyle reviews research findings from the Rush Memory and Aging Project, which has tracked about 4,000 older adults from the Chicago area annually since 1987. One lesson from this analysis is that financial and health literacy decline with age, and the rates of decline are related to poorer financial and health decision making, greater scam susceptibility, and decreased psychological well-being.

Particularly striking were the results from a fraudulent marketing campaign. Panel members were informed by a non-existent entity that their retirement savings accounts had been hacked and that the caller requested the last four digits of their Social Security numbers. Most (69%) of the participants did not engage with the campaign, yet 16% of the participants fully engaged with the campaign, and provided the information requested without skepticism. Those who did fully engage were the least financially literate and least aware of scams, while the most skeptical group had the highest cognitive function.

The authors also conclude that having difficulty making financial choices and understanding the factors at play are indicators of potential adverse health outcomes in the future, including dementia or other cognitive issues. Their main lesson is that educational opportunities would help protect older adults from financial fraud, perhaps via community initiatives.

## Spending and Dissaving in Later Life

Understanding how people spend their money in retirement is another area in which behavioral research has focused in recent years. The chapter by Michael D. Hurd and Susann Rohwedder (Chapter 10) examines findings from a series of studies tracking spending patterns among older Americans, as well as from a microsimulation model they developed, to estimate how spending patterns change with age. They set normalized spending at age 65 and find that spending declines rather substantially by about age 80. The largest rate of spending decline is among those with the lowest initial wealth (at age 65); spending paths were flatter for those with higher initial wealth, and this group also lived longer than their poorer counterparts. Some of this pattern is driven by worsening health at older ages. For example, younger retirees spend more on trips, vacations, and leisure activities; however, as they age and their health declines, their health spending doubles (from 8% to 16% of the household budget) and their vacation and leisure spending declines. Interestingly, spending on gifts and donations also rises with age for both married and single households as their time horizons shorten and mortality risk increases.

The authors also assess poverty among older households, using household consumption as a yardstick instead of more conventional income measures, on the argument that consumption-based poverty assessment is more accurate than measures that rely on income since older households finance consumption with their savings. Of note, they find that consumption-based poverty rates among older households are about half of income-based poverty rates. They go on to assess whether older individuals have sufficient economic resources to finance their retirement consumption, and they conclude that around two-thirds are adequately prepared, although singles and people of color are less well off. Moreover, non-Hispanic white individuals are better prepared than non-Hispanic Black and Hispanic individuals.

The chapter by Arna Olafsson and Michaela Pagel (Chapter 11) also examines why wealth declines slowly in retirement. A natural explanation is that retirees are worried about late-life expenses and medical health risk, but other explanations are still of interest. The authors study bank transactions of older people in Iceland, which is a useful setting since the nation has only three banks that its residents patronize. Moreover, few people in Iceland have credit card debt, and instead they use bank overdrafts for unsecured consumer debt. Interestingly, older persons repay their overdrafts when they retire and keep more cash (than average) in their bank accounts.

The authors conclude that the most likely explanation is that the process(es) of retirement in Iceland causes people to reconsider their financial situations and rein in spending. They also are undertaking additional research to better understand whether people are adequately prepared for retirement or if financial education and other tools would help them better achieve those goals.

In Chapter 12, John Beshears, James J. Choi, Joel M. Dickson, Aaron Goodman, Fiona Greig, and David Laibson evaluate ways for plan sponsors to reduce 'leakage' from peoples' retirement accounts, which undermines their ability to accumulate retirement wealth. In the US, many plans permit workers to borrow against their retirement saving, which they must then repay over the next few years. Using data from the Vanguard Group, they find that the median loan taker is in his or her early 40s and earns an annual income of around $55,000.

They consider a policy where plan sponsors could actively encourage or even automatically implement a higher contribution rate for employees taking these withdrawals. They report that workers do not change their elective contributions during loan repayment, leading them to conclude that participants taking emergency withdrawals would likely show a similar capacity to maintain their previous elective contributions. They can also repay the emergency loans over a reasonable time frame. Their study concludes that most people could probably do this within 12–18 months with a two-percentage point increase in their contribution rate. The authors also compared plan borrowers with a control group taking no loans or hardship withdrawals in the same six-month pre-period. Relative to this control group, crowding out of retirement saving for the borrowers was small, particularly for the lowest-income participants. They conclude that when plan participants are not forced to reduce their contributions after a liquidity-based distribution, they continue contributing.

R. Anton Braun and Karen A. Kopecky (Chapter 13) turn to the topic of long-term care in America, which is the second largest risk facing Americans (after earnings risk). They note that one in three 50-year-olds spend more than 100 days in a nursing home before they die, with an expected duration of three years and at an annual cost about $85,000, and that one in 10 retirees will have out-of-pocket expenses exceeding $200,000. Against that backdrop, only about 10% of persons age 62+ have private long-term care insurance (LTCI), and take-up rates are low even for higher-wealth individuals. This potentially very large expense in old age is exacerbated by severe frictions in the long-term care marketplace, including the fact that it is small, policies offer very incomplete coverage, and is quite expensive. Those with low wealth and little income can seek social insurance coverage through Medicaid, which is means-tested (usually assets must be below $3,000), and it can be tapped only after people have exhausted their private LTCI benefits, spent down their assets, and depleted Social Security and other retirement income.

The authors explore policy alternatives in a model featuring adverse selection, where individuals have private information about their health that would qualify as a risk for nursing home entry; high administrative costs for insurers, with broker fees exceeding 100% of the first year's premium; and underwriting and claims processing expenses averaging 20% of premiums. Using this quantitative framework, they conclude that an LTC Partnership Program Asset Exemption (PPAE) program would be preferred to the current system, as it enhances social welfare and would spur a vibrant private LTCI market while preserving the safety net provided by Medicaid for low-income individuals.

## Conclusions

This chapter has underscored some of the significant advancements in behavioral research on financial decision making over the past decade, highlighting contributions from diverse fields such as economics, finance, psychology, and sociology. The insights gathered in this volume illuminate the complexities of designing and sustaining effective retirement plans, acknowledging the dual reality of individuals' efforts to maximize self-interest while often achieving suboptimal outcomes due to mental and emotional constraints. By delving into how consumers navigate saving, investing, and spending, this research offers valuable implications for plan sponsors and policymakers. The chapter emphasizes the importance of creating retirement plans that are not only financially robust but also attuned to participants' behavioral tendencies, so as to ensure better economic security in old age.

## References

Jiang, Z., C. Peng, and H. Yan (2024). 'Personality Differences and Investment Decision-Making.' *Journal of Financial Economics*, 153: 103776.

# Part I

# What Helps and Hinders Retirement Saving?

Chapter 2

# Noncognitive Determinants of Retirement Saving Behavior

*Gianpaolo Parise and Kim Peijnenburg*

Research on household finance has traditionally centered on understanding how cognitive abilities and financial literacy impact individuals' preparedness for retirement. The primary emphasis has been on gauging how well people grasp financial concepts and information, linking these cognitive skills to their readiness for the retirement phase. Nevertheless, a recent shift in research focus recognizes that factors beyond cognitive capabilities also play a crucial role in determining effective savings habits and successful retirement planning.

Noncognitive skills can directly and indirectly impact retirement preparedness via different channels. Research has shown that income differences are driven in part by noncognitive abilities (Heckman et al. 2006; Lindqvist and Vestman 2011). Using household survey data from the Netherlands, we find that these 'character' skills influence household financial well-being beyond the income differences they cause (Parise and Peijnenburg 2019). In this chapter, we explore the direct causes of limited retirement readiness.

This emerging attention to noncognitive abilities offers a more detailed understanding of the complexities involved in retirement decisions. Moreover, the interaction between cognitive and noncognitive factors provides an opportunity to refine and rethink existing interventions, paving the way for a more comprehensive approach to fostering retirement preparedness. In what follows, we first review different types and measurements of noncognitive abilities. Next, we explore the relation between noncognitive traits and decisions important for retirement preparedness, in particular saving, investments, and retirement planning. We conclude with a discussion of potential policy implications.

Gianpaolo Parise and Kim Peijnenburg, *Noncognitive Determinants of Retirement Saving Behavior.* In: *Retirement Saving, Investment, and Spending.* Edited by: Olivia S. Mitchell and Nikolai Roussanov, Oxford University Press.

DOI: 10.1093/oso/9780197845752.003.0002

## Setting the Stage

### Noncognitive Abilities

Noncognitive abilities, also labeled personality traits, are enduring characteristics that shape peoples' responses and behaviors across diverse situations. Noncognitive abilities refer to a set of characteristics and skills that are distinct from cognitive skills, focusing on aspects of individuals' psychological and emotional makeup. These traits often include conscientiousness, emotional intelligence, resilience, and locus of control. Unlike cognitive skills, which involve intellectual capabilities such as IQ, knowledge, and financial literacy, noncognitive abilities encompass the interpersonal, emotional, and motivational aspects of individuals' functioning. The importance of noncognitive abilities in the financial arena lies in their influence on how individuals approach challenges, interact with others, and make decisions, all of which ultimately contribute to their overall success and well-being.

### Measurement Challenges of Noncognitive Abilities

The measurement of noncognitive abilities presents a formidable challenge due to the inherent complexity and subtlety of these traits. Several measurement methods have been devised, each with their own strengths and limitations; these methods include self-report surveys, peer evaluations, and situational judgment tests. The reliance on self-reporting introduces potential biases, as individuals may not accurately assess or may intentionally modify their noncognitive attributes. In particular, self-reported measures introduce the risk of social desirability bias, as individuals may provide responses they perceive as socially acceptable rather than reflecting their true behavioral tendencies. Moreover, the contextual nature of noncognitive abilities complicates the development of universally applicable measurement tools.

Among the various models used to conceptualize noncognitive abilities, the Big Five personality traits stand out as a widely accepted framework (Heckman et al. 2013). These traits cover openness, conscientiousness, extraversion, agreeableness, and emotional stability. Each trait encompasses a broad range of behaviors, tendencies, and dispositions that collectively contribute to an individual's noncognitive profile. The challenge lies not only in defining and operationalizing these traits but also in accurately measuring them to gain meaningful insights into an individual's noncognitive capacity.

In seeking alternative measures for noncognitive abilities, grit has gained prominence (Duckworth et al. 2007). Grit describes the tendency to persevere and having a passion for long-term goals. This noncognitive skill is regarded as a valuable predictor of success. Measurement tools for grit often include scales with items assessing individuals' commitment to long-term goals and their perseverance in the face of setbacks. For instance, respondents may be asked to rate statements like 'Setbacks don't discourage me,' 'I don't give up easily,' or 'I finish whatever I begin.' Grit's focus on sustained effort and resilience offers a distinct perspective on noncognitive traits beyond the Big Five framework.

Beyond the Big Five personality traits and grit, 'locus of control' is another frequently used measure of noncognitive abilities. Locus of control refers to individuals' beliefs about the extent to which they can control events in their lives. Internal locus of control indicates a belief in personal agency, while external locus of control suggests attributing events to external forces. Measurement often involves Likert-scale items gauging agreement with statements like 'I feel I am in control of my life' or 'Luck plays a significant role in determining life outcomes.' (Ng et al. 2006). Other measures, such as self-efficacy and emotional intelligence assessments, add further dimensions to the challenging task of comprehensively capturing noncognitive abilities in empirical research.

## Conscientiousness

In what follows, we measure conscientiousness using the Big Five personality trait questionnaire. Conscientiousness describes the tendency to be organized, practical, persistent, self-disciplined, and achievement oriented (e.g., McAdams 2008). We focus on the personality trait conscientiousness due to previous work that consistently shows this trait is a major determinant of financial choices. For instance, Parise and Peijnenburg (2019) showed that conscientiousness is an important determinant of financial distress. Figure 2.1 illustrates that those in the bottom quintiles of conscientiousness and emotional stability have an almost tenfold higher probability to be in financial distress compared to people in the top quintiles of these two noncognitive traits.

We measure conscientiousness using ten questions specifically designed to measure this personality trait, following Goldberg (1992). Examples of questions include: 'I am always prepared,' 'I pay attention to details,' and 'I like order.' Importantly, these questions are asked without reference to any context, which could limit the risk of mechanical correlations. For example, a respondent would be more likely to answer that she gets stressed easily about her retirement preparedness if her financial situation is poor, thereby inducing a mechanical correlation in the data. To circumvent this, respondents receive the following instruction: 'Please use the rating scale below to describe how accurately each statement describes you: (1) very inaccurate, (2) moderately inaccurate, (3) neither inaccurate nor accurate, (4) moderately accurate, (5) very accurate.' Subjects are not informed what the questions are intended to measure, and the ordering of the questions is random. We summarize responses related to conscientiousness into one measure by using factor analysis.

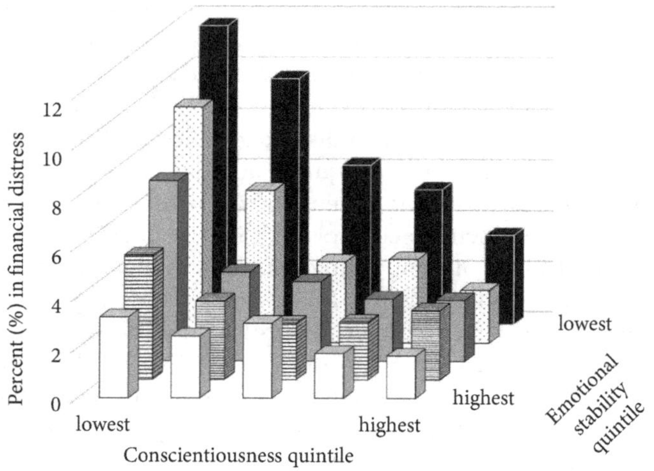


**Figure 2.1** Noncognitive abilities and financial distress

*Notes:* This figure displays the percentage of households in financial distress by quintile of emotional stability and conscientiousness. Financial distress is measured as being delinquent on mortgage payments, rent payments, utility bills, or other bills.

*Source:* Parise and Peijnenburg (2019).

## Data from the Netherlands

The present study utilizes data from the Longitudinal Internet Study for the Social Sciences (LISS) panel, a representative household survey conducted by CentERdata at Tilburg University in the Netherlands. This panel, operational since October 2007, spans the years 2008–2017 and includes 13,145 individuals randomly drawn from the population register by Statistics Netherlands. Attrition and the addition of new individuals imply that each cross-section comprises around 7,000 respondents at any given time.

The survey is computer-based, enabling subjects to participate from home, and efforts are made to mitigate selection bias by providing computers and internet connections to those who could not participate otherwise. To incentivize participation and retention, subjects receive compensation for each completed survey. This dataset is particularly well suited for our research, since one of the annual survey modules includes standard questions measuring noncognitive abilities following the Big Five personality framework. Additionally, the dataset encompasses various measures of financial distress, along with an extensive array of demographic controls, preferences, and cognitive ability variables.

## Noncognitive Abilities and Savings

Next, we discuss the empirical relationships between noncognitive abilities and savings. We provide evidence using our own calculations and build on prior work. Figure 2.2 summarizes the relation between noncognitive abilities and savings. For ease of interpretation, we standardize the noncognitive ability variable to have a mean of zero and a standard deviation of one. The y-axis shows peoples' financial wealth buffer, defined as deposit accounts plus savings plus equity investments, and the x-axis shows the standardized noncognitive ability measure. The curve is fitted using kernel-weighted polynomial smoothing (this is a statistical technique to estimate a curve as the weighted average of neighboring observed data), and the gray shading represents 95% confidence intervals. We clearly see that people with higher noncognitive abilities have higher savings buffers. The magnitudes are also sizeable: people with noncognitive abilities falling two standard deviations below the mean have financial wealth levels of approximately €43,000, compared to €70,000 for those with noncognitive abilities two standard deviations above the mean.

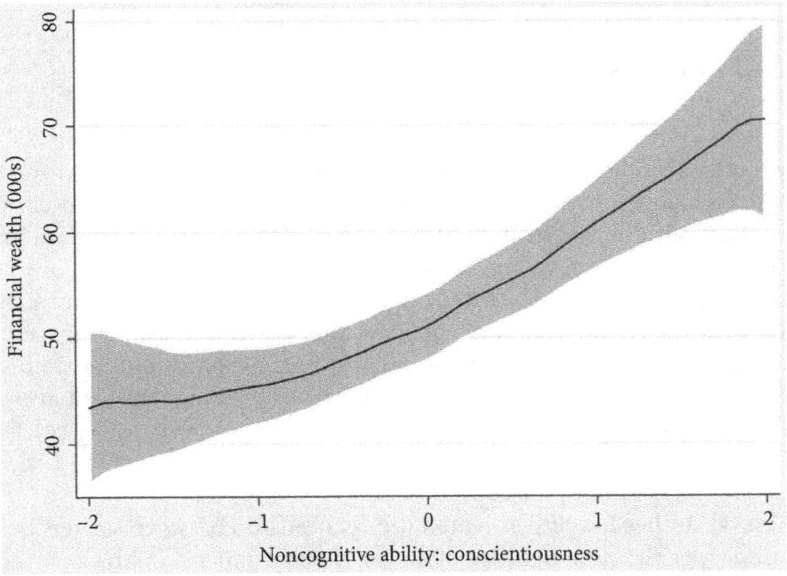


**Figure 2.2** Noncognitive abilities and financial wealth buffer

*Notes:* This figure displays the fitted curve from a local polynomial regression. The dependent variable is 'financial wealth,' and the independent variable is 'conscientiousness.' Conscientiousness is standardized to have a mean of zero and a standard deviation of 1. Conscientiousness is restricted from −2 standard deviations to +2 standard deviations around the mean. The shaded area represents the 95% confidence interval. The data are sourced from the LISS panel spanning the period 2008–2017.
*Source:* Authors' calculations.

TABLE 2.1 Noncognitive Abilities and Financial Choices

| | Financial wealth buffer | Savings | Unsecured debt |
|---|---|---|---|
| | (1) | (2) | (3) |
| *Conscientiousness* | 0.217*** (0.037) | 0.045*** (0.004) | −0.035*** (0.005) |
| Controls | Yes | Yes | Yes |
| N | 24,306 | 47,918 | 10,695 |

*Notes:* This table shows the results of an OLS regression (column 1) and probit regressions (columns 2 and 3). In column 1, the dependent variable is the log of financial wealth. In column 2, the dependent variable is equal to 1 if the respondent consumes less than her income. In column 3, the dependent variable is equal to one if the respondent has one or more of the following: a loan from a family member, debit card debt, credit card debt, a personal loan, a student loan, or some other unsecured loan. All models include a constant term and controls for risk aversion (lottery and self-reported), ambiguity aversion, numeracy, trust, optimism, financial literacy, agreeableness, openness, extraversion, male, children living at home, age, age squared, home ownership, education, partner, residence in a rural area, missing data dummies, and year dummies when indicated. The controls are suppressed for brevity. The table reports marginal effects. Standard errors are clustered by household and appear in parentheses. The data are sourced from the LISS panel spanning the period 2008–2017.

*p < .1; **p < .05; ***p < .01.

*Source:* Authors' calculations.

We test this relation more formally in Table 2.1. Here we report the estimated association between conscientiousness and three financial choices: financial wealth buffer, savings, and unsecured debt. Controls are included for risk aversion (lottery and self-reported), ambiguity aversion, numeracy, trust, optimism, financial literacy, agreeableness, openness, extraversion, male, children living at home, age, age squared, home ownership, education, partner, residence in a rural area, missing data dummies, and year dummies when indicated. The results are from ordinary least squares and probit regressions. The evidence confirms that people with lower conscientiousness also have lower financial wealth buffers, are less likely to save, and are more likely to have unsecured debt.

Several studies have investigated the relationship between savings behavior and specific noncognitive abilities. For instance, Cobb-Clark et al. (2016) showed that those with an internal locus of control save more. Those people feel that much of what happens in life stems from their own actions. Similarly, Hurd et al. (2012) found that conscientiousness relates to higher levels of wealth accumulation. Duckworth and Weir (2010) explore the impact of grit—the noncognitive trait associated with perseverance and passion for long-term goals—on savings habits. Their findings suggested that individuals with higher levels of grit tended to exhibit more consistent and disciplined saving practices. Letkiewicz and Fox (2014) examined the role of financial self-efficacy—the noncognitive factor reflecting an individual's belief in their ability to manage financial matters. Their research indicated a positive correlation between higher financial self-efficacy and increased savings behaviors. Nyhus and Webley (2001) assessed the influence of future time perspective (a noncognitive factor reflecting an individual's orientation toward the future) on savings behavior. Their results suggested that individuals with a longer-term perspective were more likely to adopt prudent saving habits.

These outcomes underscore the pivotal role of noncognitive skills in shaping financial behaviors that directly impact peoples' readiness for retirement and welfare during the retirement phase.

## Noncognitive Abilities and Investments

Several authors have posited that noncognitive abilities can impact investment decisions. Akin to cognitive abilities, persons with lower noncognitive abilities might make classic portfolio choice mistakes. These errors include non-participation in the stock market, having little financial wealth allocated to equity, being home-biased, and underdiversifying investments. This is because people with low conscientiousness are potentially less able to collect information about stock investments, process this information, and make optimal portfolio choices.

Figure 2.3 illustrates the relation between conscientiousness and the fraction of financial wealth people allocate to equity, offering insight into the relationship between noncognitive abilities and investment decisions. As expected, we find a positive relation between noncognitive skills and the fraction of financial wealth allocated to equity. This is further confirmed by Jiang et al. (2024), who showed that noncognitive traits are predictive of participation in the stock market. Their research, focusing on the measurement of noncognitive abilities with the Big Five personality traits, effectively reinforces the notion that these traits play a pivotal role in influencing individuals' decisions regarding stock market participation.

Lindqvist et al. (2018) provided similar findings. Using data incorporating test scores derived from Swedish military rolls, their findings affirmed the pervasive impact of noncognitive abilities on portfolio choices. These collective insights underscore the robustness of the identified relation, substantiating its relevance across diverse datasets and methodologies. These portfolio choice mistakes can have large welfare consequences due to the sizeable equity premium left on the table.

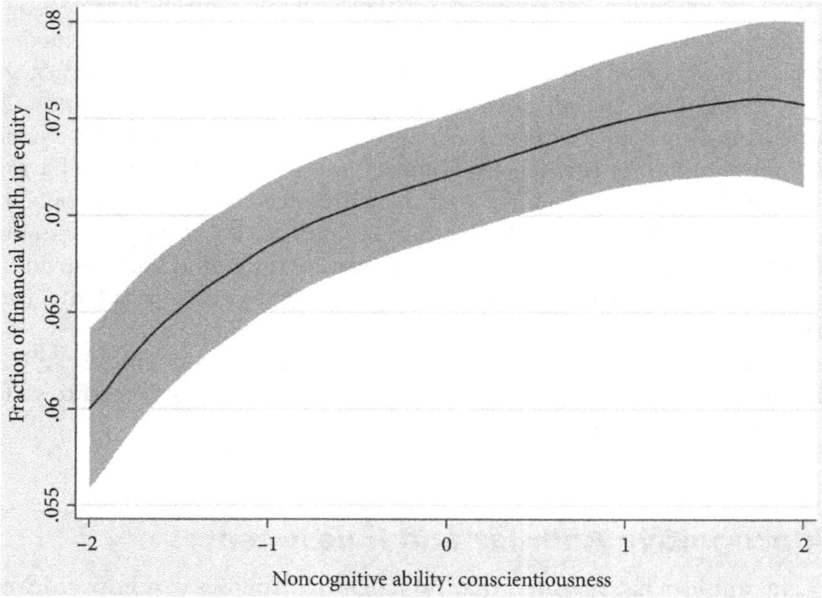


**Figure 2.3** Noncognitive abilities and the fraction allocated to equity

*Notes:* This figure displays the fitted curve from a local polynomial regression. The dependent variable is 'fraction in equity,' and the independent variable is 'conscientiousness.' Conscientiousness is standardized to have a mean of zero and a standard deviation of 1. Conscientiousness is restricted from −2 standard deviations to +2 standard deviations around the mean. Fraction in equity is calculated as the fraction of total financial wealth invested in equity. The shaded area represents the 95% confidence interval. The data are sourced from the LISS panel spanning the period 2008–2016.
*Source:* Authors' calculations.

## Noncognitive Abilities and Retirement Planning

Planning is important to ensure sufficient retirement income, reduce uncertainty, and avoid negative surprises (Van Rooij et al. 2012). It is therefore helpful that at regular intervals people take stock of their savings, expected income needs during retirement, and expected retirement dates. These calculations are complicated for many people as they require an understanding of pension statements, an ability to project savings and retirement expenses, and an awareness of the impact of retiring early or later on their pension income. We hypothesize that conscientious people are better equipped to plan for their retirement. To generate a measure for retirement planning in our empirical analysis, LISS respondents were given the

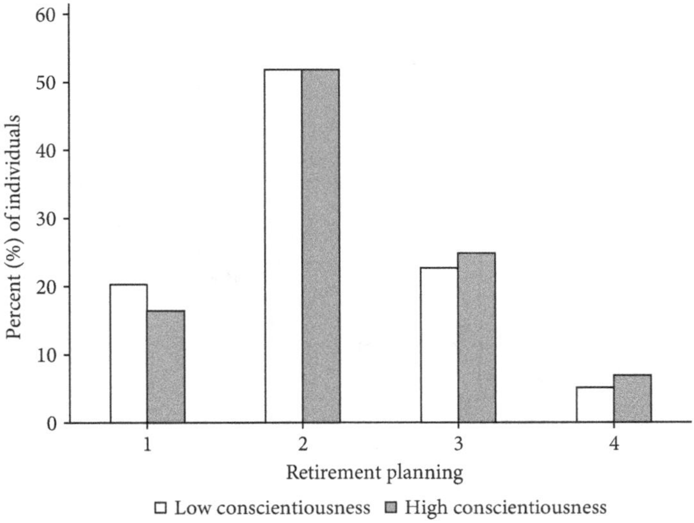


**Figure 2.4** Noncognitive abilities and retirement planning

*Notes:* This figure illustrates the percentage of individuals indicating various levels of retirement planning, ranging from minimal planning (level 1) to extensive planning (level 4). The left panel presents retirement planning for individuals with below-median conscientiousness scores, while the right panel depicts retirement planning for those with above-median conscientiousness scores. The data are sourced from the LISS panel spanning the period 2008–2015.
*Source:* Authors' calculations.

following preamble: 'The following questions are about the financial needs of you (and your partner/spouse) during retirement. Please assume for all the questions that prices of the things you spend your money on remain the same in the future as today; that is, please answer the questions as if there will be (no inflation).' A question on retirement planning is posed afterward, as follows: 'How much have you thought about retirement: (1) hardly at all, (2) a little, (3) some, (4) a lot.'

Figure 2.4 shows the retirement planning variable for below and above average level of conscientiousness. We see that 20% of those with below-median conscientiousness have thought 'hardly at all' about retirement, compared to 16% of those with above-median conscientiousness. Planning can have a large impact on pension preparedness as it allows people to adjust their savings and investments well before retirement.

Figure 2.5 demonstrates the relation between conscientious and peoples' desire for flexibility in pension savings and investments. In particular, respondents answer: 'I would like to take some responsibility for my old-age

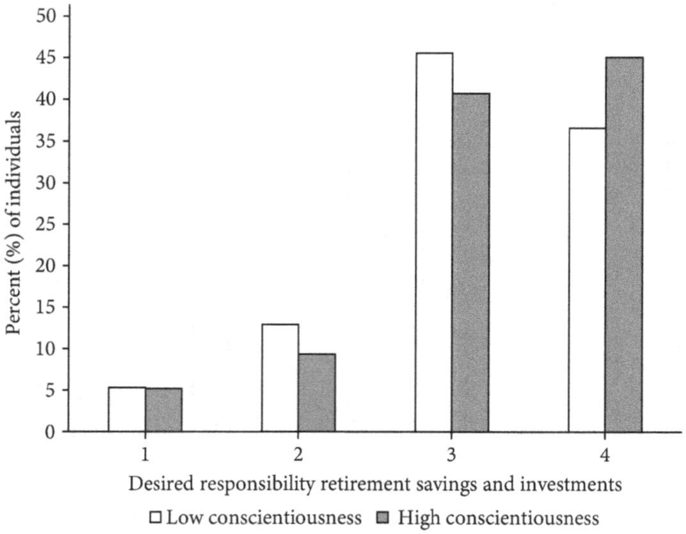


**Figure 2.5** Noncognitive abilities and desired retirement responsibility

*Notes:* This figure illustrates the percentage of individuals indicating various levels of desired retirement responsibility, ranging from minimal planning (level 1) to extensive planning (level 4). The left panel presents desired retirement responsibility for individuals with below-median conscientiousness scores, while the right panel depicts retirement desired retirement responsibility for those with above-median conscientiousness scores. The data are sourced from the LISS panel spanning the period 2008–2017.
*Source:* Authors' calculations.

provision—for example, to decide how much to save and how to invest my savings.' Answers ranged from (1) definitely not, to (4) yes, definitely. A greater degree of flexibility in savings and investment decisions is valued mostly by conscientious people. Thus, 44% of people with above-median conscientiousness would like to have more flexibility, compared to 36% of people with below-median conscientiousness. Increased flexibility and responsibility could be welfare-improving, particularly given that the people who value increased responsibility are also those more likely able to handle the responsibility.

## Noncognitive Abilities and Pension Default Investment Behavior

Default pension funds often serve as the choice for individuals entering government mandated defined contribution pension plans such as in Sweden, and in employer plans as in the US. Understanding the factors that influence people's decisions to deviate from the default option is crucial for policymakers, financial analysts, and researchers alike.

Lindqvist et al. (2018) investigated the relationship between cognitive and non-cognitive skills, and the decision to opt out of the Swedish government mandated default pension system (launched in 2000). Surprisingly, the results reveal that at the time of the plan's inception, non-cognitive rather than cognitive skills were influential in predicting people's decisions to opt out of the default fund. For those who opted out, cognitive skills were associated with increased activity in terms of reallocating investments between funds.

The positive correlation between non-cognitive skills and opting out of the default was attributed to the intense information and advertising campaigns during that period, reflecting what Cronqvist and Thaler (2004) termed a 'pro-choice' culture. Within this context, the term refers to an environment marked by intense information and advertising campaigns that strongly encourage individuals to actively make choices regarding their pension fund allocations. The persuasive nature of these campaigns likely influenced Swedish workers with higher non-cognitive skills, who in response to the proactively presented alternatives demonstrated a greater propensity to opt out of the default fund.

## Are Noncognitive Abilities Malleable?

Much behavioral evidence suggests that noncognitive abilities exhibit a certain degree of permanence, influenced by early life experiences and genetic endowments. Several studies indicate that over half of noncognitive abilities may be heritable, with only a limited impact of the external environment on these traits after childhood (e.g., Bouchard and Loehlin 2001; Bouchard and McGue 2003). To what extent noncognitive abilities are influenced by genetics remains an active area of research. A comprehensive review of over 150 longitudinal studies underscored that noncognitive abilities tend to exhibit increasing stability with age (Roberts and DelVecchio 2000). Notably, abilities measured for the same individuals from six to 30 years later are correlated from 60%–80% with the original measurements (Costa Jr. and McCrae 1994); in other words, these skills do not change much during adulthood. This is important since it mitigates potential concerns regarding reverse causality.

## Why Do Noncognitive Abilities Impact Financial Choices?

It is also important to understand the mechanisms by which noncognitive abilities influence financial choices. One approach would be to incorporate noncognitive skills in an economic model, which could provide insight for policymakers on whether (and how) noncognitive abilities can be improved. Parise and Peijnenburg (2019) showed that character skills do influence the productivity of effort as well as the cost of effort for financial decision making. For example, more conscientious people are not only better at gathering and processing information about different investment opportunities but also at making more informed decisions. More emotionally stable people can decide how to invest pension wealth more calmly. Accordingly, noncognitive abilities can be usefully incorporated in an economic framework as these factors influence the cost of effort and the productivity of effort in financial decision making.

## Conclusions

This research investigates the association between noncognitive skills, particularly conscientiousness, and retirement preparedness using data from Dutch households. We show that individuals with higher noncognitive skills display specific financial behaviors, including increased savings out of income and larger financial buffers. Notably, conscientiousness correlates positively with participation in the stock market, enhancing the likelihood of accumulating sufficient retirement savings. Furthermore, individuals with better noncognitive skills are more likely to plan for retirement and prefer flexibility in their savings and investment decisions. These findings contribute to the understanding of retirement readiness, by emphasizing the role of noncognitive factors in addition to cognitive abilities in shaping financial decisions.

The identified relationships between conscientiousness and various financial choices underscore the importance of considering noncognitive aspects when designing interventions to enhance retirement preparedness. This insight has implications for policymakers, financial analysts, and researchers, emphasizing the need for a comprehensive understanding of how cognitive and noncognitive factors interact in influencing individuals' financial trajectories as they consider and plan for retirement.

## References

Bouchard, T. J. Jr. and J. C. Loehlin (2001). 'Genes, Evolution, and Personality.' *Behavior Genetics*, 31(3): 243–273.

Bouchard, T. J. Jr. and M. McGue (2003). 'Genetic and Environmental Influences on Human Psychological Differences.' *Journal of Neurobiology*, 54(1): 4–45.

Cobb-Clark, D. A., S. C. Kassenboehmer, and M. Sinning (2016). 'Locus of Control and Savings.' *Journal of Banking and Finance*, 73: 113–130.

Costa, P. T. Jr. and R. R. McCrae (1994). 'Set Like Plaster? Evidence for the Stability of Adult Personality.' In T. F. Heatherton and J. L. Weinberger, eds., *Can Personality Change?* Washington, DC: American Psychological Association, pp. 21–40.

Cronqvist, H. and R. H. Thaler (2004). 'Design Choices in Privatized Social-Security Systems: Learning from the Swedish Experience.' *American Economic Review*, 94(2): 424–428.

Duckworth, A. L., C. Peterson, M. D. Matthews, and D. R. Kelly (2007). 'Grit: Perseverance and Passion for Long-Term Goals.' *Journal of Personality and Social Psychology*, 92(6): 1087–1101.

Duckworth, A. and D. Weir (2010). 'Personality, Lifetime Earnings, and Retirement Wealth.' Michigan Retirement Research Center Research Paper No. 2010–2235.

Goldberg, L. R. (1992). 'The Development of Markers for the Big-Five Factor Structure.' *Psychological Assessment*, 4(1): 26–42.

Heckman, J., R. Pinto, and P. Savelyev (2013). 'Understanding the Mechanisms Through Which an Influential Early Childhood Program Boosted Adult Outcomes.' *American Economic Review*, 103(6): 2052–2086.

Heckman, J. J., J. Stixrud, and S. Urzua (2006). 'The Effects of Cognitive and Noncognitive Abilities on Labor Market Outcomes and Social Behavior.' *Journal of Labor Economics*, 24(3): 411–482.

Hurd, M. D., A. L. Duckworth, S. Rohwedder, and D. R. Weir (2012). 'Personality Traits and Economic Preparation for Retirement.' Michigan Retirement Research Center Research Paper No. 2012-279.

Jiang, Z., C. Peng, and H. Yan (2024). 'Personality Differences and Investment Decision-Making.' *Journal of Financial Economics*, 153: 103776.

Letkiewicz, J. C. and J. J. Fox (2014). 'Conscientiousness, Financial Literacy, and Asset Accumulation of Young Adults.' *Journal of Consumer Affairs*, 48(2): 274–300.

Lindqvist, E., F. Paues, and R. Vestman (2018). 'The Role of Cognitive and Non-Cognitive Skills for Investment Behavior.' Stockholm University Working Paper No. 2018-11.

Lindqvist, E. and R. Vestman (2011). 'The Labor Market Returns to Cognitive and Noncognitive Ability: Evidence from the Swedish Enlistment.' *American Economic Journal: Applied Economics*, 3(1): 101–128.

McAdams, D. P. (2008). *The Person: An Introduction to the Science of Personality Psychology*. New York: John Wiley and Sons.

Ng, T. W. H., K. L. Sorensen, and L. T. Eby (2006). 'Locus of Control at Work: A Meta-Analysis.' *Journal of Organizational Behavior*, 27(8): 1057–1087.

Nyhus, E. K. and P. Webley (2001). 'The Role of Personality in Household Saving and Borrowing Behaviour.' *European Journal of Personality*, 15(S1): S85–S103.

Parise, G. and K. Peijnenburg (2019). 'Noncognitive Abilities and Financial Distress: Evidence from a Representative Household Panel.' *Review of Financial Studies*, 32(10): 3884–3919.

Roberts, B. W. and W. F. DelVecchio (2000). 'The Rank-Order Consistency of Personality Traits from Childhood to Old Age: A Quantitative Review of Longitudinal Studies.' *Psychological Bulletin*, 126(1): 3–25.
van Rooij, M. C. J., A. Lusardi, and R. J. M. Alessie (2012). 'Financial Literacy, Retirement Planning and Household Wealth.' *Economic Journal*, 122(560): 449–478.

Chapter 3

# Subjective Beliefs, Saving, and Spending for Retirement

*Rawley Z. Heimer*

Expectations about future events are essential to the decisions that individuals make every day, requiring that people make a range of forecasts about key economic variables. Many economic models posit that individuals have rational expectations, which means that people base their decisions on the information available to them when they make these decisions. Nevertheless, behavioral economists are willing to relax the assumption of individuals' reliance on available data, such as historical averages, drawing instead on psychological research to incorporate *systematic* patterns of belief formation.

Perhaps the most well-known theoretical model of decision making in behavioral economics is cumulative prospect theory (CPT), developed by Amos Tversky and Daniel Kahneman (1992). One crucial aspect of CPT is based on the observation that people assign excessive weight to events with low probabilities and insufficient weight to events with high probabilities. This chapter explores a specific *systematic* error in beliefs that many people make: they overestimate the probability of dying soon when young but overestimate the probability of living very long when old. This miscalibration in beliefs has potentially important effects on the financial decisions we make over our lifetimes since the benefits and costs of investing in human capital, saving, investing, and spending depend on one's projected lifetime.

In what follows, we first describe a simple life-cycle model and the role of subjective beliefs in the model, developing an explanation for miscalibrated mortality beliefs—namely the salience of different causes of death at different ages. We then characterize the types of financial decisions analysts can expect to observe when individuals have systematic errors in mortality beliefs. First, we discuss other variables crucial to long-term financial decision making that are prone to systematic biases in beliefs.

Rawley Z. Heimer, *Subjective Beliefs, Saving, and Spending for Retirement*. In: *Retirement Saving, Investment, and Spending*. Edited by: Olivia S. Mitchell and Nikolai Roussanov, Oxford University Press. © Pension Research Council, The Wharton School, The University of Pennsylvania (2026). DOI: 10.1093/oso/9780197845752.003.0003

## Subjective Beliefs in Life-Cycle Economic Models

Economists use life-cycle models to understand the financial decisions that people make at different ages. That is, model consumers must decide how much to consume today and how much to save for tomorrow, as they seek to maximize the utility of lifetime consumption. Such models assume that consumption today is more valuable than consumption tomorrow due to the individual's time discount factor. In this light, a life-cycle model is used to describe the inter-temporal tradeoff between consumption and saving that people make at different ages.

A version of the model that includes precautionary savings proves to generate a realistic pattern of hump-shaped consumption over the life cycle (e.g., Skinner 1988). People forego some consumption when young, so as to save for retirement; this leads wealth to peak around retirement age, after which households draw down their savings. Such models can also incorporate a desire to leave an inheritance—termed a 'bequest motive'—which can explain rising saving at all ages and a level of wealth remaining on death. To include additional realism, analysts have extended their models to include uncertain lifetime income streams, as well as endogenous decisions to work (e.g., Catherine 2022). Income stabilizes upon retirement because it comes from Social Security and other retirement assets, such as a pension. Many authors have also embedded the possibility of saving and investing in several options (Gomes 2020), leading to a portfolio choice problem where the individual can invest in either a risk-free asset (e.g., Treasury bills) or a risky asset (equities) or some combination thereof. The consumer can also make housing choices in some settings, such as whether to take out a mortgage or allow for unsecured debt such as credit cards (Cookson et al. 2022).

Typically, the decision maker in such models is assumed to be forward-looking, making decisions based on forecasts of future factors including expected asset returns (e.g., the risk and return of a diversified portfolio), retirement benefits, and the anticipated probability of survival. In practice, many research studies tend to use historical averages to calibrate peoples' expectations. For example, a model might project an expected return on a diversified portfolio of equities using historical returns since the 1950s. For survival tables, it could use statistics from the Centers for Disease Control and Prevention (CDC). Nevertheless, historical statistics might misestimate what people actually believe, instead leading some to use people's stated beliefs elicited through surveys.

## Subjective Mortality Beliefs

Several behavioral finance studies have examined subjective mortality beliefs, finding that these tend to be pessimistic for the young but become optimistic as people approach and pass retirement age. One such influential study by Hamermesh (1985) surveyed 650 white male economists and compared them to a sample of 975 people chosen randomly from a telephone directory in the Midwest. More recently, such beliefs have been studied in representative surveys in the US, Europe, and Australia (Elder 2013; Wu et al. 2015). For instance, Hurd and McGarry (1995), using US data, also reported survival pessimism among the young and optimism among the old; however, they also showed that individuals were reasonably informed about their expected longevity. For example, individuals with higher socioeconomic status expected to live longer, while smokers expected to live shorter lives.

Measuring people's distorted beliefs about mortality is not straightforward since eliciting survival beliefs in survey data is not standardized. For example, Payne et al. (2013) reported that peoples' responses differed depending on whether researchers used a 'live-to' or 'die-by' framing. That is, responses to surveys differed depending on whether respondents were asked the age to what age they expected to live (e.g., 80 years old), versus or how likely it was that they would live another 10 years (e.g., with 90% probability).

In prior research (Heimer et al. 2019), we developed a way to survey subjective mortality beliefs and used it to connect directly with life-cycle models. Specifically, we first elicited subjective beliefs about a person's probability of living a specific number of additional years. Next, we used those beliefs to estimate a function for the probability of surviving until a terminal age of 95 years. Figure 3.1 compares the resulting subjective survival function to actuarial statistics from the Social Security Administration (SSA). The figure shows that 30-year-olds had an objective chance of 12% of surviving to 95, while they believed their chances of surviving to 95 were close to zero. The error in subjective beliefs flipped as they aged: on average, 70-year-olds had about a 15% chance of surviving to 95, though people believed their chances were closer to 20%.

## Salience Theory as an Explanation for Subjective Mortality Beliefs

To explain why people might make systematic errors in judgment regarding survival, Taylor and Thompson (1982: 175) propose salience theory, which 'refers to the phenomenon that when one's attention is differentially directed to one portion of the environment rather than to others, the information

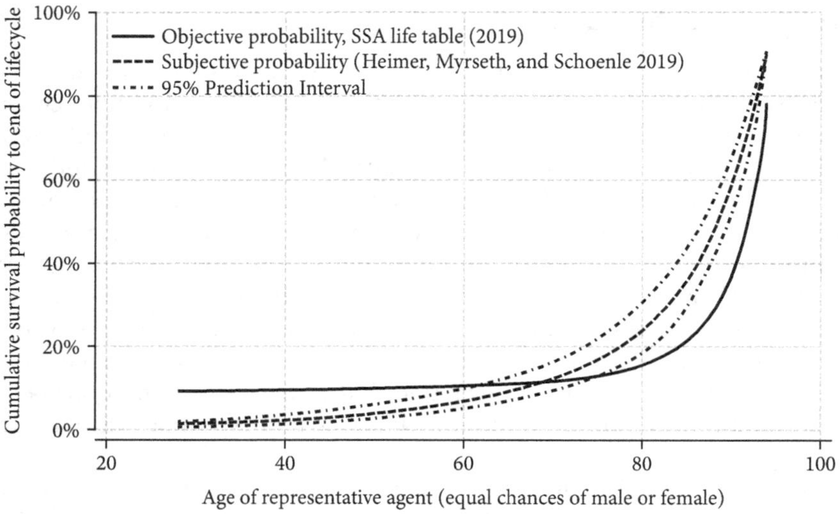


**Figure 3.1** Survival beliefs over the life cycle

*Source:* Author's calculations based on data from Heimer et al. (2019).

contained in that portion will receive disproportionate weighting in subsequent judgments.' Salience theory can thus explain why some individuals exaggerate the likelihood of experiencing extreme events, and it is useful in describing the errors in people's subjective mortality beliefs over the life cycle (Bordalo et al. 2022). Specifically, Heimer et al. (2019) showed that decision weights assigned to mortality events varied as people aged (see Figure 3.2). That is, younger people were more attuned to rare events, natural disasters, and plane crashes. Conversely, older individuals focused on health risks and natural aging.

These different foci translate into different subjective survival rates by age. One reason is that people often exaggerate the likelihood of dramatic risk factors (e.g., Hertwig et al. 2004). For instance, many television shows and movies discuss the possibility of shark attacks (e.g., the 1975 movie *Jaws* or the television event *Shark Week*), yet cows kill roughly 20 times more people per year and are not nearly as commonly feared as sharks (Forrester et al. 2018). Since young people overestimate the likelihood of rare events, they also underestimate their chances of survival to old ages.

As people age, rare events lose their salience, perhaps due to experience. Consequently, older individuals devote more attention to health risks and the natural course of aging when formulating beliefs about survival. Nevertheless, many health risks are difficult to visualize. For instance, the leading cause of death for people over the age of 75 is heart disease, and such deaths

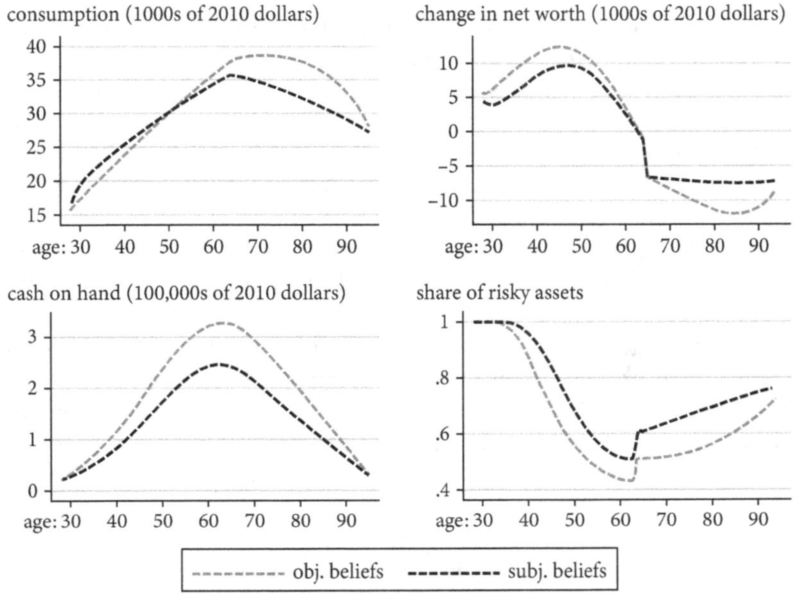


**Figure 3.2** Effects of subjective mortality beliefs in a life-cycle model
*Source:* Author's derivation from Heimer et al. (2019).

are often slow and lingering as opposed to sudden and vivid. Also, many people are averse to preventative measures and receiving treatment (Taber et al. 2015; Utkus and Mitchell 2025). Moreover, the natural course of aging might be difficult for many people to conceptualize. As such, older people may tend to overestimate their chances of survival to very old ages.

## Quantifying the Effects of Subjective Mortality Beliefs on Retirement Savings

Economic life-cycle models tend to deliver hump-shaped consumption over the course of the life cycle. The young forgo some consumption to save for retirement, and their wealth peaks around retirement age. Thereafter, they draw down their savings to nearly zero upon death. Such models can also incorporate a desire to leave an inheritance, which increases the levels of wealth at death. Most of the life-cycle literature uses actuarial statistics to determine the expected likelihood of surviving from year-to-year.

Our quantitative life-cycle model describes how these subjective mortality beliefs could affect people's consumption, savings, and portfolio choices. That approach assumes that people seek to maximize their lifetime utility of consumption, and current consumption is more valuable than future consumption, depending on the individual's time discount factor. Nonetheless, people can save year-to-year by investing in a risk-free asset (e.g., Treasury bills) or a risky asset (e.g., a diversified portfolio of US equities). People have uncertainty over their income each year of their working lives. Upon retirement, their income tends to be more stable because it comes from Social Security and other retirement assets such as a pension.

Our work suggests that peoples' financial decisions are more likely to embed subjective mortality beliefs instead of the objective survival probabilities of survival. Indeed, we found that with these subjective beliefs, consumption was higher among the young, resulting in less retirement savings, and while in retirement, people with subjective beliefs consumed less.

In addition, the difference in mortality beliefs affected the portfolio choices that people made. Because of undersaving by the young due to their subjective mortality beliefs, they later had to find ways to catch up on their savings. Such people are induced to take more risks by investing more in stocks, which persists later in life. Between overconsumption and the increased allocation to stocks, people with subjective mortality beliefs behave as though they believe in YOLO (you only live once).

Several other scholars have also studied the effects of mortality beliefs on a wide range of life-cycle financial decisions. Bloom et al. (2007) found that a higher subjective probability of survival contributed to greater wealth accumulation. Others have examined the relation between survival expectations and decisions to retire and claim Social Security. Hurd et al. (2004) showed modest effects of low subjective survival beliefs on the decision to retire earlier and claim Social Security. De Bresser (2021) studied these decisions within the context of a life-cycle model and obtained different results based on the choice of whether to use subjective or objective probabilities.

A variety of authors have also examined the decision to purchase annuities and how it relates to subjective mortality beliefs. As a benchmark, economic theory generally predicts that many people should purchase fairly priced annuities, though few people actually do so in practice. A possible explanation for this is that those with pessimistic mortality beliefs fail to demand annuities (Inkmann et al. 2011; O'Dea and Sturrock 2023; Teppa and Lafourcade 2013;). More recently, Hurwitz et al. (2021) examined mortality beliefs in the context of the global pandemic. The pandemic shortened millions of lives around the world and introduced a new and uncertain health shock into peoples' psyches. The study found that perceptions of the chances of contracting COVID-19 correlated with survival optimism. Relatedly, Heimer et al. (2020) showed that overconfidence was an important driver of peoples' perceptions of the risks of transmitting COVID-19. Overconfident people were less likely to believe that they would get sick, which in turn could have affected their forecasts of survival.

It is also of interest to learn whether subjective survival beliefs are 'hard-wired,' or whether information interventions can help correct peoples' biases. Heimer et al. (2019) found no evidence that presenting people with actuarial statistics about survival probabilities affected peoples' expectations of their own survival. By contrast, Hurwitz et al. (2022) reported that prompting people to think about financial decisions did alter their perceptions regarding their own survival. Given these opposing findings, more research is needed on methods to help guide people toward holding more accurate beliefs and toward making better financial decisions.

## Conclusions and Extensions

This chapter focuses on one factor influencing people's financial decision making over the life cycles, namely their beliefs about future events. Some analysts have examined expectations about expected work lives and retirement ages as well as their effects on financial decisions and welfare over the life cycle. One often hears people say that they 'delayed' retirement, implying that such people incorrectly estimated their actual retirement ages (Ingale and Paluri 2025). Moreover, Caliendo et al. (2023) reported that underestimating lifetime labor market participation can cost people tens of thousands of dollars in later life. An and Sachdeva (2024) studied uncertainty in retirement expectations, and those authors reported that people systematically underestimated how long they would work. Of course, individual beliefs can diverge from expected outcomes in other ways (Kosar and O'Dea 2023).

There is also research on planned versus actual bequests. For instance, some people say that they plan to leave an inheritance to their offspring and other charitable causes, yet many people overestimate the value of the inheritances actually bequeathed (Heimer and Li 2024). In the life-cycle context, economists seeking to calibrate these outcomes to data must assign a larger utility to bequests, resulting in higher savings rates at all ages.

Making financial decisions also requires people to develop forecasts of key macroeconomic variables. For instance, Das et al. (2020) reported that peoples' socioeconomic status affected their forecasts about business conditions, employment rates, and stock market returns, while Kuchler and Zafar (2019) documented that people overweighted their own experiences when developing forecasts of housing prices and employment. Some authors have also found that beliefs about housing affect decisions in the housing market: for instance, Armona et al. (2019) noted that larger price growth expectations affected a range of economic decisions such as the likelihood of making investments in the home, while Bottan and Perez-Truglia (2025) reported that expectations of larger house price growth reduced the probability of selling a home.

In conclusion, learning more about how people formulate their expectations regarding saving, investment, and spending in old age, while simultaneously understanding how these affect key retirement-related outcomes, will continue to be a high priority for future behavioral finance research.

## References


An, B. J. and K. Sachdeva (2024). 'Missing the Target? Retirement Expectations and Target Date Funds.' SSRN Working Paper No. 4763984.

Armona, L., A. Fuster, and B. Zafar (2019). 'Home Price Expectations and Behaviour: Evidence from a Randomized Information Experiment.' *Review of Economic Studies*, 86(4): 1371–1410.

Bloom, D. E., D. Canning, M. Moore, and Y. Song (2007). 'The Effect of Subjective Survival Probabilities on Retirement and Wealth in the United States.' In R. L. Clark, N. Ogawa, and A. Mason, eds., *Population Aging, Intergenerational Transvers and the Macroeconomy*. Northampton MA: Edward Elgar, pp. 67–100.

Bordalo, P., N. Gennaioli, and A. Shleifer (2022). 'Salience.' *Annual Review of Economics*, 14: 521–544.

Bottan, N. L. and R. Perez-Truglia (2025). 'Betting on the House: Subjective Expectations and Market Choices.' *American Economic Journal: Applied Economics*, 17(1): 459–500.

Caliendo, F. N., M. Casanova, A. Gorry, and S. N. Slavov (2023). 'Retirement Timing Uncertainty: Empirical Evidence and Quantitative Evaluation.' *Review of Economic Dynamics*, 51: 226–266.

Catherine, S. (2022). 'Countercyclical Labor Income Risk and Portfolio Choices over the Life Cycle.' *Review of Financial Studies*, 35(9): 4016–4054.

Cookson, J. A., E. P. Gilje, and R. Z. Heimer (2022). 'Shale Shocked: Cash Windfalls and Household Debt Repayment.' *Journal of Financial Economics*, 146(3): 905–931.

Das, S., C. M. Kuhnen, and S. Nagel (2020). 'Socioeconomic Status and Macroeconomic Expectations.' *Review of Financial Studies*, 33(1): 395–432.

de Bresser, J. (2021). 'The Role of Heterogeneous Expectations in Life Cycle Models.' CentER Discussion Paper No. 2021–034.

Elder, T. E. (2013). 'The Predictive Validity of Subjective Mortality Expectations: Evidence from the Health and Retirement Study.' *Demography*, 50(2): 569–589.

Forrester, J. A., T. G. Weiser, and J. D. Forrester (2018). 'An Update on Fatalities Due to Venomous and Nonvenomous Animals in the United States (2008–2015).' *Wilderness & Environmental Medicine*, 29(1): 36–44.

Gomes, F. (2020). 'Portfolio Choice Over the Life-Cycle: A Survey.' *Annual Review of Financial Economics*, 12: 277–304.

Hamermesh, D. S. (1985). 'Expectations, Life Expectancy, and Economic Behavior.' *Quarterly Journal of Economics*, 100(2): 389–408.

Heimer, R. Z. and X. Li (2024). 'The Motives for Bequests: Empirical Facts and Life Cycle Implications.' Presentation at the Nova School of Business and Economics Finance Seminar.

Heimer, R. Z., H. Liu, and X. Zhang (2020). 'Are People Overconfident about Avoiding COVID-19?' *Liberty Street Economics.* libertystreeteconomics.newyorkfed.org/2020/10/are-people-overconfident-about-avoiding-covid-19/

Heimer, R. Z., K. O. R. Myrseth, and R. S. Schoenle (2019). 'YOLO: Mortality Beliefs and Household Finance Puzzles.' *Journal of Finance,* 74(6): 2957–2996.

Hertwig, R., G. Barron, E. U. Weber, and I. Erev (2004). 'Decisions from Experience and the Effect of Rare Events in Risky Choice.' *Psychological Science,* 15(8): 534–539.

Hurd, M. D. and K. McGarry (1995). 'Evaluation of the Subjective Probabilities of Survival in the Health and Retirement Study.' *Journal of Human Resources,* 30: S268–S292.

Hurd, M. D., J. P. Smith, and J. M. Zissimopoulos (2004). 'The Effects of Subjective Survival on Retirement and Social Security Claiming.' *Journal of Applied Econometrics,* 19(6): 761–775.

Hurwitz, A., O. S. Mitchell, and O. Sade (2021). 'Longevity Perceptions and Saving Decisions during the COVID-19 Outbreak: An Experimental Investigation.' *AEA Papers and Proceedings,* 111: 297–301.

Hurwitz, A., O. S. Mitchell, and O. Sade (2022). 'Testing Methods to Enhance Longevity Awareness.' *Journal of Economic Behavior & Organization,* 204: 466–475.

Ingale, K. K., and R. A. Paluri. (2025). 'Retirement Planning: A Systematic Review of Literature and Future Research Directions.' *Management Review Quarterly,* 75: 1–43.

Inkmann, J., P. Lopes, and A. Michaelides (2011). 'How Deep Is the Annuity Market Participation Puzzle?' *Review of Financial Studies,* 24(1): 279–319.

Kosar, G. and C. O'Dea (2023). 'Expectations Data in Structural Microeconomic Models.' In R. Bachmann, G. Topa, and W. van der Klaauw, eds. *Handbook of Economic Expectations.* London: Academic Press Elsevier, pp. 647–675.

Kuchler, T. and B. Zafar (2019). 'Personal Experiences and Expectations About Aggregate Outcomes.' *Journal of Finance,* 74(5): 2491–2542.

O'Dea, C. and D. Sturrock (2023). 'Survival Pessimism and the Demand for Annuities.' *Review of Economics and Statistics,* 105(2): 442–457.

Payne, J. W., N. Sagara, S. B. Shu, K. C. Appelt, and E. J. Johnson (2013). 'Life Expectancy as a Constructed Belief: Evidence of a Live-To or Die-By Framing Effect.' *Journal of Risk and Uncertainty,* 46(1): 27–50.

Skinner, J. (1988). 'Risky Income, Life Cycle Consumption, and Precautionary Savings.' *Journal of Monetary Economics,* 22(2): 237–255.

Taber, J. M., B. Leyva, and A. Persoskie (2015). 'Why Do People Avoid Medical Care? A Qualitative Study Using National Data.' *Journal of General Internal Medicine,* 30(3): 290–297.

Taylor, S. E. and S. C. Thompson (1982). 'Stalking the Elusive "Vividness" Effect.' *Psychological Review,* 89(2): 155–181.

Teppa, F. and P. Lafourcade (2013). 'Can Longevity Risk Alleviate the Annuitization Puzzle? Empirical Evidence from Survey Data.' De Nederlandsche Bank Working Paper No. 302.

Tversky, A. and D. Kahneman (1992). 'Advances in Prospect Theory: Cumulative Representation of Uncertainty.' *Journal of Risk and Uncertainty,* 5: 297–323.

Utkus, S. and O. S. Mitchell (2025). 'Extending Healthspan in an Aging World.' Pension Research Council Working Paper WP2025-04.

Wu, S., R. Stevens, and S. Thorp (2015). 'Cohort and Target Age Effects on Subjective Survival Probabilities: Implications for Models of the Retirement Phase.' *Journal of Economic Dynamics and Control*, 55: 39–56.

Chapter 4

# Does It All Add Up?

## New Experimental Evidence for Undersum Bias as an Impediment to Precautionary Saving

*Shane Timmons and Féidhlim McGowan*

Increasing life expectancy is a testament to advancements in health care, technology, nutrition, and overall living standards in multiple countries (e.g., Mathers et al. 2015). With aging populations and declining birth rates, however, come multiple challenges for policymakers, employers, and society as a whole. Maintaining a desired quality of life later in life necessitates not just investing in one's health early in life but also in one's finances. Unfortunately, human psychology is poorly equipped to prioritize long time horizons, particularly when doing so also requires integrating complex numeric information with multiple uncertainties. In this chapter, we present new evidence from lab and field experiments for a cognitive bias that can demotivate pension saving: the 'undersum bias,' a systematic tendency to underestimate straightforward accumulation.

We are not the first to explore a behavioral phenomenon that impedes pension saving. Others have examined the implications of inertia (e.g., Choi et al. 2002), present bias, and temporal discounting (e.g., Beshears et al. 2022; Hastings and Mitchell 2020); over-optimism (e.g., Mitchell and Utkus 2004); subjective beliefs (Heimer this volume); and noncognitive determinants (Parise and Peijnenburg this volume). Some of these phenomena are not unique to pension saving, yet others are particularly relevant. One that is strongly linked to our thesis here is exponential growth bias. When tasked with predicting the future value of exponentially growing quantities (e.g., compounding interest), naïve consumers tend to project linear growth (Stango and Zinman 2009; Wagenaar and Sagaria 1975). Even sophisticated consumers who appreciate sources of nonlinearity make insufficient upward adjustments in their linear projections (Christandl and Fetchenhauer 2009; Wagenaar and Timmers 1979). Exponential growth bias leads consumers to underappreciate the effect of compound interest,

Shane Timmons and Féidhlim McGowan, *Does It All Add Up?*. In: *Retirement Saving, Investment, and Spending*. Edited by: Olivia S. Mitchell and Nikolai Roussanov, Oxford University Press. © Pension Research Council, The Wharton School, The University of Pennsylvania (2026). DOI: 10.1093/oso/9780197845752.003.0004

meaning they underestimate both the consequences of failing to repay debt with high interest rates and the benefits of saving (Levy and Tassoff 2017; Stango and Zinman 2009).

Exponential growth bias has clear implications for retirement savings, with consumers failing to appreciate the importance of starting to save earlier in life to exploit compound interest (Goda et al. 2019). There have thus been multiple attempts at designing interventions to help individuals better estimate exponential growth. These include instructions on heuristics to apply (Eisenstein and Hoch 2005), diagrams to use on pension benefit statements (McGowan and Lunn 2020), and financial education (Song 2020).

Nevertheless, one assumption in much of the research on exponential growth bias is that underestimation occurs when consumers must contend with exponential functions. If, for example, growth was linear, less cognitive effort would be required and, it is assumed, most consumers would be able to anticipate growth in linear contributions with reasonable accuracy. Testing this assumption is our goal in this chapter. If there are biases that precede or exacerbate exponential growth bias, these can have implications for retirement saving. To investigate this question, we first briefly review the evidence on 'number sense' (i.e., the mental representations of numerosity).

## Number Sense

People have an innate ability to form judgments of numerosity—but often imperfectly. Intuitive estimates of magnitudes tend to be noisy, with representations that become increasingly compressed as the objective magnitude increases (Dehaene 1992). As a result, approximations of numerosity of both visual stimuli and mental representations of numbers (e.g., digits) follow a concave response function; estimates are biased downward, with the strength of bias increasing as the degree of magnitude increases (Anobile et al. 2012; Dehaene et al. 2008).

Despite evidence from psychophysics research showing underestimation in judgments of the numerosity of visual stimuli (e.g., Burr et al. 2018; Dahaene 1992), evidence for whether similar effects occur when people must integrate a series of numbers has only recently emerged. In perhaps the first empirical investigation of intuitive summation of numbers (excluding the impact of compound interest), Scheibehenne (2019) tasked participants with estimating the cumulative cost of grocery items. In a lab experiment, participants saw a series of trials, each with 24 grocery items and individual cost. Results showed that participants underestimated the total bill in two-thirds of trials. The lab experiment was followed by a field experiment with greater ecological validity: shoppers in a supermarket were asked to estimate the total bill of their cart while waiting in line to pay. Given the real-world implications for underestimating a shopping bill and the experience shoppers likely had with grocery shopping (perhaps purchasing very similar items every week), this experiment presented a more stringent test of intuitive summation. Again, however, the majority underestimated the total.

While Scheibehenne (2019) did not refer to this tendency as 'undersum' bias, Goswami et al. (2021) provided a thorough exploration of the bias, replicating it across 10 experiments. They showed that the bias emerged in multiple domains, not just shopping environments, and it emerged even under lessened cognitive load—persisting even if overestimation was incentivized.

In the remainder of this chapter, we present recent evidence from lab and field experiments designed to inform policy on the implications of undersum bias for precautionary saving behavior. We first review the evidence for the implications of undersum bias on retirement saving. Conclusions are similar to Scheibehenne (2019) and Goswami et al. (2021), in that they pertain to a downward bias for intuitive summation. We also present evidence for how undersum bias might also extend to people's perceptions of the accumulation of risk, which may further inhibit motivations to save. We conclude with evidence for scalable interventions that seek to overcome these biases, and we point to avenues for future research.

## Evidence for Undersum Bias

This section summarizes several experiments relevant for the concept of undersum bias.

### Summation

The experiments described in Scheibehenne (2019) were, we believe, the first to demonstrate a bias toward underestimation when people tried to integrate sequences of monetary amounts. The field experiment is particularly convincing, as consumers are likely to have experience making similar purchases on a regular basis and might reasonably be expected to have an incentive to accurately estimate their grocery bill. Even more convincing is to see the same effect replicated independently, in supermarkets that served higher- and lower-income consumers when shoppers were offered cash incentives for accuracy (Goswami et al. 2021).

Our own work (McGowan et al. 2022) set out to further replicate and extend these key findings. In one experiment, online participants saw a series of monetary amounts and were incentivized to provide approximations of their totals. The monetary amounts were presented to participants as slot machine payouts or bills (e.g., utility bills). Participants were tasked with a more difficult task (estimating the totals) as in Scheibehenne (2019), or a simpler task of choosing whether the total of the sequence they had just seen was higher or lower than a referent amount. We varied also the length of the sequences, with either six or 12 amounts presented per trial. The experimental design was thus a 2 (framing: slot machine payouts or familiar household bills) x 2 (task order: judgments first or estimates first) x 2 (series length: six or 12) mixed design, with the first two factors varying between-groups and the final varying within. Following a couple of practice trials, participants completed 24 incentivized trials.

Results demonstrated consistent underestimation of the total. On average, two-thirds of the incentivized trials were underestimated, similar to the inaccuracy observed in Scheibehenne's (2019) first experiment. Underestimation occurred in both the familiar frame (the bills) and the unfamiliar frame (slot machine payouts). Underestimation was also observed for both the difficult estimation task and the simpler forced-choice task, and regardless of series length (although with some evidence for exacerbation on longer trials). Thus, our first experiment provided independent replication of Scheibehenne's central finding of a bias toward underestimating the accumulation of monetary amounts.

Our second experiment sought to replicate the first and further tested whether specific contextual factors could attenuate the undersum bias. Although there was no attenuation of the bias in the familiar compared to unfamiliar framing (i.e., bill versus slot machine), we suspected that other framings might matter. Specifically, we tested two additional ones: unfamiliar household bills (the cost to feed exotic pets), and a savings frame (for a vacation). Results closely replicated the first experiment, with underestimation again observed in two-thirds of the trials. Thus, we observed consistent underestimation of accumulation in a controlled environment, on a relatively simple task, with clear instructions and incentives.

The motivation for testing undersum bias under these simplified conditions resulted from experiments we had previously run to inform pension policy, funded by Ireland's Pensions Authority. There, we set out to test the accuracy of estimations of money growth from regular saving and lump sum investments (McGowan et al. 2019). These studies provided evidence that undersum bias also manifested when consumers had to contend with compound interest.

In one case, participants were presented with two straightforward saving settings. In the lump sum scenario, they were told that they had transferred €1,000 to an investment fund that generated a return of 5% per year. They were told to assume that no fees or other deductions would occur, and they were asked to estimate the growth of the fund. In the regular saving scenario, the only change was to incorporate saving an additional €1,000 every year. Results showed that for the lump sum scenario, participants tended to linearize the growth and estimated the amount after 20 years as 84% of the total. Underestimation was more striking when participants had to also consider the accumulation of regular savings: they estimated just 60% of the actual total.

In second case, we sought to more closely align with decisions individuals make when considering how much to save per month when they start saving for their pension. In this 'match task' experiment, participants again saw hypothetical scenarios. They received three pieces of information on a hypothetical character's retirement fund: the age at which he started to save, his monthly contribution, and the annual interest rate (e.g., saving €130 per month from age 22 at 3% interest). Again, the task was simplified to ignore any fees, taxes, and so on. They were then informed about a different individual who began saving at an older age (e.g., age 27) in a fund with the same interest rate and asked how much this second individual would need to save per month in order to have the equivalent fund as the first saver at age 65. This was a difficult task, and accuracy was incentivized in a performance-weighted lottery system.[1] Results showed that participants tended to underestimate how much extra the older saver would need to save per month in order to reach the same total by 65, suggesting that they again underestimated the total amount saved by the younger individual.

This evidence for consistent underestimation of summation has at least two critical implications for retirement saving. First, and perhaps most obviously, people tend to underestimate the importance of beginning to save early, even with small amounts. They are likely to judge doing so as being less effective than waiting until they can save a bit more per month, as they fail to appreciate how much they will accumulate by retirement. This underappreciation is indeed well documented but has typically been attributed to exponential growth bias (e.g., Goda et al. 2019).

By contrast, we argue that undersum bias interacts with exponential growth bias but is distinct from it. In McGowan et al. (2019), we calculated the implied retirement fund from each response in the money-match task and plotted these as cumulative distributions, shown in Figure 4.1. If responses were noisy but unbiased, we would expect half the responses to lie below the dotted horizontal line denoting 'correct response' in each condition and half to lie above. In fact, only in the lump sum 3% condition is the split close to even. In the other three conditions, the majority of responses reflect underestimation. Moreover, the magnitude of underestimation is greater for regular saving (RS) compared to lump sum saving (LS) and greater for the higher interest rate (7%) versus the lower interest rate (3%). The magnitude and prevalence of underestimation in the 7% RS condition is notably greater than the 7% LS condition, and the difference between 7% RS and 3% RS is greater than the difference between both LS conditions. This interaction effect, confirmed in regression analyses, implies that

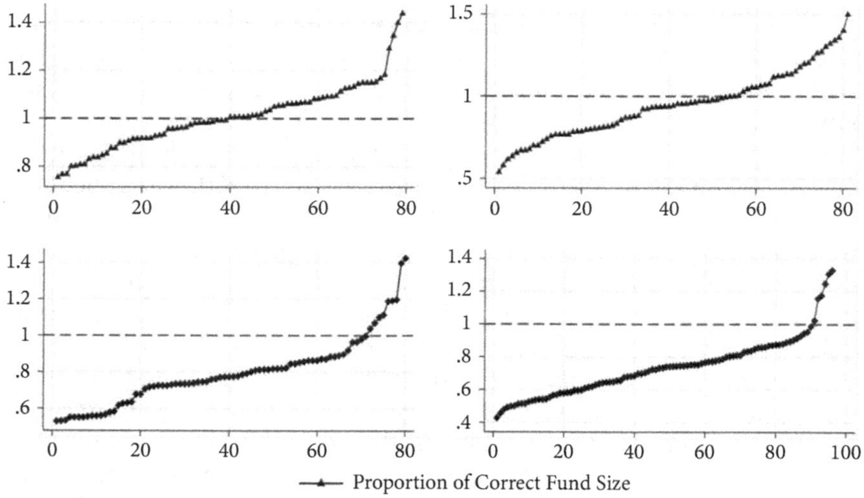


**Figure 4.1** Four cumulative distributions of fund sizes derived from responses in the money-match task

*Notes:* Left column is lump sum (LS) conditions, right is regular saving (RS). Top row is 3% interest rate condition; bottom row is 7%. The difference between the two LS lines can be attributed solely to exponential growth bias. The RS lines illustrate more prevalent and severe underestimation, which can be attributed to undersum bias.
*Source:* Authors' calculations.

individuals are likely to delay initiating retirement savings or to contribute inadequately, missing out on the opportunity to harness the potential of both accumulation and compound interest.

The second implication concerns how consumers might forecast their retirement expenditures (Hurd and Rohwedder this volume). Accurately estimating future financial requirements is a daunting challenge for many trying to plan for retirement, and our evidence suggests that when consumers attempt to do so, they tend to underestimate the expenses they will face. This may become particularly problematic as an increasing proportion of the population carry mortgages into retirement (e.g., Mayer 2017). Relatedly, undersum bias might interfere with peoples' consideration of unexpected expenses that can arise during retirement (such as unexpected health care costs or requiring additional help at home).

## Risk

Next, we speculate on the role of undersum bias with respect to the probability of facing a financial shock. We have less direct evidence for its existence specifically with respect to saving behavior, but many have documented that people struggle to estimate risk accurately. People often underestimate the probability of bad outcomes while simultaneously overestimating their ability to handle ones that arise (Jefferson et al. 2017; Shepperd et al. 2017). A related literature links overconfidence regarding financial capabilities to early withdrawals from retirement funds (Lee and Hanna 2020). If these tendencies also apply when considering the need to save for retirement, it is likely consumers will underestimate the likelihood of experiencing a financial shock when they are close to or in retirement.

That said, financial shocks tend to be low-probability events (Caldara et al. 2016), so misjudging the likelihood of any one individual shock might be detrimental for only a small minority of consumers. Nevertheless, concern arises when considering the accumulation of multiple low-probability shocks. For example, the probability of needing to finance home repairs in any one year of retirement may be low, but the risk accumulates over time. Moreover, the individual probabilities of, for example, facing a market downturn that significantly devalues assets or of losing one's job in the years approaching retirement may be low, but these individual probabilities add up, leading people to be more likely to face at least one of them. The same logic applies to all possible shocks. In other words, the disjunctive probability that at least one financial shock will be experienced is far higher than is likely to be perceived (where disjunctive probability is the probability that at least one of several events occurs).

There is a wealth of literature from psychology showing that estimates of cumulative risk are inaccurate and often biased (Kahneman and Tversky 1982; Knäuper et al. 2005; McCloy et al. 2010). Disjunctive probabilities, in particular, tend to be underestimated (Bar-Hillel 1973; Brockner et al. 2002). For example, people often fail to realize that although the probability of pregnancy when using contraceptives is very low, it accumulates and hence rises over time (Doyle 1997). Evidence on intuitions about cumulative risk confirms that people's judgments are closer to an averaging of risk rather than a summation (Carlson and Yates 1989).

Underestimating the accumulation of financial shock probabilities thus poses an additional challenge for motivating retirement saving. Individuals may perceive their future financial security as less vulnerable than it is and therefore save too little. For example, when deliberating about whether to make additional pension contributions today versus relying on future Social Security payments, consumers may reason that such Social Security payments will suffice to maintain a reasonable standard of living. Yet if they fail to accurately estimate the probability of facing at least one financial shock, they will be left with less than expected for day-to-day needs. Even if they recognize future financial shocks, undersum bias may then lead them to reason that they can procrastinate about making additional pension contributions and that saving a bit extra later in life is the equivalent to saving a bit less now.

## Interventions to Overcome Undersum Bias

What if anything could be done to improve savers' estimates? To address this question, in a different experiment, we tested the efficacy of a potential debiasing tool (McGowan et al. 2019). For the main task in the experiment, participants were again presented with two individuals, but this time the task was easier. They were shown full information (the age at which both individuals began saving and their monthly contributions), and participants were told the annual interest rate was 5%. For example, they were told that John started saving €280 per month at age 32, whereas Charlie started saving €560 per month at age 44; both had no withdrawals, fees, or deductions. Their task was to judge whether John or Charlie was likely to have saved more by age 65. Consistently choosing the older saver (who always saves more per month) would be evidence of undersum bias (with exponential growth bias).

Before completing this task, half the participants were randomized to use a computerized, interactive calculator designed to debias their estimates of money growth. On one side of the screen, participants could input a starting age and monthly contribution amount. On the other side, they could input an (older) age only, and the calculator generated the monthly amount required for both saving plans to have the same fund size at 65. Hence, the calculator answered the question: 'If I start saving later, how much would I need to save per month?' Participants were walked through some examples before given free access to the tool for a set amount of time.

Our results showed strong bias toward thinking that saving more per month later in life would generate a higher total, compared to saving less but starting earlier. Overall, 81% of responses were correct when the older saver was the correct response, but accuracy fell to 70% for 'younger correct' trials.[2] Figure 4.2 shows that the gap narrowed most dramatically on the difficult trials whereas the easy trials were subject to a ceiling effect in performance.

Nevertheless, participants who had used the debiasing tool prior to engaging with the task did display less bias. This is illustrated in Figure 4.2, which plots the proportion of trials answered correctly by difficulty level for the control and the calculator conditions. The trials where the older saver had more saved at age 65 are marked by squares, and circles denote the proportion correct when the younger saver had more at 65. One message from the figure is that people consistently underestimate the final fund size, as the 'older correct' trials have a consistently higher hit rate. The level of accuracy was generally high, with 2,448 of the 3,240 trials answered correctly. We attribute this to a combination of exponential growth bias and undersum bias. The second message is that the money calculator reduced the bias, as shown by the smaller gap in the figure (older correct—younger correct).

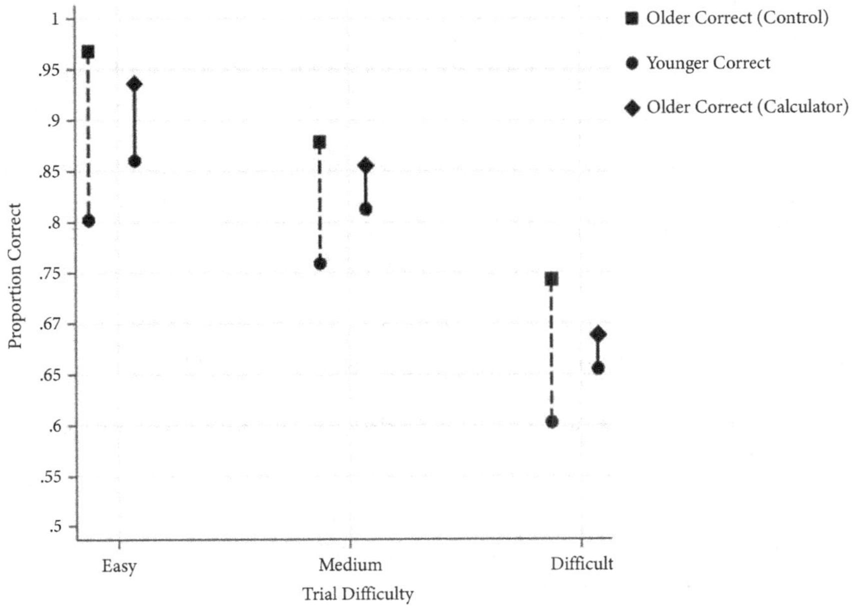


**Figure 4.2** Proportion correct by trial type and trial difficulty for control and money calculator conditions

*Note:* The money calculator reduced the extent of underestimation, as illustrated by the higher proportion correct on younger correct trials.
*Source:* Authors' calculations.

Although the tool did not fully mitigate people's tendency to underestimate, just a few minutes of using our interactive calculator more than halved the bias.

The interactive debiasing calculator was designed for scalable implementation as it could be easily adapted on any consumer website. To test whether the tool would work in the real world, we set out to test the tool in a field trial (Timmons et al. 2022). The aim here was to encourage precautionary saving (i.e., 'rainy day' saving), and it was conducted on a sample of over 160,000 retail bank customers in Ireland.[3] Following a review of relevant literature and analysis of existing survey microdata, we settled on two interventions that sought to motivate precautionary saving.

The first incorporated our debiasing calculator (McGowan et al. 2019). The target account was the bank's 'GoalSaver' account. Similar to a pension saving account, the account required customers to set up an automatic monthly payment (i.e., direct debit) of between €20 and €2,000. There were two arms to the trial. The first was a communications campaign, in which customers who had consented to receiving communications from the bank received emails to encourage saving (we discuss these communications in greater detail below). The second was a test of 'organic' traffic to the account's web application form (i.e., customers who accessed the form unprompted). For both arms, we tested a 'behaviorally enhanced' version of the bank's existing application form.

We made minor changes to the form, including changing the order in which questions were asked (e.g., we moved the savings start date question to earlier in the form) and incorporating basic financial advice on relevant questions (e.g., to choose to start saving soon after a regular pay date). The primary change, however, was to add the debiasing calculator. Consumers had to first input their target savings total (i.e., their goal), following financial advice to aim to save to cover three months of expenses. Consumers randomized into the treatment group were asked whether they would like to use the interactive calculator to help them figure out how much to save per month. Those who opted in were asked to input into the calculator either a target date for reaching their goal or how much they were considering saving per month. The calculator then generated the missing value (i.e., how much to save per month or when they would reach their savings goal, respectively), factoring in the low level of annual interest at the time of the study (0.25%). Consumers could use the calculator as much as they liked.

Results showed a positive effect of the enhanced application form on the number of accounts opened over the six-month trial period. In the sample of over 160,000 who received the email communication, 0.29% of the control group opened the target savings account, but this increased to 0.37% of those with access to the enhanced savings form (i.e., a 28% increase in accounts opened).[4] The effect was even stronger among organic traffic to the web application form: the enhanced form boosted the conversion rate from 3.4% to 4.7% (a 38% increase). Google Analytics data from the web form showed that significantly more of those who ultimately opened the account had used the debiasing calculator (63.0%) compared to those who did not ultimately open the account (56.5%).

We were further able to test whether the treatment influenced the amount saved per month. Although intuitively an intervention to mitigate undersum bias should result in consumers showing greater appreciation for saving more per month, our (pre-registered) hypothesis for this analysis was non-directional. We reasoned that although the enhanced form should increase appreciation for the importance of saving, an increase by some participants could be offset by growth in the proportion of lower-income consumers (who were a target population) completing the form, or indeed from consumers who otherwise might have procrastinated saving from realizing the benefits of starting to save lower amounts earlier. In other words, increasing the participation rate could reduce the average amount saved because lower-income individuals are less likely to be able to save. Indeed, results from the communications campaign arm showed a slight but non-significant increase in monthly deposits among the treatment group (€250 per month versus approximately €225 per month). In the organic arm, however, those who accessed the enhanced form saved *less* per month (€200 per month versus €280 per month among the control).

Available socio-demographic data provided some insight into this tendency toward lower monthly deposits. An examination of the association between consumer income and treatment group showed that the enhanced form had substantially stronger effects on lower-income consumers: there was a 120% increase in account openings among the lowest income group, with the strength of the effect declining monotonically to zero for the higher income group. Hence the reason for lower deposits in the organic traffic is explained by consumers having less disposable income to save.

The communications arm of the trial also tested an intervention designed to overcome our more speculative manifestation of undersum bias: the tendency to understate the accumulated risk of financial shocks. This treatment was based solely on informing consumers about the risk of financial shocks. We developed an infographic to communicate the risk of facing a financial shock in a given year based on principles from the psychological literature on risk communication (e.g., Spiegelhalter 2017). The infographic was assigned at random to half of the bank customers in the communications arm, and it featured three animated GIFs. The first GIF employed natural frequencies to communicate the proportion of the public who face a financial shock in a given year (six in 10). The second showed a grid of people experiencing different types of shocks via icons (e.g., a car icon to indicate car problems). The end sequence of the animation showed that only a minority had avoided any financial shock. The third GIF illustrated that three in 10 face more than one shock per year. The data for the infographic were accurate and based on responses to a 1,000-person survey run to inform the trial. The email ended with a call to action to open a savings account. Cookies allowed us to track whether customers randomized into the treatment group accessed the savings form at a later date. The control communication was the bank's planned email about the importance of saving for financial well-being, which also incorporated GIFs relevant to saving but did not feature information on the risk of financial shocks.

The risk accumulation treatment was manipulated orthogonally to the application form treatment, in a 2 (form: behaviorally enhanced versus control) x 2 (email: cumulative risk versus financial well-being) between-group design in the communications arm. This design allowed us to isolate the effect of this novel communication treatment. Results showed that compared to the control group, those who received the risk accumulation communication were significantly more likely to have opened a savings account by the end of the trial. The effect size was comparable to the effect of the debiasing calculator, albeit slightly weaker (20% increase in uptake; 0.35% of treated customers opened an account versus 0.29% in the control group). Although we hoped for an additive effect of the treatments (i.e., a stronger effect among those who received the risk communication and accessed the enhanced application form), none was observed. This perhaps indicated a ceiling in the potential for behavioral interventions to increase savings account uptake.

Of course, it was important in the trial to not just assume customers had benefitted from increased savings account uptake, so we further assessed the evidence in the trial for negative spillovers. We had access to indicators of debt in the partner bank (i.e., any credit products or arrears on their current accounts) as well as any other savings accounts held with the same bank. Importantly, the partner bank offered the highest interest rate at the time of trial, meaning participants were unlikely to open accounts at other institutions. Fortunately, we observed no evidence of negative spillovers. In fact, there was suggestive evidence that participants in the treatment groups were less likely to hold any form of debt at the end of the six-month period, perhaps implying that the precautionary savings account was functioning as intended.

Both of our treatments (the debiasing calculator and the cumulative risk communication) targeted undersum bias, albeit different manifestations of it. To our knowledge, these treatments are the first to successfully increase precautionary savings rates in a country with widespread access to banking infrastructure. Of further note is that the relative effect sizes we observed are far larger than typical for successful 'nudge' type interventions. That is, we observed increases in account uptake of between 20% and 40%, compared to a standard relative effect size of just 8% (DellaVigna and Linos 2022).

These interventions are also the first to target undersum bias in the field. We provide evidence that the debiasing calculator is beneficial for consumers, although we cannot perfectly isolate its effect given the combination of lighter-touch interventions. We also show that underestimating the cumulative probability of a financial shock leads to undersaving—a novel idea not tested previously in a financial context.

## Conclusions and Opportunities for Future Research

Ensuring desired quality of life in retirement requires consumers to estimate the kinds of expenses they will face in later life and to evaluate how to accumulate sufficient pension assets to cover those expenses. Bias in these estimates produces asymmetric risk: if consumers apply a precautionary principle and save too much, they could afford more luxuries later in life at the expense of present needs and wants. Nevertheless, saving too much does not appear to be a prevalent policy problem. Instead, many consumers around the world appear to save too little, and we present evidence for a bias that can help explain why.

Undersum bias describes the systematic tendency to underestimate accumulation. We show that it matters not only for estimating the accumulation of expenses and the potential for financial shocks but also for how regular savings accumulate. Consumers are thus likely to underestimate their expenses later in life, and they also reason that saving earlier will have less of an impact than it in fact does, even without incorporating compound interest. We present real-world evidence for interventions to help people overcome the bias, including a boost to help consumers figure out how much to save per month in the form of an interactive online calculator, and a communication tool to help them more accurately estimate the risk of facing financial shocks.

The behavioral economics literature on pension saving has thus far focused on complex psychological phenomena such as hyperbolic discounting and exponential growth bias. The cognitive ability to intuitively generate accurate approximations of summation seems deceptively simple by comparison, so undersum bias appears to have been overlooked. Evidence for its existence has emerged relatively recently, with much work still in progress. Interestingly, there is almost a 'multiple discovery' component to undersum bias whereby evidence has emerged independently from different research teams over the recent past.

This evidence offers several avenues for future research. First, and perhaps most straightforwardly, there is considerable scope for further exploration of the implications of undersum bias for saving behavior. Scheibehenne (2019) investigated only shopping behaviors, while McGowan et al. (2022) and Goswami et al. (2021) mainly focused on spending behaviors. McGowan et al. (2019) explored undersum bias in pension saving, but this was not the authors' primary target. Our conclusion is that further studies are required to explicitly investigate the implications of undersum bias for saving behavior. Multiple potential angles are available, such as asking whether undersum bias demotivates saving due to consumers underestimating forecasted expenditure needs, underestimating forecasted saving accumulation, or both.

Second, and relatedly, our thesis that undersum bias may also apply to how people consider the risk of financial shocks has important implications for precautionary saving, but the evidence is still circumstantial. Direct testing of this hypothesis using controlled diagnostic laboratory studies is needed.

Third, there is considerable scope for developing interventions to help consumers overcome the bias. McGowan et al. (2019) and

Timmons et al. (2022) showed that interactive calculators can help, but their effect diminishes (rather than entirely mitigates) the bias. Policymakers and other stakeholders interested in helping consumers make welfare-improving decisions would thus benefit from investing in research to develop boosts and other tools to help mitigate undersum and other relevant biases (e.g., Hertwig and Grüne-Yanoff 2017). Such interventions could also benefit from controlled diagnostic experiments to identify relevant psychological mechanisms (Lunn 2019).

## Acknowledgments

The authors thank their collaborators Pete Lunn, Deirdre Robertson, and Eleanor Denny for many useful conversations on these topics. They also acknowledge research funding by independent commissions from the Pensions Authority of Ireland, the Competition and Consumer Protection Commission, and a grant from the Irish Research Council (GOIPG/2019/66). They are also grateful to Bank of Ireland for facilitating the savings field trial.

## Notes

1. Specifically, for each response in the top half of the sample in terms of accuracy, the participant got an extra draw into the lottery for a €50 voucher.
2. The average accuracy rate on easy trials was 89%, for medium trials it fell to 82%, and was 67% for the difficult trials where the smaller fund size was approximately one-tenth smaller than the larger one at age 65.
3. The trial was commissioned by Ireland's Competition and Consumer Protection Commission, which had identified undersaving as a target behavior for improving financial well-being in Ireland. We partnered with a high-street retail bank, Bank of Ireland, to implement the trial.
4. Although saving rates are low, we were assured by our partners at the bank that such absolute effects are normal for communications campaign; we could not know, for example, how many customers had even opened the email.

## References

Anobile, G., G. M. Cicchini, and D. C. Burr (2012). 'Linear Mapping of Numbers onto Space Requires Attention.' *Cognition*, 122(3): 454–459.

Bar-Hillel, M. (1973). 'On the Subjective Probability of Compound Events.' *Organizational Behavior and Human Performance*, 9(3): 396–406.

Beshears, J., J. Choi, D. Laibson, and P. Maxted (2022). 'Present Bias Causes and Then Dissipates Auto-enrollment Savings Effects.' *AEA Papers and Proceedings*, 112: 136–141.

Brockner, J., S. Paruchuri, L. C. Idson, and E. T. Higgins (2002). 'Regulatory Focus and the Probability Estimates of Conjunctive and Disjunctive Events.' *Organizational Behavior and Human Decision Processes*, 87(1): 5–24.

Burr, D. C., G. Anobile, and R. Arrighi (2018). 'Psychophysical Evidence for the Number Sense.' *Philosophical Transactions of the Royal Society B: Biological Sciences*, 373(1740): 20170045.

Caldara, D., C. Fuentes-Albero, S. Gilchrist, and E. Zakrajšek (2016). 'The Macroeconomic Impact of Financial and Uncertainty Shocks.' *European Economic Review*, 88: 185–207.

Carlson, B. W. and J. F. Yates (1989). 'Disjunction Errors in Qualitative Likelihood Judgment.' *Organizational Behavior and Human Decision Processes*, 44(3): 368–379.

Choi, J. J., D. Laibson, B. C. Madrian, and A. Metrick (2002). 'Defined Contribution Pensions: Plan Rules, Participant Choices, and the Path of Least Resistance.' In J. M. Poterba, ed., *Tax Policy and the Economy, Volume 16*. Cambridge, MA: MIT Press, pp. 67–113.

Christandl, F. and D. Fetchenhauer (2009). 'How Laypeople and Experts Misperceive the Effect of Economic Growth.' *Journal of Economic Psychology*, 30(3): 381–392.

Dehaene, S. (1992). 'Varieties of Numerical Abilities.' *Cognition*, 44(1–2): 1–42.

Dehaene, S., V. Izard, E. Spelke, and P. Pica (2008). 'Log or Linear? Distinct Intuitions of the Number Scale in Western and Amazonian Indigene Cultures.' *Science*, 320(5880): 1217–1220.

DellaVigna, S. and E. Linos (2022). 'RCTs to Scale: Comprehensive Evidence from Two Nudge Units.' *Econometra*, 90(1): 81–116.

Doyle, J. K. (1997). 'Judging Cumulative Risk.' *Journal of Applied Social Psychology*, 27(6): 500–524.

Eisenstein, E. M. and S. J. Hoch (2005). 'Intuitive Compounding: Framing, Temporal Perspective, and Expertise.' Unpublished manuscript.

Goda, G. S., M. Levy, C. F. Manchester, A. Sojourner, and J. Tasoff (2019). 'Predicting Retirement Savings Using Survey Measures of Exponential-Growth Bias and Present Bias.' *Economic Inquiry*, 57(3): 1636–1658.

Goswami, I., A. Greenberg, D. Schley (2021). 'Undersum Bias.' dx.doi.org/10.2139/ssrn.3954282

Hastings, J. and O. S. Mitchell (2020). 'How Financial Literacy and Impatience Shape Retirement Wealth and Investment Behaviors.' *Journal of Pension Economics & Finance*, 19(1): 1–20.

Hertwig, R. and T. Grüne-Yanoff (2017). 'Nudging and Boosting: Steering or Empowering Good Decisions.' *Perspectives on Psychological Science*, 12(6): 973–986.

Jefferson, A., L. Bortolotti, and B. Kuzmanovic (2017). 'What is Unrealistic Optimism?' *Consciousness and Cognition*, 50: 3–11.

Kahneman, D. and A. Tversky (1982). 'Variants of Uncertainty.' *Cognition*, 11(2): 143–157.

Knäuper, B., R. Kornik, K. Atkinson, C. Guberman, and C. Aydin (2005). 'Motivation Influences the Underestimation of Cumulative Risk.' *Personality and Social Psychology Bulletin*, 31(11): 1511–1523.

Lee, S. T. and S. D. Hanna (2020). 'Financial Knowledge Overconfidence and Early Withdrawals from Retirement Accounts.' *Financial Planning Review*, 3(2): e1091.

Levy, M. R. and J. Tasoff (2017). 'Exponential-Growth Bias and Overconfidence.' *Journal of Economic Psychology*, 58: 1–14.

Lunn, P. D. (2019). 'Nudger Beware: Diagnosis Precedes Remedy.' *Journal of Behavioral Economics for Policy*, 3(S): 23–26.

Mathers, C. D., G. A. Stevens, T. Boerma, R. A. White, and M. I. Tobias (2015). 'Causes of International Increases in Older Age Life Expectancy.' *The Lancet*, 385(9967): 540–548.

Mayer, C. J. (2017). 'Housing, Mortgages, and Retirement.' In L. Fennell and B. J. Keys, eds., *Evidence and Innovation in Housing Law and Policy*. Cambridge: Cambridge University Press, pp. 203–230.

McCloy, R., R. M. J. Byrne, and P. N. Johnson-Laird (2010). 'Understanding Cumulative Risk.' *Quarterly Journal of Experimental Psychology*, 63(3): 499–515.

McGowan, F., E. Denny, and P. Lunn (2022). 'Consistent Underestimation in the Intuitive Summation of Monetary Amounts.' dx.doi.org/10.2139/ssrn.4021708

McGowan, F. P. and P. D. Lunn (2020). 'Supporting Decision-Making in Retirement Planning: Do Diagrams on Pension Benefit Statements Help?' *Journal of Pension Economics & Finance*, 19(3): 323–343.

McGowan, F. P., P. Lunn, and D. A. Robertson (2019). 'Underestimation of Money Growth and Pensions: Experimental Investigations.' Economic and Social Research Institute Working Paper No. 611.

Mitchell, O. S. and S. P. Utkus (2004). 'Lessons from Behavioral Finance for Retirement Plan Design.' In O. S. Mitchell and S. P. Utkus, eds., *Pension Design and Structure: New Lessons from Behavioral Finance*. Oxford: Oxford University Press, pp. 3–41.

Scheibehenne, B. (2019). 'The Psychophysics of Number Integration: Evidence from the Lab and from the Field.' *Decision*, 6(1): 61–76.

Shepperd, J. A., G. Pogge, and J. L. Howell (2017). 'Assessing the Consequences of Unrealistic Optimism: Challenges and Recommendations.' *Consciousness and Cognition*, 50: 69–78.

Song, C. (2020). 'Financial Illiteracy and Pension Contributions: A Field Experiment on Compound Interest in China.' *Review of Financial Studies*, 33(2): 916–949.

Spiegelhalter, D. (2017). 'Risk and Uncertainty Communication.' *Annual Review of Statistics and Its Application*, 4: 31–60.

Stango, V. and J. Zinman (2009). 'Exponential Growth Bias and Household Finance.' *Journal of Finance*, 64(6): 2807–2849.

Timmons, S., D. Robertson, and P. Lunn (2022). 'Combining Nudges and Boosts to Increase Precautionary Saving.' The Economic and Social Research Institute Working Paper No. 722.

Wagenaar, W. A. and S.D. Sagaria (1975). 'Misperception of Exponential Growth.' *Perception & Psychophysics*, 18: 416–422.

Wagenaar, W. A. and H. Timmers (1979). 'The Pond-and-Duckweed Problem: Three Experiments on the Misperception of Exponential Growth.' *Acta Psychologica*, 43(3): 239–251.

Chapter 5

# Deepening Our Understanding of Savings Automation in Retirement and Nonretirement Contexts

*Alycia Chin, Heidi Johnson, and Brianna L. Middlewood*

Savings are essential for weathering financial shocks and planning for the future. Although Americans' personal savings rates have varied substantially over the last 60 years, many people today lack sufficient savings. In 2023, only 57% of households in the United States had enough savings to cover at least three months of living expenses (Financial Health Network 2023). The Employee Benefit Research Institute (2023) reported that only one in five Americans felt confident they would have enough money to live comfortably in retirement, and only 27% of retirees felt very confident that they would live comfortably throughout their retirement years. These statistics suggest that a significant number of Americans are neither prepared for short-term shocks nor for retirement, which could lead to lower financial well-being, delayed retirement, and an increased strain on public pension and welfare systems.

For years, researchers have worked to identify barriers to saving, to test interventions to increase saving, and to examine the long-term benefits of those interventions. A common factor driving these interventions is automating part of the savings process. By 'automating,' we mean that an aspect of the savings process happens without the consumer needing to take action. The specific implementation of automation may vary—with different variations addressing different consumer tendencies.[1]

In the retirement space, automation often includes *automatic enrollment* into a defined contribution retirement savings plan (e.g., Beshears et al. 2010). With automatic enrollment, employees are included in a program that deducts money from their paychecks and places it into a 401(k) or similar type of tax-advantaged retirement account unless they opt out. Automatic enrollment of employees into retirement savings programs can boost enrollment by as much as 86% (Derby et al. 2023) and push overall participation rates up to 91% (Clark

Alycia Chin, Heidi Johnson, and Brianna L. Middlewood, *Deepening Our Understanding of Savings Automation in Retirement and Nonretirement Contexts.* In: *Retirement Saving, Investment, and Spending.* Edited by: Olivia S. Mitchell and Nikolai Roussanov, Oxford University Press. © Pension Research Council, The Wharton School, The University of Pennsylvania (2026). DOI: 10.1093/oso/9780197845752.003.0005

and Young 2021). Automatic enrollment is often paired with *automatic escalation*, which increases the amount deducted from paychecks over time. Hence, as time passes, retirement contributions can rise. Both forms of automation increase savings in a way that requires little consumer effort.

To automate savings outside of employer provided retirement plans, consumers have to take some action. Depending on their financial institution's capabilities, consumers can set up *automatic transfers* from their paychecks or from one account to another, including automatic investment purchases, or opt for *automatic rebalancing* of investment account assets to achieve a given asset allocation. Using these means, the effort to save is greatly reduced because consumers make an automation decision once. As long as automation remains in place, consumers will continue to save with no additional effort required.

The 2022 Setting Every Community Up for Retirement Enhancement (SECURE) 2.0 Act is evidence that policymakers now recognize the power of automation. The Act aims to extend the reach of automation features to improve retirement savings by requiring that many retirement plans (including many new 401(k) and 403(b) plans, multiple employer plans, and pooled employer plans) automatically enroll employees in these plans. It also imposes default contribution rates at a minimum of 3% of salaries and automatic escalation of contributions at 1% annually, capping at 15% after 2025. The SECURE 2.0 Act may also boost Americans' liquid emergency savings, as it permits employers to automatically enroll employees into emergency savings accounts linked to their retirement plan.[2] Emergency savings accounts—perhaps especially emergency savings accounts with automatic transfers—may increase employees' chances of weathering a financial shock and reduce the need to make costly withdrawals from retirement savings or take on debt.

Importantly, however, the regulatory requirements of the SECURE 2.0 Act do not apply to every employer-sponsored retirement plan and do not guarantee retirement plans for every individual. For an increasing number of Americans working at jobs where retirement plans are not available—including some part-time workers and independent contractors—the corresponding benefits of expanded savings automation will not be realized. Given the emphasis on savings automation in the SECURE 2.0 Act, but also in recognition of the limitations of this intervention, our discussion aims to foster research and thinking regarding saving in the presence and absence of automation for different types of savings and consumer groups. To this end, we discuss:

- The benefits of savings automation (see Reuter this volume) and recent findings that suggest a smaller, though still positive, benefit of automation.
- Variation in the effects of automation by demographic and psychological characteristics, including an extension of previous work on time preferences.
- The need for research examining nonretirement savings automation, long-term retirement outcomes, wealth inequalities, and the impact of policies like SECURE 2.0.

## The Rationale for Savings Automation

As a behavioral intervention, savings automation can help consumers save more by circumventing several well-documented consumer tendencies including status quo bias and present bias. Consumers show a tendency to maintain the status quo (Samuelson and Zeckhauser 1988), so those not currently saving may require strong motivation to start or processes that make saving easier. With automation, consumers can save with reduced effort, as they do not need to repeatedly act. This reduction in effort is important for present-biased consumers, whose tendency to prioritize the present means they may never set aside the time or money to save for the future (Ashraf et al. 2006; Meier and Sprenger 2010) and may spend their income before making the decision to save. For those with disposable income available to save but who are present focused, the reduction in effort for saving introduced by automation may be especially helpful. Once the initial enrollment decision is made, people are unlikely to stop saving for the same reason it was difficult to start—inertia.

Automation may also lead to inattention that can be beneficial for long-term investments, such as those used for retirement saving. Specifically, research on individual consumers finds that those who trade the most tend to have lower returns than those who adopt a 'set it and forget it' strategy with their investments (Barber and Odean 2001). In addition, investors are rarely successful at 'timing' the market—that is, buying low and selling high—thereby achieving superior returns (Barber and Odean 2013). For these reasons, both academic research and popular advice tend to suggest that people invest in passive indexes rather than actively managed funds (Choi 2022). Although there may be a downside to inattention inherent in automation (e.g., account abandonment; discussed below), in the context of trading, it may also help investors avoid overtrading and suboptimal market timing. The chapter by Reuter (this volume) elaborates on the portfolio management mistakes targeted by investment-related interventions.

## Savings Automation Benefits Participation, Contribution Rates, and Net Saving

Consistent with the behavioral rationale just discussed, recent research (summarized in Table 5.1) generally shows a positive relationship between automation interventions and consumer outcomes.[3] For example, researchers find that automatic enrollment in employer-sponsored retirement plans significantly increases employees' participation in those plans, contributions, and net savings (Beshears et al. 2022; Cribb and Emmerson 2021; Falk and Karamcheva 2023; Derby et al. 2023). Furthermore, automatic escalation helps raise contribution rates for automatically enrolled participants (Beshears et al. 2017; Clark and Young 2021). Although the literature on nonretirement savings is smaller, a quasi-experiment in the UK found that automatic enrollment increases this kind of saving (Berk et al. 2022). Automation also appears to be associated with greater nonretirement savings for those with very low income (Newmeyer et al. 2021).

## Not All Consequences of Savings Automation Are Positive

Despite the power of automating steps in the savings process, it is not necessarily a sufficient response to mitigate savings challenges. In this section, we discuss ways in which initial participation rates or savings amounts typically examined in prior research (see Table 5.1) may provide an overly simplistic view of the benefits of savings automation.

Automatic savings into retirement accounts could lead to saving either too little or too much. Starting with the risk of saving too little, a potential challenge is that participants frequently perceive the default choice of contribution rate as a recommendation from their employer (Madrian and Shea 2001). This means that the path of least resistance in automation may include signing up at a contribution rate lower than what an individual might have selected without a default. Indeed, in a study by Clark and Young (2021) of newly hired employees eligible for 520 different retirement plans in 2017, 2018, and 2019, the average retirement contribution rate after three years for plans with no automatic enrollment (i.e., no default contribution rate) was 7.6%, in contrast to 6.6% for plans with automatic enrollment (and no automatic escalation). The average contribution rate for plans with automatic enrollment was therefore lower, despite plan participants having higher median income than employees participating in the voluntary enrollment plans (Clark and Young 2021).

The problem of lower savings rates with automatic enrollment may be mitigated by pairing automatic enrollment with automatic savings escalation, which has been effective at increasing contribution rates

TABLE 5.1 Review of Recent Literature on Savings Automation and Associated Financial Welfare Outcomes

| Authors | Behavioral constraint or strategy | Design or methodology | Outcomes examined | Subgroups examined for differential effectiveness of strategy (if any) | Selected results |
|---|---|---|---|---|---|
| **Retirement** | | | | | |
| Burke et al. (2015) | AE in DC plan | Survey data from Health and Retirement Survey (HRS), (2008 and 2010 survey waves) (employee AE is self-reported) | Participation, contribution, opt out from AE plans | • Age<br>• Marital status<br>• Income<br>• Education<br>• Wealth | AE is associated with an 11-percentage point increase in plan participation and is effective at encouraging lower-income and less educated individuals to participate. Participants who opt-in are more likely than AE individuals to continue making contributions. |
| Goda et al. (2020) | AE in Thrift Savings Plan for employees of the US Office of Personnel Management | Merged survey and administrative data. Survey collected in April 2017 | Participation, contributions (including contributions at default rate) | • Long-term discounting<br>• Present bias<br>• Financial literacy<br>• Exponential growth bias | AE increases savings among individuals with low financial literacy. Present bias predicts keeping the default contribution rate under AE. |
| Quinby et al. (2020) | AE in OregonSaves, an individual retirement account (IRA) program | Administrative data (2018 to 2019) (no comparison group) | Participation, preretirement withdrawals | None | Participation rate in OregonSaves is estimated at 48%–67%. Twenty percent of employees made at least one pre-retirement withdrawal ($1,000 on average). |

*Continued*

Table 5.1 *Continued*

| Authors | Behavioral constraint or strategy | Design or methodology | Outcomes examined | Subgroups examined for differential effectiveness of strategy (if any) | Selected results |
|---|---|---|---|---|---|
| Chalmers et al. (2025) | AE in OregonSaves, an IRA program | Administrative data (2018–2020) (no comparison group) | Participation, contributions, amount saved, opt-out rates | • Positive Balance<br>• Age | Younger employees in larger firms are less likely to opt out of OregonSaves. Overall, 34.3% of workers had positive account balances. |
| Cribb and Emmerson (2021) | AE in pension plan in the UK | Comparison of AE and non-AE employees in 4/2016 using panel survey data from annual survey of hours and earnings (data between 2012 and 2016). All employees work for 'small employers,' or those with between two and 29 employees (in 2012). | Participation, contribution rates | • Gender<br>• Earnings<br>• Age<br>• Years with employer | AE increases pension participation to 70% (from 26%) among small employers. There are larger gains for younger employees and those with shorter job tenures. |
| Hung et al. (2021) | AE in company-sponsored DC retirement plans | Vanguard record-keeping data of employees hired between 2010 and 2013, excluding those in plans that changed from voluntary enrollment to AE after employees were hired. | Taking a cash distribution, rolling over balances, and aggregate retirement savings (net of distributions) after job separation | None | Workers who separate from their jobs and were automatically enrolled are 19 percentage points more likely to take a cash distribution than those who enrolled in an opt-in plan. Those in AE plans are more likely to have at least $500 in retirement savings balances after job separation (by 42 percentage points). |

| | | | | | |
|---|---|---|---|---|---|
| Clark and Young (2021) | AE in DC plan sponsors (voluntary enrollment plans versus AE plans) | Vanguard record keeping data (2017 to 2020). Sample consists of newly hired, eligible employees between 1/1/2017 and 12/31/2019 who were still employed by the plan sponsor as of 6/30/2020. | Participation, contribution, default portfolio allocation, loans from the plan | • Income<br>• Age<br>• Gender | AE increases participation to 91%, compared to 28% under voluntary enrollment. 90% of participants increase contribution rates over time and 86% under AE remain invested in the default fund (compared to 66% of individuals in voluntary enrollment). |
| Beshears et al. (2022) | AE in TSP for civilian employees of the US Army | Comparison of pre-AE employees (hired 8/1/2009 to 7/31/2010) and post-AE employees (hired 8/1/2010 to 7/31/2011). Semi-annual credit bureau data available 6/2007 to 12/2014. | Debt, auto debt, first mortgage debt, contributions, savings | • Low income<br>• Age <30<br>• High school education<br>• Black<br>• Hispanic<br>• Credit score <620 | AE increases cumulative contributions by 4.1% of annual salary. AE causes no significant change in credit scores, debt balances excluding auto debt and first mortgages. |
| Falk and Karamcheva (2023) | AE and employer match in TSP | Comparison of non-AE and AE employees hired before and after 8/2010. Administrative panel data from the TSP, which covers federal civilian workers (data available between 2008 and 2014). | Participation, contribution rates, portfolio allocations, balance, and balance-to-pay ratio | • Education level<br>• Race<br>• Gender<br>• Earnings | AE increased participation by 14%. It is associated with a larger increase in participation rates and contribution rates among men than women. The positive effect is stronger for bottom earning workers (vs. middle or top earners), less-educated workers (vs. more-educated), and for Black and Hispanic workers (vs. white). AE increased the balance-to-pay ratio for these groups. |

*Continued*

TABLE 5.1 *Continued*

| Authors | Behavioral constraint or strategy | Design or methodology | Outcomes examined | Subgroups examined for differential effectiveness of strategy (if any) | Selected results |
|---|---|---|---|---|---|
| Derby et al. (2023) | AE in company-sponsored DC retirement plans | Comparison of AE and non-AE employees, with date of AE varying by employer; sample is 2 years pre-AE and 1 year post-AE. Administrative data (available between 2010 and 2016). | Participation, contributions, savings rate, withdrawals, and net savings | Firms with 4 years of pre auto-enrollment data and 4 years post auto-enrollment adoption | AE increases participation by 86% and contributions by 51%. Employees are 33% more likely to take a nonrollover withdrawal. The estimated increase in net savings (i.e., after accounting for withdrawals) is 37%. |
| Beshears et al. (2024) | AE in the UK. | Comparison of AE and non-AE employees, with date of AE varying by employer. Sample covers approximately 649,000 individuals from 160,000 'small' employers (2–29 employees each) in the UK. Administrative data links pensions and credit files (three cross sections in 2016, 2017, and 2018). | Pension savings, unsecured debt, having a mortgage, mortgage balance | • Income<br>• Credit score<br>• Age | Each additional month after AE increases the average employee's pension savings by £32–£38, unsecured debt by £7, the likelihood of having a mortgage by 0.05 percentage points, and mortgage balances by £118. The additional savings generated through AE are partially offset by increases in unsecured debt (by £7). The net savings effects of automatic enrollment seem more positive for higher-income, those with higher credit scores, and older individuals. |

| | | | | | |
|---|---|---|---|---|---|
| **Nonretirement** | | | | | |
| Middlewood et al. (2018) | Automation of deposits into nonretirement savings account | Survey data from Consumer Financial Protection Bureau's National Financial Well-Being Survey (collected between October and December of 2016). | Liquid savings, Financial Well-Being, confidence in ability to raise $2000, difficulty of paying bills | • Time preferences ('doer' vs. 'planner') | Impatient consumers have less liquid savings, lower financial well-being, less confidence in their ability to raise $2000, and more difficulty paying bills, compared to those with stronger planner preferences. These differences between consumers with doer and planner preferences largely disappear for those who automate savings deposits. |
| Newmeyer et al. (2021) | Automation of deposits into nonretirement savings account and liquid savings account | **Study 1**: Survey data (Consumer Financial Protection Bureau's National Financial Well-Being Survey (collected between October and December of 2016) (no comparison group).<br>**Study 2**: Survey data from SSI, a consumer panel. | Reported saving (yes/no), amount of liquid savings | • Income level<br>• Personal savings orientation (PSO) level | **Study 1**: Savings automation is correlated with liquid savings for individuals with annual household income under $200,000.<br>**Study 2**: Savings automation is positively correlated with liquid savings for respondents with annual household income of $35,000 or less. For higher incomes, automation has no relationship with savings for those with low PSO levels and a negative relationship for those with high PSO levels. |
| Berk et al. (2022) | AE in payroll savings plan for new hires in the UK | Comparison of AE and non-AE employees hired before and after 11/1/2021. Administrative data (November 2020 to June 2022). | Participation, amount saved | • Age<br>• Gender<br>• Starting pay<br>• Role | AE increases participation in savings plan by 50 percentage points and balances by £68. Post-AE workers appear to follow a similar participation pattern regardless of age, gender, and starting pay. |

*Notes:* AE = automatic enrollment. PSO = personal savings orientation. TSP = Thrift Savings Plan.
*Source:* Authors' compilations.

(Benartzi and Thaler 2013; Thaler and Benartzi 2004). Automatic escalation is common in employer-provided retirement plans with automatic enrollment: Clark and Young (2021) reported that seven in 10 plans with automatic enrollment included an automatic annual increase in contribution rates. After three years, plans with both automatic enrollment and escalation had an average contribution rate of 7.9%, exceeding the 7.6% average contribution rate of plans without automatic enrollment. In addition, researchers examining data from 2017 to 2020 from a state-sponsored auto-IRA program, OregonSaves, demonstrated that increases in savings from the 5% default contribution rate to 6%–7% occurred as a direct result of the program's 1% annual automatic escalation (Chalmers et al. 2025).

A second reason for accumulating 'too little' retirement money could be that plan participants select overly conservative portfolio allocations. To address the effort and knowledge barriers that plan participants need to choose appropriate investments and rebalance them over time, many plans now automatically enroll participants in target date funds. These funds establish a combination of assets that automatically change to align the fund's risk level with the time remaining to an estimated retirement year. Target date funds are nearly universally the default allocation for employers who use automatic enrollment for their retirement plans. According to Clark and Young (2021), 99% of automatic enrollment plans had a target date fund as the default allocation. This is important because their data also showed that the default portfolio investment is sticky: 86% of participants who were automatically enrolled remained entirely invested in the default option. For a more complete discussion of target date funds, please refer to the chapter by Reuter (this volume).

An alternative challenge to retirement saving as a result of automation is that some consumers may save 'too much,' with a variety of downstream consequences. Recent literature has explored three outcomes: lower 401(k) balances due to early withdrawals and loans, higher levels of debt, and reduced contributions in subsequent jobs. Some early withdrawals from a 401(k) may not be the result of oversaving—instead reflecting the complexity of executing a rollover when workers leave their employers or an intentional strategy to use a retirement account to cover precautionary savings. Nevertheless, a traditional 401(k) can be a much more expensive option for precautionary savings than many other savings vehicles, as there are typically fees and penalties associated with early withdrawals.[4] In a study of an employer's implementation of automatic enrollment, Beshears et al. (2018) found that the share of plan participants who had taken at least one nonrollover withdrawal within eight years of being hired was higher for employees who were automatically enrolled in the retirement plan (58.6% of plan participants) versus employees who were not automatically enrolled (43.2%).[5]

Another option for people who need to access their retirement accounts for liquidity is to take a loan from the account, which must be repaid over time. Clark and Young (2021) reported a higher incidence of loans among those who were automatically enrolled (24%) versus those who enrolled voluntarily (20%). After taking withdrawals and loans into account, there is evidence that automatic enrollment continues to show an overall benefit to retirement savings. Beshears et al. (2018) claimed that after withdrawals and plan loans, 60% of savings remained, whereas Derby et al. (2023) estimated that automatic enrollment increased net savings by 1.02 percentage points (37%).

There is also mixed evidence that automatic enrollment increases debt. Beshears et al. (2022) explored whether consumers with retirement savings respond to liquidity shocks through other forms of borrowing. They found no evidence that automatic enrollment increased borrowing for most types of credit, before and after automatic enrollment took effect, with the exception of auto loan and first mortgage balances (in some cases). The net welfare effects for these types of loans are less clear, as people who take on auto and mortgage debt could be financially savvy. A study of automatic enrollment in the UK by Beshears et al. (2024) similarly found that it increased employees' likelihood of holding a mortgage and therefore mortgage debt, although there were no differences in auto loan balances. For other types of debt, the UK results differed from the US study in that unsecured debt, such as personal loans and bank overdrafts, did increase. Measures of credit health, however, improved over time, with credit scores increasing and loan defaults falling (Beshears et al. 2024).

Finally, we note that there are other ways for consumers to offset saving too much. Choukhmane (2024) argued that job switchers who saved too much responded by reducing their retirement plan contributions in subsequent jobs. Hung et al. (2021) also documented that among workers who separated from their jobs and were eligible to keep their retirement savings in their previous employer's plan, those who were automatically enrolled into their plan were more likely to cash out their balances than those who had enrolled in an opt-in plan. More research is needed to understand the impact of job switching on savings over time, especially given that job switches frequently coincide with a temporary loss of income and withdrawn savings as consumers manage transitions between jobs.

The benefits of automation are effectively erased for consumers who forget about their savings altogether. Recent work suggests that automatic enrollment may increase account abandonment (Goodman et al. 2023). The problem appears to be concentrated among smaller accounts, which are more prevalent for those with lower incomes and for people of color (John et al. 2021a). Worryingly, Rosen and Sade (2022) examined interventions to help consumers find lost or forgotten accounts, concluding that those interventions had little success. With estimates for abandoned savings as high as $1.65 trillion (Capitalize 2023), institutions and consulting firms have begun to explore institution- and policy-level solutions. For example, policies could require automatic portability of retirement accounts from one employer to another. Alternatively, John et al. (2021b) have discussed the benefits of a national retirement dashboard to consolidate information from all of a consumer's retirement plans in a single, centralized account.

Thus far, existing research on automation suggests that the net gain is still positive, though there may be some attenuation of retirement savings benefits due to the need to make withdrawals or to the increased odds of abandoning accounts. The SECURE 2.0 Act and certain industry-driven campaigns are encouraging increased automation into emergency savings accounts (and nonretirement investment accounts). If these are successful, such efforts could increase the number of individuals with emergency savings they can tap during shocks, thereby limiting the need to draw down retirement savings.

## The Benefits of Automation Vary Across Demographic Groups

Recent research shows that the effects of automatic enrollment in retirement saving vary across different types of consumers. The fifth column of Table 5.1 shows demographic subgroups examined by researchers, with gender, age, race, and education differences being the most often explored. Overall, the literature is fairly consistent in finding that the effects of automatic enrollment are stronger for consumers found in more vulnerable financial positions. For instance, Beshears et al. (2022) showed that the effects were larger for those with low incomes, younger individuals, and Black and Hispanic workers. Similarly, Cribb and Emerson (2021) found that the impact of automatic enrollment on pension participation was larger for those who typically had lower participation—younger employees and those with shorter job tenures. For example, automatic enrollment led to an estimated 35.8% increase in participation for those 40 years of age and above, compared to an estimated 54.3% increase for those age 22 to 39. Clark and Young (2021) and Derby et al. (2023) both reported that automatic enrollment raised participation rates more for young and low-income workers compared to older and higher-income workers. Falk and Karamcheva (2023) found that automatic enrollment led to a larger increase in participation and contribution rates among men than for women (e.g., a 13.9 percentage point increase in participation for men verses a 11.2 percentage point increase for women). The effects of automatic enrollment were also larger for lower-income workers (in the bottom earnings tercile).

Finally, younger consumers and those with lower incomes were slower to opt out of contribution rate defaults (Beshears et al. 2016).

## Time Preferences and Implications for the Benefits of Automation

Little empirical work on savings automation to date has explored consumer heterogeneity beyond demographic subgroups. To supplement the literature, we examined one source of heterogeneity (Middlewood et al. 2018) by asking whether automation would be more helpful for relatively present-focused 'doers' as opposed to relatively future-focused 'planners.' This framework, posited by Shefrin and Thaler (1988), argues that behavioral constraints like savings automation would be more effective for individuals who do not naturally have future-oriented tendencies. In what follows, we briefly review our earlier research and extend our literature review to include the most recent work on how automation benefits heterogeneous consumers.

Previously, we used the Consumer Financial Protection Bureau's (CFPB) National Financial Well-Being Survey to test an implication of the behavioral life-cycle hypothesis (Shefrin and Thaler 1988) that a behavioral process like automation would be especially helpful for those with 'doer' tendencies. To measure automation, we used a survey question in which respondents confirmed whether they had 'money automatically transferred' into a retirement savings account, a nonretirement savings account, both, or neither. The analysis examined consumers who automated their *non*retirement savings; next, we expand that analysis to include retirement savings (see Figure 5.1).

We operationalized doer and planner tendencies using a measure that asked participants to indicate whether they would prefer to have $816 now or $860 in three months. Those who selected $816, the smaller-sooner amount, were classified as 'doers,' whereas those who selected $860, the larger-later amount, were classified as 'planners.'[6] Combining this measure of present bias with the automation question resulted in four groups: doers who automated, doers who did not, planners who automated, and planners who did not.

We compared these four groups in terms of several financial health outcomes: financial well-being as defined by the CFPB Financial Well-Being Survey (CFPB 2015), self-reported liquid savings, self-reported ease in covering monthly expenses, and confidence in one's ability to raise $2,000 in 30 days.[7] Across the four metrics, the evidence was in line with expectations. Overall, planners had better financial health than doers. Furthermore, although automation was helpful for both groups, the gap in financial

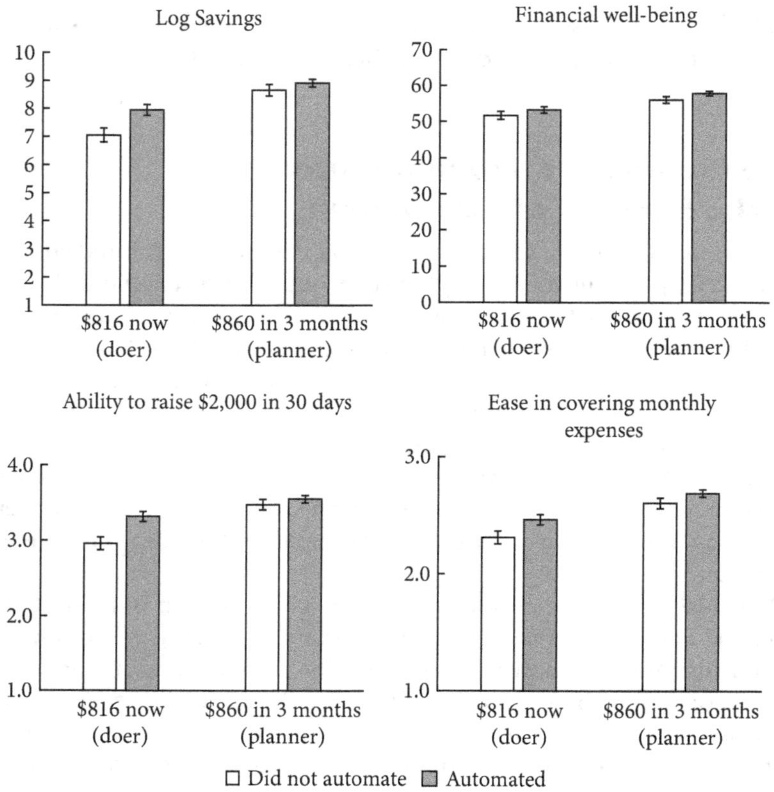


**Figure 5.1** Financial welfare outcomes by doer and planner preferences and retirement savings automation

*Notes:* Figure displays the means from unweighted regression analysis using a regression that also includes controls for nonretirement savings automation, time preferences, and demographic characteristics. 'Doer' refers to respondents who, in response to a survey question, reported preferring $816 now over $860 in three months. 'Planner' refers to those who preferred $860 in three months. Error bars show 95% confidence intervals around the means.
*Source:* Authors' calculations of the CFPB Financial Well-Being Survey.

health between those who did and did not automate was larger for doers. We interpreted this as evidence that the benefits of nonretirement savings automation were larger for doers than for planners.

Next, we examine a similar set of outcomes for doers and planners who reported automatically transferring money into *retirement*-related savings accounts. Using the same dataset, we found that 39% of the US population reported automating savings into a retirement savings account, and a similar proportion reported automating savings into a nonretirement savings account. A comparison of those with both types of accounts suggests that there were differences in automation behavior across accounts, with more than 20% of the US population choosing to automate deposits into one type of account but not the other. In other words, there is limited evidence of an 'automater' personality.

We then examined whether financial health outcomes were related to retirement savings automation and time preferences using the same analytical framework as previously employed. That is, we explored average outcomes for the four groups (doers and planners, who do or do not automate), controlling for individual demographic characteristics (e.g., income, age, employment status). Here, we omitted survey respondents who reported being retired, as it is not entirely clear how these respondents answered the question about automating retirement savings.

Results showed that retirement savings automation was correlated with having greater liquid savings and being better able to absorb a shock, as demonstrated by the interaction between time preferences and automation (left panels of Figure 5.1). Planners had higher overall levels of both variables, but the gap between planners and doers was smaller for doers who also automated their retirement savings. These results held even when controlling for the decision to automate nonretirement savings. This pattern suggests that retirement savings automation may be especially helpful for doers, who may struggle more than planners to save without the aid of interventions that circumvent their tendency to focus on the present rather than the future.

Unlike savings automation into a nonretirement account, however, there was no significant relationship between retirement automation and time preferences on financial well-being or perceived ease of covering monthly expenses (right panels of Figure 5.1). In addition, retirement-related outcomes like expected retirement age and Social Security claiming age were unrelated to automation and time preferences (not shown). The survey sample size for the two latter outcomes was smaller, however, as expected retirement age was only provided for nonretirees, and the Social Security claiming age was provided only for those age 61 to 71. Nevertheless, it is surprising that retirement savings automation did not relate to these and other long-term financial outcomes that one might expect to be improved by automation.

Goda et al. (2020) used matched survey and retirement plan data to estimate the relationship between time preferences (both present bias and discount rates) and retirement savings behavior. Under an automatic enrollment regime with 3% matching, the authors concluded that present-biased individuals were more likely to stick with the default. In our research, we find no relationship between time preferences and the decision to automate savings, for either retirement or nonretirement accounts.

## Beyond Time Preferences? Understanding Further Heterogeneity in Automation

Time preferences are only one dimension by which automation effects may vary. Yet as noted earlier, there is relatively little research on how the benefits of retirement savings automation vary by subgroup, particularly when looking beyond demographic characteristics. In this section, we address other aspects of consumer psychology and structural factors that may represent interesting dimensions of heterogeneity.

### Differences in Financial Skill, Socialization, and Knowledge

In Middlewood et al. (2018), we explored the characteristics of who was more likely to automate nonretirement savings. Results showed that those with higher financial skill measured using the CFPB 10-item financial skill scale (CFPB 2018), which included items such as 'I know when I need advice about my money' and 'I know how to make myself save,' were more likely to automate nonretirement savings. We also found that those with higher financial socialization (measured using positive responses to seven statements such as 'While growing up at home, did your family do any of the following?') were more likely to automate nonretirement savings. When we examined retirement savings, automation was positively related to financial socialization and financial skill.

Using a 10-item scale (Houts and Knoll 2020) with items such as 'If the interest rates rise, what should happen to bond prices,' we found no relationship between automating savings into nonretirement accounts and financial knowledge, Perhaps surprisingly, automation into retirement accounts was negatively related to financial literacy in a regression that controlled for several other variables.[8] Possibly, this negative relationship was due to the confounding effects of compliance with auto-enrollment in retirement plans among those with low levels of financial literacy. Mrkva et al. (2021) found that across several choice contexts, people with lower financial literacy were more likely to stick with default options; in the specific context of retirement savings, they showed that people with less financial sophistication and financial experience who were automatically enrolled into their employers' retirement plans were less likely to change either the contribution amounts or the investment allocations to which they were assigned by default. Other work comparing opt-in and automatic enrollment regimes seems to align, finding that financial literacy is more predictive of saving under opt-in regimes while present bias is more predictive of saving under automatic enrollment (Goda et al. 2020).

## Attitudes Toward Saving

The concept of personal savings orientation (PSO) (Dholakia et al. 2016) adds more nuance to the relationship between financial literacy and savings behavior. This construct refers to the extent to which savings is a lifestyle and not merely goal oriented. Questions about PSO ask respondents to rate statements such as: 'The goal of saving money is always at the back of my mind,' and 'Putting money into personal savings is a habit for me.' In their research, Dholakia et al. (2016) found that financial literacy only predicted savings for those with a higher PSO. Newmeyer et al. (2021) built on this work to show that the relationship between automating savings and liquid savings varies significantly by PSO and income level.

## Heterogeneity in Access to Accounts

Much research on automation focuses on retirement accounts and relies primarily on employer-sponsored plan data, whereas few studies explore how consumers pursue retirement savings outside of employer-based plans, and whether automated deposits into those accounts also yield the same retirement benefits. Many people lack access to employer-sponsored retirement programs and therefore must save for retirement on their own (Glasner 2023; John et al. 2022). This section explores ownership of retirement accounts and the implications of these differences.

We analyzed CFPB data from the National Financial Well-Being Survey (CFPB n.d.) to explore how ownership of retirement accounts varies across the US population. As shown in Table 5.2, 30% of the US population reported not having a retirement account in 2018.[9] Table 5.3 highlights the different demographic composition of retirement account owners and nonowners. In particular, account ownership is more prevalent among men, non-Hispanic, and white respondents, and those with higher levels of educational attainment. Account ownership is also more prevalent for those working full time, suggesting differences by employment status. Owners also reported roughly double the amount saved ($30,000 versus $15,000), as well as less usage of products and services like prepaid cards or check cashing. These patterns are largely consistent with nonretirement account evidence (Middlewood et al. 2018).

Even though we analyze 'retirement accounts,' defined by the survey respondents, heterogeneity in retirement account ownership shown in Table 5.3 could also reflect differences in who has access to employer-sponsored retirement plans. More Hispanic, Black, and Asian workers report not having access to an employer-sponsored retirement plans than do non-Hispanic white workers (John et al. 2022).[10] In addition, only 30% of workers earning below $37,000 a year have access to an employer plan,

TABLE 5.2 Automation Behavior in Retirement and Nonretirement Savings Accounts

| | | Nonretirement Savings Account | | | |
|---|---|---|---|---|---|
| | | Do not automate | Automate | I do not have this | Row Totals |
| **Retirement Savings Account** | Do not automate | 20.69% | 8.46% | 1.17% | 30.32% |
| | Automate | 12.67% | 23.32% | 3.40% | 39.39% |
| | I do not have this | 3.94% | 6.35% | 20.00% | 30.30% |
| | Column Totals | 37.30% | 38.14% | 24.57% | 100% |

*Notes:* $N = 6246$. Table shows the proportion of respondents providing each set of responses. Survey weights result in a sample that is representative of the US population.
*Source:* Authors' calculations using data from the CFPB Financial Well-Being survey.

and of those with access, only 19% participate (Glasner 2023). Further compounding the retirement savings result, low-income households face barriers to building and maintaining their retirement savings balances, as they switch jobs more frequently than high-income households do, on average (US Government Accountability Office [GAO] 2023). Low-income households are also more likely to make early withdrawals from their employer-sponsored retirement plans (Argento et al. 2015; GAO 2023), potentially incurring a 10% tax penalty and income taxes.

To the extent that retirement account access and ownership are unevenly distributed across the US population and are correlated with existing wealth, increased automation into these accounts may exacerbate these underlying differences. In other words, retirement savings automation could help increase retirement security and net worth for those who use these accounts, but it could leave behind those who are already the most financially insecure. With the advent of the SECURE 2.0 Act, as well as the extension of automation benefits to nonretirement savings through employer-sponsored programs, differential access could be an increasingly important source of disparity in overall savings amounts. There may be an opportunity to mitigate these disparities through state-sponsored auto-IRA programs such as OregonSaves, which automatically enroll certain workers who lack access to employer-sponsored retirement accounts into IRAs (for a discussion of research examining the OregonSaves program, see Reuter (this volume). These plans cover a limited but increasing number of workers to date.[11]

TABLE 5.3 Demographic Composition of Retirement Account Owners and Nonowners

| | Nonowner | Owner | p-value |
|---|---|---|---|
| *Gender* | | | |
| Female | 54% | 45% | 0.089 |
| *Race* | | | |
| Non-Hispanic white | 65% | 73% | −0.080 |
| Non-Hispanic Black | 13% | 10% | 0.032 |
| Non-Hispanic other | 6% | 5% | 0.003 |
| Hispanic | 17% | 13% | 0.045 |
| *Education* | | | |
| Less than high school | 13% | 5% | 0.082 |
| High school degree | 32% | 23% | 0.097 |
| Some college | 34% | 29% | 0.057 |
| Bachelor's degree | 12% | 24% | −0.112 |
| Graduate/professional degree | 8% | 21% | −0.124 |
| *Employment Status* | | | |
| Self-employed | 9% | 8% | 0.003 |
| Work full time for an employer or the military | 20% | 47% | −0.264 |
| Work part time for an employer or the military | 12% | 8% | 0.036 |
| Homemaker | 9% | 5% | 0.035 |
| Full-time student | 8% | 3% | 0.054 |
| Permanently sick, disabled, or unable to work | 10% | 3% | 0.068 |
| Unemployed or temporarily laid off | 8% | 3% | 0.049 |
| Retired | 34% | 28% | 0.052 |
| Missing | 2% | 2% | 0.007 |
| Log of imputed income | 10.558 | 11.153 | −0.595 |
| Log of imputed savings | 6.475 | 8.699 | −2.224 |
| Imputed savings ($) | 15,468 | 31,021 | −15,553 |
| Used reloadable card not linked with checking or savings account | 11.8% | 7.6% | 0.042 |
| Used nonbank service for cashing a check or purchasing a money order | 9.4% | 5.5% | 0.038 |
| Retirement date (1 = later than planned, 0 = early or on time) | 6.2% | 5.3% | 0.008 |

*Notes:* Table displays the proportion of participants who report that they 'do not have' a retirement account (nonowners) versus that they automate or do not automate savings into a retirement account (owners). P-values represent t-tests of the differences in means.

*Source:* Authors' calculations using data from the CFPB Financial Well-Being survey.

## Discussion

Our summary of the literature on automation as a savings intervention leaves many questions unanswered. We enumerate several below.

## Is Automating Saving for Retirement and Nonretirement Outcomes Different?

One question arising from our review and prior research is whether there are differences in the benefits of automation for retirement and nonretirement savings. Empirically, we found that the relationship between time preferences and savings automation holds for fewer outcomes for retirement savings compared to non-retirement savings. Specifically, the relatively positive relationship between automation and outcomes for impatient consumers was significant only for liquid savings and the ability to absorb a shock—not financial well-being or ease in covering monthly expenses. At this juncture, we can only speculate on why these differences may occur. One factor may be the time horizon associated with the savings, with retirement being a long-term outcome for many consumers (Bruine de Bruin et al. 2024). Time horizons may affect the benefits of automation in two opposing ways. Automation is likely to have greater benefits for retirement savings accrual, as this one-time fix permits workers to accumulate benefits over the life cycle as long as they do not opt out. Yet automation may be less beneficial for those with significant liquidity constraints, who may respond to automation by taking early withdrawals from retirement accounts and paying tax penalties.

A second possible explanation for differences in the impact of automation between retirement and nonretirement accounts is how automation works. For many Americans, nonretirement savings are held in checking and savings accounts, nonbank fintech accounts (e.g., PayPal), or money market funds, and most of these accounts facilitate automate transfers. Possibly, automatic transfers that occur after workers receive their paychecks could affect budgeting and spending behavior, as consumers can observe the reduction in disposable income due to saving. This process can be contrasted with automatic enrollment and automatic escalation (more common in employer-sponsored retirement plans), and where money is not easily accessible prior to being saved. For consumers who attend less to account balances, automated transfers could result in overdraft and other fees due to insufficient funds. Future research should explore how the effects of automation differ across these different accounts, methods, and products.

Third, the automation of savings into nonretirement versus retirement accounts may also differ in intentionality. Employer-sponsored retirement saving is supported by institutional policies and practices such as employer matching of employee contributions, tax benefits, and encouragement by firm personnel departments. Future research should explore whether automation decisions made without such institutional support are more intentional on the part of consumers.

Ultimately, we identified only three papers examining automation in the context of nonretirement savings, as opposed to the 11 papers examining retirement savings. In the retirement savings arena, most papers study enrollment into employer-sponsored retirement plans as opposed to brokerage accounts used for long-term savings or IRAs. It remains an open question of how to best encourage individual consumers to automate savings outside of employer-sponsored plans, and whether state-level programs like OregonSaves could be a more promising solution.

### Does Automation of Retirement Savings Lead to More Successful Retirement?

Few authors to date have examined long-run longitudinal outcomes, as opposed to proximate behaviors (e.g., participation and initial contribution rates). The time span of data covered in Table 5.1 is, at most, 4.5 years postintervention—a long time compared to many intervention studies but likely to be insufficient if one considers that the workers must save over their entire working lives. Furthermore, to our knowledge, little research on savings automation focuses on retirement well-being—arguably the ultimate aim of such retirement savings interventions. Our correlational results on financial well-being suggest no significant relationship between automation and consumers' subjective sense of financial security. Therefore, although the interventions show promising results for crucial inputs to retirement savings (such as retirement account participation and contribution rates), it remains to be seen whether these benefits persist throughout retirement.

## Conclusions

The retirement savings shortfall facing many American households is unlikely to abate. Household expenses have risen following the COVID-19 pandemic, after a period of inflation rates as high as 9.1% in June 2022 (Bureau of Labor Statistics [BLS] 2023b). Although the gap between wage growth and inflation is now narrowing, American workers are still feeling the repercussions of the highest price increases since 1981 (BLS 2022). With housing making up approximately one-third of Americans' annual expenses (BLS 2023a), households are paying significantly more for rent and mortgages, and wages have not increased at the same rate (National Low Income Housing Coalition 2023). Many households also carry substantial debt, the payments for which can interfere with households' ability to save. Student loan debt is also pervasive across age groups (US Department of Education 2023), and credit card balances have recently topped $1 trillion (Federal Reserve Bank of New York 2023). Americans are also living longer

(Medina et al. 2020), making retirement savings more important, even as the shift from defined benefit to defined contribution retirement plans has put more responsibility on individual consumers to save.

As a policy response, the SECURE 2.0 Act does help encourage retirement and nonretirement savings through savings automation programs. Our review of the literature, drawing on automation interventions predating the implementation of the SECURE 2.0 Act, paints a generally positive picture regarding the possible benefits of savings automation. In particular, automation appears to reliably increase participation rates and contributions into retirement accounts, and it is correlated with positive outcomes, particularly for people who tend to be present focused.

Nevertheless, the literature also suggests that an emphasis on near-term outcomes may be short-sighted, as automation can have long-term downsides. Individuals with automated savings may forget about their savings (Goodman et al. 2023) and make withdrawals from 401(k) accounts when facing financial shocks (Beshears et al. 2018). Not all Americans have access to employer-sponsored retirement accounts, especially those in low-income and vulnerable groups, meaning that automation may exacerbate existing wealth disparities. Without the retirement savings infrastructure provided in many conventional full-time positions, policymakers and advocates may need to widen avenues for retirement savings outside the workplace. The rising number of state-sponsored auto-IRAs warrants further evaluation of this changing landscape and how to alleviate potential disparities.

## Acknowledgments

We thank Alexsandra Galanis and Nettie Silvernale for research assistance, and Katie Carman, Angela Fontes, Melissa Knoll, Danielle Specce, and Caroline Ratcliffe for comments on earlier versions of this chapter. We also thank Olivia S. Mitchell and participants in the 2024 Pension Research Council Symposium for their helpful comments.

## Disclosure

This chapter was prepared by staff of the Office of the Investor Advocate at the Securities and Exchange Commission (SEC) but does not necessarily reflect the views of SEC, the commissioners, or other members of the staff. The reported research was done independently from, and does not represent, the views of any of the authors' affiliations. All findings, interpretations, and conclusions of this paper represent the views of the authors and not those of the Wharton School or the Pension Research Council.

## Notes

1. Newmeyer et al. (2021) lists specific actions the authors consider automation.
2. See section 801 of the Employee Retirement Income Security Act of 1974 (ERISA), which allows for 'a pension-linked emergency savings account' and the ability to 'automatically enroll an eligible participant in such account pursuant to an automatic contribution arrangement.' Furthermore, such accounts are not allowed to have any fees or charges for at least the first four withdrawals of funds in a plan year.
3. For a review of work published prior to 2015, and therefore not included in Table 5.1, see O'Neill (2007), Burke et al. (2015), and CFPB (2020).
4. There are no penalties for withdrawing contributions from a Roth 401(k), but few people use these plans. According to Fidelity, 80% of their plans offer a Roth 401(k) but only about 15% of those eligible make use of one (Fidelity 2024).
5. Withdrawal rates may be higher for other types of automatic enrollment programs. Quinby et al. (2020) found that 20% of employees in the OregonSaves program—a state-sponsored auto-IRA—made at least one withdrawal during the 12-month study period, with an average withdrawal amount of $1000. The authors suggest that the structure of the program as a Roth IRA—in which contributions can be withdrawn without the 10% tax penalty—may mean that withdrawals are more likely relative to traditional defined-contribution plans. For a summary of the OregonSaves program and other auto-IRAs, see Pew Charitable Trusts (2021).
6. Such time-amount tradeoff questions are commonly used to assess whether someone is willing to defer gratification to earn higher rewards in the future (e.g., Hardisty et al. 2013). As described in Middlewood et al. (2018), the implied rate of return for this tradeoff is approximately 23.4%, well above what one could expect to earn from investing. Therefore, selecting the smaller amount sooner suggests that the respondent prefers present consumption over future returns.
7. Our estimating equation was: $Y_i = \beta_0 + \beta_1 Doer_i + \beta_2 Automated_i + \beta_3 Doer_i * Automated_i + \gamma X_i + \varepsilon_i$, where $Y_i$ represented one of the four financial welfare outcomes, Doer was a variable representing whether the respondent was classified as a doer (1/0), Automated represented whether the respondent automated savings (1/0), and X represented a vector of demographic characteristics (age, gender, income, education, race/ethnicity, and presence of children in the household).
8. These variables included time preferences, financial socialization, financial skill, gender, age, race/ethnicity, educational attainment, employment, and reports of having a retirement account from other questions in the survey. In addition to those patterns highlighted in the text, there were positive associations with income, working full time or part time, or being a homemaker. There were negative relationships with being Hispanic or retired.
9. The measure analyzed in this table does not distinguish between employer-sponsored retirement accounts and nonemployer-sponsored retirement accounts.
10. Approximately 64% of Hispanic workers, 53% of Black workers, and 45% of Asian workers lack access to an employer-sponsored retirement plan, as compared to 42% of white non-Hispanic workers (John et al. 2022).

11. More states are enacting auto-IRA programs to provide coverage for those who lack access to an employer-sponsored plan (Pew Charitable Trusts 2022). There were 15 states that had enacted such programs as of May 2024 (Center for Retirement Initiatives 2024), which have enrolled fewer than one million workers out of the 56 million who lack access to employer-sponsored retirement plans (Olson 2023).

## References

Argento, R., V. L. Bryant, and J. Sabelhaus (2015). 'Early Withdrawals from Retirement Accounts During the Great Recession.' *Contemporary Economic Policy*, 33: 1–16.

Ashraf, N., D. Karlan, and W. Yin (2006). 'Tying Odysseus to the Mast: Evidence from a Commitment Savings Product in the Philippines.' *Quarterly Journal of Economics*, 121(2): 635–672.

Barber, M. and T. Odean (2001). 'Boys Will Be Boys: Gender, Overconfidence, and Common Stock Investment.' *Quarterly Journal of Economics*, 116(1): 261–292.

Barber, M. and T. Odean (2013). 'The Behavior of Individual Investors.' In G. M. Constantinides, M. Hallis, and R. M. Stulz, eds., *Handbook of the Economics of Finance*. Oxford: North Holland, pp. 1533–1570.

Benartzi, S. and R. H. Thaler (2013). 'Behavioral Economics and the Retirement Savings Crisis.' *Science*, 339(6124): 1152–1153.

Berk, S. H., J. Beshears, J. Choi, and D. Laibson (2022). 'Automating Short-Term Payroll Savings: Initial Evidence from a Large U.K. Experiment.' NBER Working Paper No. 32581.

Beshears, J., S. Benartzi, R. Mason, and K. L. Milkman (2017). 'How Do Consumers Respond When Default Options Push the Envelope?' dx.doi.org/10.2139/ssrn.3050562

Beshears, J., M. Blakstad, J. J. Choi, C. Firth, J. Gathergood, D. Laibson, R. Notley, J. D. Sheth, W. Sandbrook, and N. Stewart (2024). 'Does Pension Automatic Enrollment Increase Debt? Evidence from a Large-Scale Natural Experiment.' NBER Working Paper No. 32100.

Beshears, J., J. J. Choi, D. Laibson, and B. C. Madrian (2018). 'Potential vs. Realized Savings Under Automatic Enrollment.' TIAA Institute Research Dialogue 148.

Beshears, J., J. J. Choi, D. Laibson, B. C. Madrian, and W. L. Skimmyhorn (2022). 'Borrowing to Save? The Impact of Automatic Enrollment on Debt.' *Journal of Finance*, 77(1): 403–447.

Beshears, J., J. J. Choi, D. Laibson, B. C. Madrian, and B. Weller (2010). 'Public Policy and Saving for Retirement: The "Autosave" Features of the Pension Protection Act of 2006.' In J. Siegfried, ed., *Better Living Through Economics: How Economic Research Improves Our Lives*. Cambridge, MA: Harvard University Press, pp. 274–290.

Beshears, J., J. J. Choi, D. Laibson, B. C. Madrian, and S. Y. Wang (2016). 'Who Is Easier to Nudge?' Unpublished manuscript.

Bruine de Bruin, W., A. Chin, D. Zimmerman, and W van der Klaauw (2024). 'Everything In Its Own Time: Planning Horizons Vary Across Financial Domains.' Presentation at the University of Southern California.

Bureau of Labor Statistics (BLS) (2022). *Consumer Price Index: June* 2022. USDL-22-1470. Washington, DC: BLS.

Bureau of Labor Statistics (BLS) (2023a). *Consumer Expenditures: 2022.* USDL-23-1943. Washington, DC: BLS.

Bureau of Labor Statistics (BLS) (2023b). *Consumer Price Index: April 2025.* USDL-25-0786. Washington, DC: BLS.

Burke, J., A. Hung, and J. Luoto (2015). 'Automatic Enrollment in Retirement Savings Vehicles: Evidence from the Health and Retirement Study.' RAND Corporation Working Paper No. WR-1117.

Capitalize (2023). *The True Cost of Forgotten 401(k) Accounts.* New York: Capitalize. www.hicapitalize.com/wp-content/uploads/2023/06/The-true-cost-of-forgotten-401k-accounts-2023.pdf

Center for Retirement Initiatives (2024). 'State Programs 2024: Optimism More Programs Enacted While Several Newer Programs Will Partner with Existing Programs to Launch in 2024.' cri.georgetown.edu/states/

Chalmers, J, O. S. Mitchell, J. Reuter, and M. Zhong (2025). 'Evidence on Auto-Enrollment Retirement Plan Efficacy from OregonSaves.' *Journal of Public Economics,* 246: 105379.

Choi, J. J. (2022). 'Popular Personal Financial Advice Versus the Professors.' *Journal of Economic Perspectives,* 36(4): 167–192.

Choukhmane, T. (2024). 'Default Options and Retirement Saving Dynamics.' Unpublished manuscript.

Clark, J. W. and J. A. Young (2021). *Automatic Enrollment: The Power of the Default.* Malvern, PA: Vanguard Research.

Consumer Financial Protection Bureau (CFPB) (2015). *Financial Well-Being: The Goal of Financial Education.* Washington, DC: CFPB. www.consumerfinance.gov/data-research/research-reports/financial-well-being/

Consumer Financial Protection Bureau (CFPB) (2018). *Measuring Financial Skill: A Guide to Using the Bureau of Consumer Financial Protection Financial Skill Scale.* Washington, DC: CPFB. www.consumerfinance.gov/data-research/research-reports/measuring-financial-skill/

Consumer Financial Protection Bureau (CFPB) (2020). *Evidence-Based Strategies to Build Emergency Savings: Office of Research Report for the Start Small, Save Up Initiative.* Washington, DC: CPFB. www.consumerfinance.gov/data-research/research-reports/evidence-based-strategies-build-emergency-savings/

Consumer Financial Protection Bureau (CFPB, n.d.). 'National Financial Well-Being Survey Date.' www.consumerfinance.gov/data-research/financial-well-being-survey-data/

Cribb, J. and C. Emmerson (2021). 'What Can We Learn About Automatic Enrollment into Pensions from Small Employers?' *National Tax Journal,* 74(2): 377–404.

Derby, E., K. Mackie, and J. Mortenson (2023). 'Worker and Spousal Responses to Automatic Enrollment.' *Journal of Public Economics,* 223: 104910.

Dholakia, U., L. Tam, S. Yoon, and N. Wong (2016). 'The Ant and the Grasshopper: Understanding Personal Saving Orientation of Consumers.' *Journal of Consumer Research,* 43(1): 134–155.

Employee Benefit Research Institute (EBRI) (2023). *Retirement Confidence Survey, EBRI Chartbook.* Employee Benefit Research Institute and Greenwald Research Report.

Falk, J. and N. S. Karamcheva (2023). 'The Impact of an Employer Match and Automatic Enrollment on the Savings Behavior of Public-Sector Workers.' *Journal of Pension Economics & Finance* 22(1): 38–68.

Federal Reserve Bank of New York (2023). *Quarterly Report on Household Debt and Credit.* Center for Microeconomic Data Research and Statistics Group Report.

Fidelity (2024). 'Roth 401(k): Pros and Cons of a Roth 401(k).' www.fidelity.com/viewpoints/retirement/roth-401k

Financial Health Network (2023). 'Financial Health Pulse 2023 U.S. Trends Report Rising Financial Vulnerability in America.' finhealthnetwork.org/financial-health-pulse-2023-share-of-financially-vulnerable-americans-grows-to-pre-pandemic-levels/

Glasner, B. (2023). 'How Much Does Retirement Plan Coverage Vary by State and Income? An Updated Look.' *Economic Innovation Group.* eig.org/state-retirement-coverage-2023/

Goda, G. S., Levy, M. R., Manchester, C. F., Sojourner, A., and Tasoff, J. (2020). 'Who Is a Passive Saver Under Opt-In and Auto-Enrollment?' *Journal of Economic Behavior & Organization*, 173: 301–321.

Goodman, L., A. Mukherjee, and S. Ramnath (2023). 'Set It and Forget It? Financing Retirement in an Age of Defaults.' *Journal of Financial Economics*, 148(1): 47–68.

Hardisty, D. J., K. F. Thompson, D. H. Krantz, and E. U Weber (2013). 'How to Measure Time Preferences: An Experimental Comparison of Three Methods.' *Judgment and Decision Making*, 8(3): 236–249.

Houts, C. R. and M. A. Knoll (2020). 'The Financial Knowledge Scale: New Analyses, Findings, and Development of a Short Form.' *Journal of Consumer Affairs*, 54(2): 775–800.

Hung, A. A., J. Luoto, J. Burke, S. P. Utkus, and J. A. Young (2021). 'Automatic Enrollment and Job Market Turnover.' *Journal of Pension Economics and Finance*, 20: 547–557.

John, D. C., G. Enda, W. G. Gale, and M. Iwry (2021b). 'A Retirement Dashboard for the United States.' In W. G. Gale, J. M. Iwry, and D. C. John, eds., *Wealth After Work: Innovative Reforms to Expand Retirement Security.* Washington, DC: Brookings Institution Press, pp. 82–115.

John, D. C., J. M. Iwry, C. Pulliam, and W. G. Gale (2021a). *Small Retirement Accounts: Issues and Options.* Economic Studies at Brookings Policy Brief No. 20211123. Washington, DC: Brookings Institution.

John, D., G. Koenig, and M. Malta (2022). *Payroll Deduction Retirement Programs Build Economic Security.* Washington, DC: AARP. doi.org/10.26419/ppi.00164.001

Madrian, B. C. and D. F. Shea (2001). 'The Power of Suggestion: Inertia in 401(k) Participation and Savings Behavior.' *Quarterly Journal of Economics*, 116(4): 1149–1187.

Medina, L., S. Sabo, and J. Vespa (2020). *Living Longer: Historical and Projected Life Expectancy in the United States, 1960 to 2060.* Washington, DC: US Census Bureau.

Meier, S. and C. Sprenger (2010). 'Present-Biased Preferences and Credit Card Borrowing.' *American Economic Journal: Applied Economics*, 2(1): 193–210.

Middlewood, B. L., A. Chin, H. Johnson, and M. A. Knoll (2018). 'Exploring the Relationships Between Impatience, Savings Automation, and Financial Welfare.' *Financial Planning Review*, 1(3–4): e1020.

Mrkva, K., N. A. Posner, C. Reeck, and E. J. Johnson (2021). 'Do Nudges Reduce Disparities? Choice Architecture Compensates for Low Consumer Knowledge.' *Journal of Marketing*, 85(4): 67–84.

National Low Income Housing Coalition (NLIHC 2023). 'Press Release: NLIHC Releases Out of Reach 2023: The High Cost of Housing.' nlihc.org/oor

Newmeyer, C., D. Warmath, G. E. O'Connor, and N. Wong (2021). 'Is Savings Automation Helpful to Liquid Savings? It Depends on Whether You Have a Savings Habit.' *Journal of Public Policy & Marketing*, 40(2): 285–297.

Olson, K. (2023). 'Retirement Assets in State Automated Savings Programs Hit $1 Billion.' *Pew Charitable Trusts*. www.pewtrusts.org/en/research-and-analysis/articles/2023/12/22/retirement-assets-in-state-automated-savings-programs-hit-1-billion

O'Neill, B. (2007). 'Overcoming Inertia: Do Automated Saving and Investing Strategies Work?' *Journal of Family and Economic Issues*, 28: 321–335.

Pew Charitable Trusts (2021). 'OregonSaves Auto-IRA Program Works for Employers.' Pew Charitable Trusts Issue Brief. Philadelphia, PA: Pew Charitable Trusts.

Pew Charitable Trusts (2022). 'State Auto-IRAs Continue to Complement Private Market for Retirement Plans.' www.pewtrusts.org/en/research-and-analysis/articles/2022/04/state-auto-iras-continue-to-complement-private-market-for-retirement-plans

Quinby, L. D., A. H. Munnell, W. Hou, A. Belbase, and G. T. Sanzenbacher (2020). 'Participation and Pre-retirement Withdrawals in Oregon's Auto-IRA.' *Journal of Retirement*, 8(1): 8–21.

Rosen, M. H. and O. Sade (2022). 'Investigating the Introduction of Fintech Advancement Aimed to Reduce Limited Attention Regarding Inactive Savings Accounts: Data, Survey, and Field Experiment.' *AEA Papers and Proceedings*, 112: 370–375.

Samuelson, W. and R. J. Zeckhauser (1988). 'Status Quo Bias in Decision Making.' *Journal of Risk and Uncertainty*, 1: 7–59.

Shefrin, H. and R. H. Thaler (1988). 'The Behavioral Life-Cycle Hypothesis.' *Economic Inquiry*, 26: 609–643.

Thaler, R. H. and S. Benartzi (2004). 'Save More Tomorrow™: Using Behavioral Economics to Increase Employee Saving.' *Journal of Political Economy*, 112(S1): S164–S187.

US Department of Education (2023). *Direct Loan Portfolio by Borrower Age.* Washington, DC: US DOE. studentaid.gov/sites/default/files/fsawg/datacenter/library/DLPortfolio-by-Age.xls

US Government Accountability Office (GAO) (2023). *Older Workers' Retirement Account Disparities Have Increased by Income and Persisted by Race Over Time.* GAO-23-105342. Washington, DC: US GAO.

# Part II

# Investment Behavior of Retirement Savers

Chapter 6

# Plan Design and Participant Behavior in Defined Contribution Retirement Plans

## Past, Present, and Future

*Jonathan Reuter*

The debate continues about whether US households, particularly those with lower earnings, save enough for retirement.[1] Because private retirement savings in the US primarily accrue through employer-sponsored defined contribution (DC) retirement plans such as 401(k) plans, there is renewed interested by policymakers, practitioners, and academics in improving plan design and expanding access.[2] In this chapter, we review recent economic evidence on how employees have responded to changes in retirement plan design intended to boost participation rates, savings rates, and exposure to equity markets; discuss the potential impact of recent regulation on these outcomes; and highlight areas where additional research is needed.

DC retirement plans are a means to generate retirement benefits above those payable from the government Social Security program. When discussing such plans, it is often helpful to model them as a savings account in a classic economic life-cycle model.[3] Many such models make the (unrealistic) assumption that employees know and can implement their optimal savings rates and asset allocations each period. In this case, a well-designed plan would be one that provides participants with a sufficiently rich set of investment options for them to create custom portfolios based on their individual characteristics and preferences, at a reasonable cost.[4] In such a simplistic setting, those who will choose not to participate are those for whom the expected benefits of participating fall short of the costs in terms of forgone consumption or alternative savings (such as paying down student loans).

If the framework is extended to acknowledge that some employees lack the financial literacy and investment experience required to determine their optimal savings rates and asset allocations, optimal plan design becomes more complex.[5] In practice, households must decide how much to

Jonathan Reuter, *Plan Design and Participant Behavior in Defined Contribution Retirement Plans*. In: *Retirement Saving, Investment, and Spending*. Edited by: Olivia S. Mitchell and Nikolai Roussanov, Oxford University Press.

DOI: 10.1093/oso/9780197845752.003.0006

save each period, where to save (e.g., in employer-sponsored or individual retirement plans), how to invest retirement contributions throughout the accumulation phase, when to retire, when to claim government-provided Social Security, and how to manage assets during the payout phase, including the potential purchase of life annuities. The fact that these are complex decisions does not avoid the reality that households must make them, but it does suggest that less financially literate households may outsource decision making to others or even avoid saving for retirement altogether.

Accordingly, one challenge for plan sponsors is to design retirement plans that move unsophisticated employees closer to their optimal savings rates and asset allocations (compared to being left to their own devices), while simultaneously providing sophisticated employees with the investment options needed to implement their optimal saving rates and asset allocations. This is where nudges such as automatic enrollment and default investment options have come to play an important role, in practice. A second challenge for plan sponsors is to accommodate the (potentially) quite diverse needs of unsophisticated retirement savers, which can necessitate more sophisticated defaults.

In what follows, we begin by reviewing evidence on suboptimal retirement plan investment behavior in the days before automatic enrollment (AE). Next, we consider the benefits of AE and active choice relative to voluntary enrollment (VE). We also examine the intended and unintended consequences of replacing money market funds with target date funds (TDFs) as default investment options and discuss the potential value of customized defaults. Next, we review the evidence on expanding access to employer-based retirement plans and liquid savings in the UK and US. We then summarize new evidence on how households finance incremental savings under AE and how the short-run effects of AE likely overstate long-run changes in savings. We conclude by discussing potential conflicts of interest in plan design, the possible outcomes of recent regulation intended to increase participation rates and savings in the US, and areas where additional research is needed.[6]

## Evidence on Retirement Plan Suboptimal Participant Behavior

Before describing how DC retirement plans have evolved, it is helpful to review the early evidence on how some DC plan participants (mis)managed their retirement portfolios. In their widely cited '1/N' paper, Benartzi and Thaler (2001) cast doubt on the idea that plan participants construct optimal portfolios.[7] Instead, they showed that many plan participants relied upon naïve diversification strategies when deciding how to invest their retirement savings. For instance, those authors found that when more equity funds were included in the plan menu, people invested more in equity, even when there are no incremental benefits from diversification. Huberman and Jiang (2006) revisited this finding using account-level data from 640 DC plans administered by Vanguard. They did find evidence of the 1/N effect in the sense that participants typically allocated contributions equally across a small number of funds, but they did not confirm that average equity allocations rose with the fraction of equity funds in the menu.[8] They concluded that 'the absence of a relation between equity allocation and equity exposure suggests that *menu design is not important* [emphasis added] and that the data fail to reject the null hypothesis of rationality in favor of the alternative that plan menus influence participants' equity allocations' (p. 764).

Nevertheless, this was neither a particularly powerful test of investor rationality nor of the quality of DC investment menus. Using account-level data from 2004 for an even larger sample of DC plans managed by Vanguard, Tang et al. (2010) showed that approximately 94% of plans offered efficient investment menus but that 'most participants fail[ed] to construct an optimal portfolio from the menu offered to them by their plan sponsors' (p. 1080). The authors' headline estimate was that inefficiently constructed portfolios reduced retirement wealth by as much as one-fifth over a 35-year horizon.

To test for 'mental accounting,' or the cognitive process by which individuals categorize, evaluate, and keep track of financial activities by creating separate 'accounts' in their minds, Choi et al. (2009) exploited a 2003 change in how a single firm made 401(k) matching contributions. Prior to the change, participants selected their contribution allocations, and all employer matching was in company stock. After the change, participants selected the asset mix for both their own and the employer's contributions. Fully rational employees should have set a lower allocation to company stock before the change, taking into account the fact that the employer match was entirely in company stock. Instead, consistent with mental accounting, participants before the change appeared to ignore how the employer match was allocated. After the change, participants elected similar allocations to company stock for both contribution streams, implying very different allocations to company stock after six months (58.7% versus 27.4%).

There are also numerous related questions about whether some participants are willing and able to manage their retirement savings portfolios over time. One example is that people often accept the status quo, giving rise to excess inertia. Samuelson and Zeckhauser (1988) provided real-world evidence of status quo bias in a study of approximately 850,000 Teachers Insurance and Annuity Association (TIAA) participants' allocations of retirement contributions, between a fixed-income (TIAA) fund and a diversified common stock (CREF) fund. Following participants from 1981 to 1986, they showed that allocation changes each year were insignificant 'despite large variations in TIAA and CREF rates of return' (p. 32).

They also reported that fewer than 2.5% of participants remaining in the plan for at least 12 years made a change to their asset allocations in any given calendar year. That paper did not discuss whether participants transferred money between the two funds without adjusting their future asset mix, which is the more efficient way to rebalance portfolios. Further research by Agnew et al. (2003) studied trading behavior among participants in a single large 401(k) plan from 1994 to 1998. They found that extreme asset allocations were common, with 47.6% of participants allocating nothing to equity. They also documented allocation changes were relatively uncommon, with 87.6% of accounts making no trades in a given year. This study is widely cited as evidence that DC plan participants 'set it and forget it,' never revisiting their initial asset allocation choices.[9]

There is also research on whether employees hold overly concentrated positions in their employer's stock, yet Benartzi (2001) showed that approximately 25% of discretionary contributions in 401(k) plans were invested in company stock, as documented using Form 11-K data for fiscal year 1993. Moreover, allocations to company stock were higher when company stock returns had been higher, but these higher allocations did not predict higher future returns. Poterba (2003) reported an average allocation to company stock of 44.3% in the 20 largest DC plans in 2001, even though, over the same period, the average standard deviation of company stock was 35.7%, versus only 15.8% for the S&P 500 Index. His simulations confirmed that large allocations to company stock significantly reduced savers' investment performance.

Following the Pension Protection Act of 2006 allowing employees to move company stock holdings into other investments, holdings of company stock have declined. For instance, the fraction of participants with a positive allocation to company stock (among plans offering company stock), fell from 50% in 2014 to 31% in 2023 (Vanguard 2024). Collectively, this research implies that at least some participants would benefit from outsourcing their asset allocation decisions, given the status quo bias, 1/N investment allocations, and inertia they exhibit.

## Defaults Changed Everything

Over time, the widespread transition from voluntary to automatic enrollment has had enormous implications for retirement plan participant behavior.[10] When a retirement plan begins automatically enrolling new employees in its retirement plan (i.e., giving them the option to opt out instead of requiring them to opt in), they are enrolled at the default savings rate, and their contributions are invested in the default investment option. In a widely cited study, Madrian and Shea (2001) compared the choices of employees who joined a firm after the introduction of AE, to employees who joined under the previous VE regime. Their empirical setting was the 401(k) plan of a 'large, publicly traded Fortune 500 company in the health care and insurance industry' (p. 1151). The authors underscored four main findings. First, switching from VE to AE dramatically increased plan participation rates, from 49% to 86%. Second, the effects were heterogeneous: the largest increases in participation were observed among younger, lower-income, and Black and Hispanic employees. Third, conditional on participating, average employee savings rates decreased. In particular, the modal savings rate fell from 6% to 3%, and the average savings rate declined from 7.3% to 4.4%. While some of these decreases were likely driven by acceptance of the 3% default rate by employees that would not have voluntarily enrolled, there were not enough new participants to rationalize the full decline. Fourth, the fraction of employees allocating all their contributions to the (default) money market fund jumped from 6.4% to 80.0%.

These findings were consistent with those of Choi et al. (2004), who extended the analysis to include two additional large firms and followed participants for up to 48 months after the change in policy. Again, participation rates rose significantly under AE and remained high. At the same time, 65%–87% of new plan participants saved at the default contribution rate and invested exclusively in the default investment option. The authors noted that 'this percentage decline[d] slowly over time, falling to 40%–54% after two years of tenure, and to about 45% after three years of tenure (in the two companies for which data extends this far)' (p. 83). In other words, widespread acceptance of default options did boost participation, but it also reduced dispersion in participant outcomes for at least three years, relative to plans without defaults. As a result, employees who would not have participated under VE arguably benefited from the positive contribution rates under AE, despite the low-risk default investment options. By contrast, employees who would have participated at a higher contribution rate under VE or chosen to hold a riskier portfolio were potentially worse off.

It is noteworthy that Madrian and Shea (2001) and Choi et al. (2004) studied the impact of AE on 401(k) plans sponsored by employers willing to experiment with plan design. Employers offering 401(k) plans tend to pay relatively high wages and offer stable employment, and the plans often feature employer matching contributions. According to Vanguard (2024), the median participant income within 401(k) plans was $82,000 in 2023, and 96% of 401(k) plans offered an employer match.[11] Furthermore, the fact that the large firms featured in the papers cited sought to increase plan participation rates raises questions about external validity if AE were applied to a broader set of firms. A comprehensive literature review on automatic enrollment by Beshears et al. (2023), however, confirmed that automatic enrollment has similar effects in a wide variety of other DC retirement plans.

The early finding that reliance on defaults reduced asset accumulation for some participants arose from an interaction between low default contribution rates and low-risk default investment options. Indeed, the expected benefits of automating retirement (and non-retirement) savings do differ with employee demographic characteristics, financial literacy, and the extent to which households are present biased (Chin et al. this volume). This begs the question of how we should think about optimal defaults in a world with heterogeneous effects. At a minimum, as discussed below, there has been movement toward higher contribution rates and riskier default investment options.

## Voluntary Enrollment, Automatic Enrollment, or Active Choice?

The widespread acceptance of default contribution rates and default investment options in company retirement plans raises important questions about how employers should set optimal defaults. Choi et al. (2003) considered optimal default retirement savings rates when participants are assumed to be hyperbolic discounters.[12] Specifically, their model assumes that participants suffer flow welfare losses when they save too much or too little, relative to their privately optimal savings rate, but that participants must incur a one-time, time-varying adjustment cost to move away from the default contribution rate. On the one hand, when the range of privately optimal savings rates is narrow, the optimal default contribution rate is near the middle of the distribution. When the range is wide, on the other hand, such that many employees will be harmed by any particular default savings rate, the optimal default contribution rate will be close to the minimum or maximum of the distribution because extreme defaults are the most likely to trigger active choices by employees.[13] Relatedly, when Beshears et al. (2023) studied a retirement plan with a default savings rate of 12% (and minimum required rate of 4%), they found that 73% of participants chose a different savings rate within 12 months. They interpret the fact that lower-income employees are *less* likely to deviate from the default rate as evidence that they 'face higher psychological barriers to active decision making' (p. 4). Conditional on making any changes, however, the authors found that 40% of lower-income employees chose the lowest possible savings rate, versus 26% of higher-income employees.

Goda et al. (2020) asked whether predictors of retirement contribution rates varied across AE and VE choice environments. They analyzed choices pertaining to the (supplemental DC) thrift savings plan (TSP) using a combination of administrative and survey data. For employees hired before August 2010, TSP offered VE and a default contribution rate of 0%. For employees hired after this date, TSP implemented AE with a default contribution rate of 3%. The authors found higher financial literacy predicted that employees would accept the default rate under AE but contribute more under VE. Controlling for survey-based measures of long-run discount rates, present bias, and exponential-growth bias, they found that present bias (i.e., overweighting immediate benefits and costs relative to future benefits and costs) predicted acceptance of the default rate under AE, but not under VE. They concluded that 'a causal interpretation of our results suggests that auto-enrollment increases saving primarily among those with low financial literacy' (p. 314) but also cautioned against extrapolating their findings to non-government workers, who lacked DB pension benefits and faced different default contribution rates and employer matching schemes.

Carroll et al. (2009) derived conditions under which forcing employees to make active choices could dominate AE. In their model, active choice was preferred when employees have heterogeneous preferences and a strong tendency to procrastinate. This requires, however, that employees can map their preferences into savings rates and choices over asset allocations. When employees suffer from low levels of financial literacy, it may be optimal to combine active choices over contribution rates with reliance on default investment options, which allow participants to outsource portfolio management.

## Target Date Funds as Default Investment Options

Before the Pension Protection Act of 2006, it was common for retirement plans that featured automatic enrollment to offer either a money market mutual fund or a stable value fund as the default investment option. Beginning in 2007, plans were provided with a safe harbor when they defaulted participants into target date funds, balanced funds, or managed accounts (Department of Labor 2006). Of the three qualified default investment alternatives (QDIAs), TDFs have proven the most popular. According to Vanguard (2024), 98% of the retirement plans that designated a QDIA in 2023 chose to offer a TDF.

Mitchell and Utkus (2022) studied the introduction of TDFs in a large sample of Vanguard 401(k) plans. They highlighted two advice-related features of TDFs. First, participants are likely to interpret the fact that each fund name includes a target retirement year as an implicit recommendation about how they should be investing. Second, because TDFs automatically reduce portfolio risk over time in a prespecified manner (known as the 'glide path'), TDFs relieve participants of the need to rebalance portfolios as they age. The authors found that when Vanguard TDFs were introduced into plans with voluntary enrollment, 28.4% of new employees and 10.2% of existing employees invested partially or entirely in TDFs. For plans with automatic enrollment, those statistics were 78.7% and 21.7%, respectively. The authors interpreted the fact that approximately twice as many existing employees chose to invest in TDFs in plans featuring automatic enrollment as a default-related 'endorsement effect.' With respect to portfolio characteristics, they showed that transitioning to TDFs was associated with increased equity exposure and decreased idiosyncratic risk. They acknowledged, however, that decreases in idiosyncratic risk could partly reflect the fact that Vanguard TDFs invest in index funds rather than actively managed funds. Analyzing account-level data from a large US financial institution, Parker et al. (2023) found that the widespread adoption of TDFs, made possible by the Pension Protection Act of 2006, increased both the average allocation to equity and the extent to which equity allocations varied over the life cycle.

Several other studies have also highlighted the benefits of TDFs. Keim and Mitchell (2018) studied participant responses to a change in the investment menu offered by a large nonprofit institution, which eliminated 39 funds in 2012, impacting approximately half of plan participants. Only 26% of the participants with funds slated for removal actively chose from among the remaining funds during the July 1 to October 19 window; the remaining 74% were mapped into an age-appropriate TDF. In both samples of participants, there were significant reductions in expense ratios, idiosyncratic risk, and systematic risk. Chalmers and Reuter (2020) studied a retirement plan where TDFs were added for all participants, but access to one-on-one advice from brokers was eliminated for new participants. They documented that the same participant characteristics predicting demand for brokers also predict demand for TDFs. For participants with high predicted demand for advice, TDF-based portfolios held by new participants outperformed broker-recommended portfolios held by existing participants. More generally, to the extent that less sophisticated investors now outsource their portfolio management to TDFs rather than managing portfolios on their own, one can plausibly expect to see participants making fewer investment mistakes. This is an interesting area for future research. Relatedly, Blanchett et al. (2020) found that participants invested in TDFs (or managed accounts) were much less likely than others to change their retirement portfolios during 2020Q1, when COVID-19 caused a large (temporary) drop in market indices and led to spikes in volatility.

Goldin and Reck (2020) described conditions under which researchers can recover participant preferences from choices in settings with framing effects by focusing on choices against the frame. Using data on participation decisions under AE and VE, the authors concluded that most employees preferred to participate, but that for example, those employees with low job tenure did not. Adopting a similar framework, Choukhmane and de Silva (2023) used changes in default investment options within 401(k) plans to estimate the investment preferences of plan participants. Their goal was to shed new light on whether stock market non-participation is driven by preferences or frictions. They found that very few of the participants defaulted into TDFs actively chose to opt-out of stock market participation by reallocating contributions to low-risk investment options, while a significant fraction of those defaulted into money market funds actively choose to invest in equity.[14] They concluded from these patterns that in the absence of frictions, most investors would prefer to be holding risky assets in their retirement accounts. An important implication is that for many investors, money market funds were particularly poor choices for default investment options.

While some retirement plan participants could view TDFs from different asset management firms as perfect substitutes, in practice TDFs with the same target retirement date may pursue different investment strategies. Using data from 1994 to 2012, Balduzzi and Reuter (2019) documented significant differences in the investment strategies of TDFs offered by different mutual fund families. They found that the TDFs of families entering the market after the passage of the Pension Protection Act of 2006 exhibited higher levels of idiosyncratic risk, which they attributed to strategic risk-taking with the goal of attracting flows. The fact that different TDFs exhibited different levels of systematic and idiosyncratic risk raises the possibility of matching between the riskiness of a TDF suite and the riskiness of the firm sponsoring the retirement plan. Using cross-sectional data on a large sample of retirement plan investment menus in 2010, they detected little evidence of risk matching. Whether this has changed over the past 14 years is unknown.[15]

While TDFs allow participants to outsource portfolio management decisions to professionals, thereby reducing the likelihood of investment mistakes, reliance on TDFs may also have unintended consequences. Goda et al. (2019) asked whether and how federal employee behavior within the TSP changed when the default investment option for new hires was changed from a low-risk, low-return fund that invested in US government bonds to TDFs. Their main finding was that employees were less likely to make active choices about their contribution rates when the default investment option was a TDF. Because the default contribution rate was 3% and the minimum contribution rate required for an employer match was 5%, on average, total contributions fell for new hires. A broader concern is that reliance on TDFs can reduce engagement with the retirement plan because the most important function (portfolio management) has been outsourced.

Reuter and Richardson (2022) studied demand for advice within a set of retirement plans administered by TIAA-CREF, and they concluded that participants who invested solely through TDFs were significantly less likely to seek advice on both asset allocation and retirement income levels. While it is not surprising that this would be true for younger employees, it remained true throughout the age distribution, suggesting that investors in TDFs were less likely to learn whether the default savings rate best suited them.

## Customized Defaults

Moving from VE to AE boosts retirement plan participation rates, but it also replaces at least some active choice with one-size-fits-all defaults. Conceptually, it should be possible to reduce the gaps between employees' optimal choices and default choices by conditioning defaults on employee characteristics. While TDFs already offer different portfolios to employees with different target retirement dates, there is scope for improvement with respect to default investment options and other defaults.

In one study, Goda and Manchester (2013) used a regression discontinuity design empirical strategy to study the effect of defaults on the choice of retirement plan. Their empirical setting was a firm that closed its defined benefit (DB) retirement plan to new employees, and then gave existing employees a one-time, irreversible choice between the two plan types. For employees age 45+, the default was the DB plan; for younger employees, it was the DC plan. The authors estimated that employees with ages just below 45 were around 60 percentage points more likely to enroll in the DC plan, compared to workers just over age 45 at the time of plan transition. Next, they solved for the optimal age-based cutoff between the two types of plans as one that maximized aggregate pension wealth, controlling for the greater risk of DC retirement plans. Implicit in this exercise was the possibility that DC plans could be optimal for participants who were sufficiently young, so long as they were not too risk averse. Indeed, when the coefficient of constant relative risk aversion was assumed to be two, they found that the optimal age below which to default employees into the DC plan was 47, close to the age that was chosen by the firm. When the assumed coefficient of constant relative risk aversion was increased to 10, the optimal age below which to default employees into the DC plan fell all the way to 20, implying that all existing employees should be defaulted into the DB retirement plan (and reducing the expected benefit to the firm of closing the DB plan). The authors concluded that defaults that ignore key employee characteristics were likely to result in smaller welfare gains than those that internalized one or more of these characteristics.

It is conceivable, if permitted by the US Department of Labor (DOL), that employers could condition default savings rates on age, income, industry, expected employment tenure, and other characteristics, including whether the employee is currently making student loan payments. With respect to default investment options, plans could replace TDFs with managed accounts that internalized employee preferences, savings needs, and the level of other financial assets (if any). For example, Duarte et al. (2022) used machine learning algorithms to demonstrate that TDF-style glide paths depending only on investor age reduced expected consumption by 2%–3% relative to allocations that incorporated investor wealth levels and macroeconomic factors. Or, under the assumption that the value of customized advice on asset allocation and savings rates increased with age, plans could offer managed accounts as defaults for employees above a particular age. The question that employers would first need to answer is whether the expected benefits of customization outweighed any increase in fees, especially if meaningful customization required detailed input from employees.

## Automatic Escalation

As noted above, automatic enrollment is associated with decreased dispersion in employee contribution rates. In the earliest studies, default contribution rates under AE were lower than under VE because the default rates were set quite low. According to Vanguard data (2024), however, the average employee contribution rate was 7.4% in 2023, and the median was 6.2%. These higher rates reflect some combination of higher default contribution rates and automatic escalation, which was encouraged by the Pension Protection Act of 2006. Under automatic escalation, plans could set a default contribution rate of 3% but then, if participants did not opt out, raise the contribution rate by one percentage point each year, up to a maximum of 10%.[16]

Thaler and Benartzi (2004) provided the first real-world evidence that automatic escalation could be used to increase contribution rates—at least within firms actively seeking to boost contributions. They described how behavioral biases, including a lack of self-control, procrastination, and loss-aversion, could lead some workers to save too little for retirement. Then, because their paper sought to provide prescriptive savings advice, the authors tested a (trademarked) intervention named Save More Tomorrow™ (SMarT). This product set an initial contribution rate and then committed to increase the contribution rate by one or more percentage points following annual raises, with this timing chosen so that take-home pay was not reduced.

The SMarT plan was implemented differently at three firms. At the first, which they followed over four pay cycles, average contribution rates for participants joining SMarT increased from 3.5% to 13.6%, and participation rates remained high. For the entire plan, the average contribution rate increased from 4.4% to 10.6%. The implementation of SMarT at the third firm came closest to how automatic escalation is typically implemented by firms today, as it featured pre-determined contribution rate increases of one, two, or three percentage points on April 1 of each year. (In their data, 54% of participants chose one percentage point, 35% chose two percentage points, and 11% chose three percentage points.) Take-up rates were higher for those earning less than $50,000 (in 2004), but also for those with four to five years of tenure, suggesting that automatic escalation was most popular with employees having stable employment. Based on a simulation at the end of the paper, the authors concluded that when automatically enrolling workers in SMarT with a 5% baseline contribution rate and a two percentage-point annual increase (and allowing for attrition from the plan), 'the average saving rate is projected to increase from 5.0% to 10.9% within five years' (Thaler and Benartzi 2004: S184).

The magnitude of this simulated increase begs the question of how well automatic escalation works when applied to more diverse plans. While financial services firms are in an excellent position to describe the evolution of plan contribution rates in plans with and without automatic escalation by participant age and income, we are unaware of any such tabulations. In a very-recent study of the long-term effects of automatic enrollment and automatic escalation (described in more detail below), Choi et al. (2024) estimated that automatic escalation increased contribution rates by 0.2% of income per year, with fewer than half of participants accepting automatic escalation on their first escalation date.[17]

## Expanding Access to Retirement Savings: The UK Experience

The 2008 UK Pensions Act extended AE to most private sector employees, beginning in 2012. An initial assessment of the regulation by Cribb and Emmerson (2020) found that only 36% of private sector employees were active participants in an employer-sponsored retirement plan in 2012. Thereafter, AE was rolled out in waves, between 2012 and 2017, beginning with the largest employers.[18] The set of 'targeted' employees included those of working age with annual earnings above a minimum threshold (£10,000 in 2014). Until April 2018, the minimum employee contribution was 1% and the minimum employee plus employer contribution was 2%. In April 2018, the minimum contribution rates increased to 3% and 5%, and in April 2019, increased again to 5% and 8%. Employees who opted out of the program forwent the employer contributions.

Exploiting a difference-in-difference empirical strategy, Cribb and Emmerson (2020) estimated that this policy increased private sector participation rates by 36 percentage points (relative to a baseline of 49% for the large and medium-size employers studied). Furthermore, they estimated even larger effects for lowest-quartile earners (54 percentage points) than for highest-quartile earners (16 percentage points). The combined employee plus employer contribution rate was estimated to rise by 1.1% of earnings (including the 0% contribution rates of those who opted out). Interestingly, they also found modest increases in participation by employees who were not targeted by the program (e.g., based on age or income) but nevertheless eligible to participate.

In a later study, Cribb and Emmerson (2021) analyzed the short-term effect of AE on small employers; these firms had the lowest participation rates in 2012. The authors' empirical strategy exploited randomization in enrollment dates of employers with between 2 and 29 employees. There were several reasons to expect that automatic enrollment would be less successful in smaller firms. These firms pay lower wages and have higher turnover rates. Moreover, because they disproportionately lack retirement benefits, these firms may attract employees with higher discount rates. As a result, it was unclear whether smaller employers would view the introduction of an automatic enrollment retirement plan as a positive development. Nevertheless, the authors concluded that small employer participation rates increased by 44 percentage points, resulting in an overall participation rate of 70%. The largest effects were for employees below the age of 40 (54% versus 36%) and with fewer than four years of tenure (49% versus 40%). Total contributions increased by 1.8% of earnings, a bigger increase than for the larger firms studied in their earlier paper. Given their empirical strategy and data, however, the authors were unable to measure long-term effects on participation rates or retirement account balances, or to test for crowd-out among different forms of savings.

## Expanding Access to Retirement Savings: The US Experience

Many US employees still lack access to employer-sponsored retirement plans, especially lower-wage workers at smaller firms. In April 2020, 64% of private sector workers in the US had access to employer-sponsored DC retirement plans (US Bureau of Labor Statistics [BLS] 2021). Access was higher for employees of larger employers (78% of those with 100+ employees versus 53% of those with 1–99 employees), and for employees earning higher wages (84% in the top quartile of wages versus 41% in the bottom quartile). Moreover, while employees lacking access to employer-based retirement plans could open and contribute to individual retirement accounts (IRAs), very few do so (e.g., Chalmers et al. 2022).

In response to low levels of retirement savings by lower-income US households, there have been legislative movements at the state and federal levels to greatly expand access to employer-based retirement plans (Degen 2024). In 2017, Oregon introduced the first state-sponsored automatic enrollment retirement plan, requiring employers not already offering a retirement plan to automatically enroll their employees in OregonSaves (Chalmers et al. 2025). As in the UK, the program was launched in waves, beginning with the largest employers. Following a brief enrollment period during which employees could opt out of the program, the state of Oregon opened (after-tax) Roth IRAs on behalf of eligible employees. The default contribution rate was 5% of before-tax income and, unless the employee opted out of the automatic escalation provision, rose by one percentage point per year to a maximum of 10%. There was no employer match, but because employees contributed to Roth IRAs, employees could withdraw contributions without tax penalties, resulting in liquid retirement savings.[19]

According to the Center for Retirement Initiatives, 16 states have introduced automatic enrollment IRA programs (Center for Retirement Initiatives 2024), and as of March 31, 2024, some $1.38 billion was invested in automatic IRAs in California, Colorado, Connecticut, Illinois, Maryland, and Oregon. In Oregon alone, 126,234 accounts held $273.1 million, for an average account balance of $2,163 (OregonSaves 2024). Consistent with the large number of funded accounts in Oregon, Dao (2024) showed that OregonSaves boosted IRA ownership among employees without access to 401(k) plans by 2.8 percentage points (or 27%).

Both Quinby et al. (2020) and Chalmers et al. (2025) relied on administrative data ending in 2019/2020 to provide initial assessments of OregonSaves. All studies emphasized that OregonSaves targeted employees in low-wage jobs and industries, where participation rates are much lower than observed in private sector 401(k) plans with automatic enrollment. For example, taking a calendar-time perspective, Quinby et al. (2020) found that among those employees classified as actively employed, 43% had a positive contribution rate and a positive account balance. By way of comparison, for employees earning between $15,000 and $30,000, Vanguard (2024) reported participation rates of 44% under voluntary enrollment and 87% under automatic enrollment.

Taking an event-time perspective, Chalmers et al. (2025) showed that after 12 months, 50% of participants had opted out, 37% had experienced job turnover, and 69% have either opted out or experienced job turnover—though there were meaningful differences across industries. High turnover rates pose serious challenges for employees seeking to save, as well as those seeking to measure participation rates.[20] Chalmers et al. (2025) found modestly higher opt-out rates in industries with higher average incomes. At the same time, the authors found that employees with lower earnings within their industry (and within their employer) were more likely to quickly stop contributing. Chalmers et al. (2022) reported that the number one reason that employees gave for opting out of OregonSaves was a lack of income.

These authors also tracked the evolution of account balances in event time for the subset of contributors that could be followed for at least 12 months (Chalmers et al. 2025). Including the 10% of accounts that end the 12-month period with a $0 balance—but ignoring employees that never contributed—the mean account balance was $699, and the median was $348. These amounts are small by the standards of retirement accounts but large by the standards of liquid saving accounts. Because their administrative data end in April 2020, the authors could not track inflows or outflows during the pandemic, to learn whether participants tapped into the liquid savings. Quinby et al. (2020) reported that 20% of accounts with a positive balance during September 2018 experience at least one withdrawal over the next 12 months, and the withdrawal rate was highest for those that stopped working for an employer participating in OregonSaves. It is still not known if employees viewed their OregonSaves accounts as a source of liquid savings to smooth consumption between jobs or if they simply closed their accounts because they did not wish to contribute to OregonSaves again.

In the future, it will be interesting to see how participation rates and account balances in OregonSaves compare to those in CalSavers and other state-sponsored automatic IRAs.[21] One puzzling feature of the OregonSaves program is the large number of employers who enrolled employees but never directed contributions to their Roth IRAs. For example, in March 2024, 27,745 employers had uploaded employee data but only 7,514 had submitted payroll during the past 90 days (OregonSaves 2024). Because OregonSaves had not yet imposed fines on employers for non-compliance, it is unclear how many employers could be waiting for penalties to be imposed before beginning to comply (or applying for exemptions from the program). In California, employers can face penalties of up to $500 per employee for non-compliance (CalSavers Retirement Savings Program 2024).

## How Do Households Finance Savings from Automatic Enrollment?

To the extent that automatic enrollment and automatic escalation are intended to move employees closer to their optimal saving rates, there is an implicit assumption that employees will reduce consumption to accommodate the additional savings. Yet there also may be offsetting decreases in other savings or even increases in debt. A particularly concerning scenario would arise if low-income employees effectively financed retirement savings by taking on payday loans. Unfortunately, data on the behavior of retirement plan participants rarely can be linked to information on checking accounts, liquid savings accounts, other retirement accounts (if any), credit card balances, and other forms of debt. There are three notable exceptions.

Beshears et al. (2022) were the first to ask whether increased savings under automatic enrollment was financed through increased household debt, resulting in higher measured financial distress. In August 2010, newly hired civilian employees of the US Army were automatically enrolled in the TSP at a default contribution rate of 3%; those hired before that date were still subject to voluntary enrollment. The researchers observed contributions to the TSP, but not withdrawals; this was the same plan change studied by Goda et al. 2020. To measure changes in debt, they linked employee payroll records to credit bureau reports. They found little evidence that credit scores or debt balances (excluding auto loans and first mortgages) changed in response to automatic enrollment, even when focusing on employees earning under $34,000.

Scenarios in which employees finance savings through borrowing seem more likely to arise when retirement savings plans are extended to jobs with lower wages and less stable employment. To study this possibility, Choukhmane and Palmer (2024) exploited the increases in UK minimum contribution rates that took place in April 2018 and April 2019 (described above). To determine how employees responded to changes in both their contribution amounts and employer matches, they analyzed panel data from a large UK financial institution that merged retail deposit and credit account data with pension account data. The authors' empirical strategy made use of the fact that some employee and employer contributions needed to be adjusted because of the regulation, while others (already above the required minimums) did not. They found that only one-third of the decrease in monthly take-home pay was financed through decreased consumption; the rest was financed through lower deposit account balances and higher credit card balances.[22] Furthermore, the changes in consumption were concentrated in discretionary non-durable spending, including restaurants and leisure. Consistent with liquidity constraints, they also found that households with the lowest pre-existing deposit balances and the highest pre-existing credit card balances reduced their consumption the most.

Beshears et al. (2024) also asked whether increases in retirement plan contributions in the UK were offset on other margins. Like Cribb and Emmerson (2021), their empirical strategy was based on randomized enrollment dates for employers with 2–29 employees during the initial rollout, when the minimum combined contribution rate rose from 0% to 2%. The authors combined individual-level data from the National Employee Savings Trust (NEST) with individual-level credit bureau data from Experian and employer-level data on enrollment dates.[23] The (treatment-on-treated) estimates compared pension contributions and outcomes of those enrolled earlier relative to those enrolled later, over a three-year period. Among contributors, they found an additional month of enrollment increased employee contributions by £16–19 but also increased unsecured debt by £7. Accounting for employee contributions, employer contributions, and tax credits, an additional month of enrollment increased total pension contributions by £32–£38. The authors reported that the increase in unsecured debt was higher for younger and lower-paid employees, as well as those with higher credit scores. They concluded that 'automatic enrollment has complex effects across different facets of the household balance sheet' (p. 24).

## What are the Long-Term Effects of Automatic Enrollment?

In a presentation to the American Economic Association and American Finance Association titled 'Nudges are Not Enough,' Laibson (2020) argued that the long-term effects of nudges like AE were generally smaller than the short-term effects. His insight was that while large welfare effects depend on cumulative effects over long horizons, the effects of nudges often can be undone—and that this was especially likely to occur when nudges sought to overcome long-standing worker preferences or biases.[24]

Three recent papers report that the short-run effects of automatic enrollment on retirement savings overstate the long-run effects. In one, Choukhmane (2024) analyzed data from the US and UK. Using data on over 100 US 401(k) plans with a variety of default contribution rates, he found that AE boosted contribution rates initially, but that after three years of tenure, average cumulative contributions of non-automatically enrolled employees converged to those of automatically enrolled employees. Convergence occurred because automatically enrolled workers were more likely to remain at the default contribution rate, while voluntarily enrolled workers were more likely to increase their contribution rates over time. When comparing average contribution rates, however, it is important to recall that AE simultaneously increases contribution rates for employees who would not have contributed under VE and decreases the contribution rates for (some) employees who would have contributed under VE. Consequently, Choukhmane (2024) found that AE increased the savings of workers at the bottom of the savings distribution, who would not otherwise have benefited from employer matching contributions. The same study exploited the phased rollout of automatic enrollment by employer size in the UK (described above) and found that workers automatically enrolled at their prior employer were less likely to voluntarily enroll at their new (smaller) employer. This finding highlighted a limitation of behavioral nudges. The practical implications of this finding in the UK are unclear, however, because he found no difference in the likelihood of opting out if the new employer also offered automatic enrollment (now the norm).

Derby et al. (2023) used US tax data covering 745 firms to study the responses of employees and their spouses to automatic enrollment. While the authors found that AE increased retirement plan contributions by 1.28% points (a 51% increase) during the first year, the net increase at the end of the year was only 1.02 percentage points because employees subject to AE were significantly more likely to withdraw contributions following job turnover. Four years after enrollment, the net increase in savings had fallen to 0.73 percentage points. The authors did not find any evidence that spouses adjusted their retirement savings behavior in response to AE, which they attributed to the fact that savers under AE are not active savers.

Finally, Choi et al. (2024) compared the behavior of new and existing employees at nine firms that made changes to the structure of their 401(k) plans that only impacted new employees. There were three types of changes: the introduction of AE without default automatic escalation, the addition of default automatic escalation to plans that already featured AE, and the simultaneous introduction of AE and default automatic escalation. After accounting for plan withdrawals following job turnover, and removing variation due to differences in investment returns, the authors estimated that over 60 months, AE increases annualized savings by 0.6% of income, automatic escalation increased annualized savings by 0.2% of income, and that the introduction of both features boosted annualized savings by 0.8% of income.

These estimates were lower than earlier estimates for three reasons. First, as in Choukhmane and de Silva (2023), existing employees were more likely to increase savings rates on their own. Second, while the likelihood that withdrawals were reinvested in another retirement plan were similar for new and existing employees, new employees were more likely to experience leakage because they were more likely to experience job turnover. Third, while many employees did not initially opt out of automatic escalation, only 39% of employees subject to automatic escalation allowed their savings rate to increase on the first escalation date. The conclusion of all three papers is that nudges in 401(k) plans increased savings, but by less than policymakers might have hoped. It is important for future research to ask how these effects vary with employee characteristics such as income and expected job tenure, and whether there are groups of employees for whom increased savings are entirely offset by increased debt.

## Employer-Based Liquid Savings Accounts

Although many life-cycle models focus on a single portfolio, real-world savers need to decide how much to save in relatively illiquid retirement accounts versus in liquid savings accounts. The evidence suggests that in practice, many households fail to accumulate much in the way of liquid savings. Canilang et al. (2020) reported that 16% of US households stated they were unable to pay all their monthly bills, and another 12% stated that they would be unable to do so if confronted with an unexpected expense of $400. Given this evidence of financial fragility, there has been growing interest in bundling liquid savings accounts with traditional employer-sponsored retirement accounts.

In an analysis of the 2019 Survey of Consumer Finances, Berk et al. (2023a) confirmed that 25% of US households of all ages lacked emergency savings and pointed out that these patterns were consistent with present-biased preferences (Laibson 1997). The authors also established that these broad patterns held in the UK, where 34% of those surveyed reported non-pension savings of less than £250 (but there was a strong positive correlation between income and levels of liquid savings). So, how did UK workers respond to the introduction of employer-based liquid savings accounts, for which they needed to sign up? Across five UK employers that began to offer these accounts, the authors found that less than 1% of eligible employees ever activated a savings account.

In contrast, when Berk et al. (2023b) studied the introduction of employer-based liquid savings accounts with automatic enrollment, they found much higher participation rates. For example, SUEZ Recycling and Recovery UK LTD automatically enrolled new employees in a liquid savings plan with a default contribution rate of £40 per month. In a departure from automatic enrollment norms in the US and UK, SUEZ was required to receive consent from each new hire to complete the automatic enrollment. Employees were also given multiple opportunities to opt out. By month 18, 44.5% of new employees participated in the liquid savings account versus 1.3% of existing employees (who had to opt in). Notably, because the authors did not find that contributions to the retirement account decreased when contributions to the liquid savings plan began, total net savings rose by approximately one percentage point for the new hires.

## Distortions in Plan Design and Provision

Employees described in economics models are assumed to maximize their expected lifetime utility (e.g., Horneff et al. 2023). Given this objective, many employees would prefer their employers to offer a menu of low-cost investment options (conditional on investment style and quality), to pay all plan expenses, and to provide generous matching contributions. Of course, the generosity of the retirement plan—and whether one is offered at all—is determined by the competitiveness of the labor market.

From the employer's perspective, offering a traditional 401(k) plan is costly even when the employer shares plan expenses with employees and offers a limited employer match. The employer must hire a recordkeeper for the plan, oversee the creation of an investment menu, and periodically review the appropriateness of the investment options.[25] In practice, firms that provide recordkeeping services tend to be asset management firms. Pool et al. (2016) tested for potential conflicts of interest between employers and mutual fund families that serve as plan recordkeepers, using data for 1988–2009. They documented increases in the fraction of plans with mutual fund family recordkeepers (creating a potential conflict), as well as the number of mutual fund families represented on the typical investment menu (reducing the size of any such conflict). The movement toward open architecture investment menus resulted in many funds being available from both affiliated and unaffiliated recordkeepers. The authors found that the lowest-performing funds over a three-year period were about half as likely to be removed from the menus of affiliated recordkeepers over the next year as they were from the menus of other recordkeepers (13.7% versus 25.5%). Moreover, consistent with earlier evidence on plan participant inertia, they showed 'that participants are generally not sensitive to poor performance and do not undo the menu's bias toward affiliated families' (Pool et al. 2016: 1781).

More recently, however, Kronlund et al. (2021) found that participants responded to a 2012 DOL change in the disclosure of investment option fees and performance by withdrawing money from the most expensive funds. Additionally, they found that there were stronger effects in plans with larger average contribution amounts and smaller investment menus. Perhaps unintentionally, the change in disclosure also increased the sensitivity of participant flows to funds' one-year returns.

With respect to plan expenses, employers must decide what fraction of plan fees should be paid by participants, whether to offer employer matches, and whether to choose funds that provide 'revenue sharing' back to the plan. This revenue can be used to cover plan expenses or rebated back to participants. Pool et al. (2022) reported that funds paying revenue sharing were more likely to be added and less likely to be removed from retirement plans that receive indirect compensation from revenue sharing, and that participants pay higher 'all-in fees.' It is unclear, however, whether the higher all-in fees reflect conflicts of interest or conscious decisions by employers to make participants pay a greater fraction of plan costs.

Bhattacharya and Illanes (2022) evaluated how market imperfections and misalignment in employers' willingness to pay for quality could distort the investment menus provided to workers and lead some employers not to offer plans. On the one hand, offering higher-quality 401(k) plans could help with employee hiring and retention, and potentially reduce litigation risk under the Employee Retirement Income Security Act of 1974 (ERISA). On the other hand, employees might not value the time and expense required to offer a high-quality plan (or any plan at all), and employers are likely to possess limited budgets to pay for plan expenses. Analyzing data on all DC plans with at least 100 participants in 2016, Bhattacharya and Illanes (2022) estimated that large employers preferred for their plans to include an S&P 500 index option and TDFs, and to charge lower expense ratios, when compared to smaller employers. Yet the authors could not identify whether these preferences arose from differences in worker demand, differences in competitive pressures from the labor market, or differences in litigation risk. The authors also found that while both large and small firms preferred that plan expenses were paid with indirect rather than direct compensation, small firms exhibited the stronger preference for indirect compensation (e.g., by offering investment options with revenue sharing). The provocative implication for those seeking to expand access to employer-based retirement plans was that 'many small firms must be able to offer low-quality plans in order to provide them at all' (Bhattacharya and Illanes 2022: 37). Although there was no discussion of how employer willingness to pay varied across industries, it may be lowest in industries that currently provide the least access to employer sponsored retirement plans (e.g., agriculture and food services).

After discussing several possible regulatory interventions, this study concluded that regulation must directly target quality, 'either by constraining the design of plans or by subsidizing or penalizing certain plan features' (p. 42). The automatic IRA programs discussed above offer one standardized product which may be less expensive for employers. One interpretation of the relatively high opt-out rate in OregonSaves is that employers who previously chose not to offer their own retirement plans were internalizing relatively low demand from their employees.

All else equal, participants benefit from lower fees. For example, participants typically benefit when plans switch to lower cost share classes of existing funds.[26] The situation becomes more complicated when higher fees are associated with more or higher-quality services. Loseto (2023) and Yang (2025) documented significant cross-plan dispersion in the level of fees paid by 401(k) participants, but they used different models to rationalize the dispersion.[27] Loseto found that employers were only half as sensitive to fund fees as investors and tended to offer funds affiliated with their recordkeepers. Concluding that fee dispersion was driven by markups, he advocated for low-cost default investments. In contrast, Yang (2025) concluded that markups could explain only about one-quarter of the cross-plan dispersion in fees, and that the remaining dispersion could be attributed to differences in the provision of costly administrative and advisory services. As indirect evidence that recordkeeping services were not 'pure commodities,' he cited survey evidence that plan sponsors ranked 'participant readiness for retirement, plan sponsor website or tools, and participant experience' as higher priorities, on average, than the levels of recordkeeping fees and investment fees (p. 9).

## Regulatory Changes to US Savings Plans

The US recently passed two major pieces of legislation focused on retirement savings, with SECURE Act 1.0 of 2019 and SECURE Act 2.0 of 2022.[28] Below, we describe several interesting provisions from each act, offer predictions on likely outcomes based on existing research, and highlight where additional research is needed.

- Section 102 of SECURE 1.0 increased the maximum possible contribution rate under automatic escalation from 10% to 15%, beginning in 2020. Some employees may accept rising contribution rates, especially if increases in contribution rates coincide with higher salaries (Thaler and Benartzi 2004), but rising contribution rates could also trigger active choices about contribution rates, opting out from automatic escalation, or opting out from the plan (Beshears et al. 2023, Choi et al. 2024, Zhong 2021).
- Section 203 of SECURE 1.0 required retirement plans to provide savers with two lifetime income illustrations on participants' pension benefit statements at least once a year, under a set of assumptions stipulated by the DOL (2020). Specifically, the retirement plan must state the current account balance and convert this balance into both single-life and joint-life annuity payments using the prevailing 10-year Treasury rate and assuming that the participant is age 67. While we are unaware of research on how this requirement has affected contribution rates, to the extent that the annuitized monthly incomes prove to be lower than employees expect, the rule could plausibly result in higher contribution rates. Relatedly, Goda et al. (2014) ran a field experiment to study the effect of providing retirement income projections on employee contribution rates in supplemental retirement plans. They reported that treatment groups were approximately one percentage point more likely to make any changes in contribution rates than the control group; moreover, the treatment groups increased annual contributions by $85 relative to the control group (or 3.6% of the average contribution amount and 0.15% of the average salary). More provocatively, they found that changes in

contribution amounts responded to the underlying assumptions in the income projections, which they randomized. It would be interesting to compare the assumptions in Goda et al.'s (2014) field experiment to the assumptions adopted by the DOL.

Many of the provisions in SECURE 2.0 were intended to increase participation and savings rates:

- Section 101 of SECURE 2.0 required all *new* 401(k) and 403(b) plans to feature automatic enrollment and automatic escalation, with an initial contribution rate of at least 3% and a maximum contribution rate of at least 10%. This provision will eventually increase the set of retirement plans offering automatic enrollment, but the initial impact is likely to be small because existing plans are not required to do so.
- Section 110 of SECURE 2.0 allowed (but did not require) employers, from 2024, to treat student loan payments as employee retirement contributions from the perspective of employer matching contributions. It will be interesting to see what fraction of plans adopt this feature and how the rule impacts retirement savings for the large fraction of young employees with college debt. Holding employee college debt repayment strategies constant, retirement savings could rise due to the new employer matches, increasing the costs associated with offering the retirement plan, except insofar as the provision helps with recruiting and retention. Allowing for optimal responses, as modeled by Horneff et al. (2024), it is likely that net employee retirement contributions by younger employees will decline (because they are no longer required to qualify for the employer match), resulting in increased consumption rather than increased savings.
- Section 103 of SECURE 2.0 replaced a non-refundable Saver's Tax Credit with a Saver's Match beginning in 2027. The previous approach allowed lower-income households to reduce their taxes by up to $1,000 (single) or $2,000 (married), while the new approach will directly deposit up to 50% of the first $2,000 to eligible retirement accounts (eligibility for the match will still depend on household income). Ramnath (2013) showed that households adjusted their incomes to preserve the value of the Saver's Tax Credit, yet the higher credit rate did not boost individual savings contributions at the margin. It remains to be seen whether the Saver's Match proves more effective in increasing retirement savings than the Saver's Tax Credit. Notably, because Roth IRAs will not be eligible for Saver's Match contributions, state-sponsored plans like OregonSaves would need to create companion traditional IRAs for participants to receive Saver's Match contributions.
- Section 113 of SECURE 2.0 allowed employers to offer employees small financial incentives to participate in their retirement plans. It will be

interesting to see whether these incentives increase participation rates meaningfully in plans featuring voluntary enrollment.

- Section 121 of SECURE 2.0 allowed employers to offer starter 401(k) plans, which can set a default employee contribution rate between 3% and 15% and need not offer any employer match. Unlike traditional 401(k) plans, the annual employee contribution limits are the same as for IRAs. Based on estimates from Bhattacharya and Illanes (2022), we predict that take-up of these plans will be quite low, except to the extent that they allow employers to comply with automatic IRA mandates.

With respect to emergency savings:

- Section 115 of SECURE 2.0 allowed plan participants to withdraw up to $1,000 per year to cover emergency expenses. It is unclear whether this option was intended to replace small 401(k) loans or to extend the possibility of small 401(k) loans to more plans. While the need to repay 401(k) plan loans plausibly could crowd out elective plan contributions, Beshears et al. (2025) found that participants in Vanguard plans only slightly reduced their contributions when repaying loans.
- Section 127 of SECURE 2.0 went further, allowing employers to offer the type of automatic-enrollment emergency savings accounts in the UK (Berk et al. 2023b). Because the accounts must be structured like Roth IRAs, with a maximum contribution rate of 3% and maximum employee contributions of $2,500, it is an open question whether participation rates will be as high in the US as they are in the UK. It is also unclear whether employers will benefit from lower absenteeism and turnover rates when their employees gain liquid emergency savings.

In February, US Representative Richard Neal introduced the Automatic IRA Act of 2024, which would expand the automatic enrollment mandate underlying the existing state-sponsored plans to all fifty states, increasing plan portability (Degen 2024). Given the resistance by some politicians to mandates, there also has been bipartisan work on a bill that would allow workers to voluntarily enroll in a government-sponsored plan like the TSP. In either case, it will be important to study the effects of expanded access on retirement savings behavior.

## Conclusions

Defined contribution retirement plans have come a long way since the 1974 passage of ERISA, and they continue to evolve. Widespread acceptance of automatic enrollment, automatic escalation, and sensible default investment options allow workers to outsource retirement plan participation decisions, savings rates, and asset allocation decisions to their employers, simultaneously increasing savings and (likely) decreasing the extent to which participants make common investment mistakes. The potential downside, as emphasized at the outset, is that relying on a one-size-fits-all solution to complex optimization problems which depend on heterogeneous characteristics and preferences may produce far from optimal outcomes. Plan sponsors would do well to encourage active choice along those dimensions about which employees are best able to make decisions, but which otherwise relies on defaults.

It is useful to conclude this chapter by noting several open research questions. Goda and Manchester (2013) emphasized that welfare gains from defaults vary depending on employee characteristics. This raises the question as to what extent should default savings rates and asset allocation decisions vary with income, industry, job type, age, household structure, and part-time versus full-time employment status? For example, should efforts to expand access to automatic IRAs exempt certain industries or job types? Should these plans force active choices instead of relying on automatic enrollment? With respect to default asset allocations, should retirement plans continue to condition TDFs' portfolio mix only on participants' age or instead move to managed accounts that use a broader set of participant characteristics to better capture saver heterogeneity? When will the potential benefits of customization outweigh additional portfolio management fees and administrative costs? More generally, even if there are strong economic arguments for transitioning to customized defaults, doing so may raise issues of fairness. Exempting the lowest-income workers from automatic enrollment or defaulting them into a retirement plan at a lower default savings rate may make sense given their financial constraints, but doing so is likely to increase wealth inequality. Finally, it is important to address whether the rise of automatic enrollment has implications for the choice of non-default investment options, for instance, by reducing the likelihood that unsophisticated participants use these options to construct their own portfolios. Questions such as these require answers if plan sponsors and policymakers are to move ahead with new plan designs.

As researchers continue to combine data on household assets and liabilities, it will be critical to gain an even deeper understanding of the various ways that households respond to automatic enrollment.[29] This is particularly important when studying programs like OregonSaves that extend retirement savings to lower-paid and high turnover jobs. Given the potential concerns about crowd out, we need to learn more about whether such automatic IRA programs continue to emphasize their dual role as retirement savings and liquid savings. More broadly, it will also be critical to determine whether the extension of automatic enrollment to liquid savings increase the fraction of households with meaningful precautionary savings.

Finally, while the research discussed focuses on asset accumulation, decisions around asset decumulation are at least as difficult. Default investment options structured to provide annuity income—such as those introduced by TIAA in 2023 and recently announced by Blackrock—are one potentially valuable development in this area. Horneff et al. (2023) made an important contribution by studying when retirees benefit from using DC assets to purchase annuity income versus using them to delay the claiming of Social Security benefits; nevertheless, more research on optimal decumulation is needed.

## Acknowledgments

The author thanks Vivek Bhattacharya, James Choi, Taha Choukhmane, Tim de Silva, Gopi Shah Goda, Clemens Sialm, Andrew Stichman, James Veneruso, and participants at the Pension Research Council 2024 Symposium for helpful questions and comments. He thanks Jinyoung Kim for excellent research assistance. Any errors and all opinions are his own.

## Notes

1. On the one hand, many households that earn low wages are reliant upon Social Security benefits for retirement income. On the other, Social Security replacement rates are the highest for this group of workers (assuming steady employment histories); see the Investment Company Institute (2023) Figure 8.3.
2. According to the Investment Company Institute (2023: 99), assets 'earmarked for retirement' totaled $33.6 trillion at the end of 2022.
3. The review by Gomes et al. (2021) of the literature on household finance links life-cycle model considerations to the literature on retirement savings and financial advice.
4. In their review of the literature on financial advice, Reuter and Schoar (2024) emphasized the difficulty of identifying optimal portfolios in real-world data.
5. Lusardi and Mitchell (2023) provided an up-to-date review on the literature on the benefits of financial literacy. For example, Clark et al. (2017) documented higher participation and savings rates within the thrift savings plan (TSP) for employees with higher levels of financial literacy. They also demonstrated that employees who completed a learning module about retirement planning were more likely to start contributing and less likely to stop contributing. Heimer (this volume) highlights the role subjective beliefs play in consumption, savings, and consumption decisions.
6. Readers interested in learning more about the heterogeneous effects of automating retirement and non-retirement savings should read the chapter authored by Chin et al. (this volume), while those interested in learning more about how and why consumption and savings vary over the life cycle may consult Heimer (this volume) and Olafsson and Pagel (this volume).

7. An optimal portfolio would offer the highest expected return for a given level of portfolio risk. For any specific investor, the optimal portfolio would depend on the employee's risk tolerance, investment horizon, wealth level, riskiness of labor income, health status, and other factors.
8. Consistent with Benartzi and Thaler (2001), Brown et al. (2007) showed that within-plan, time-series variation in the fraction of equity funds on the investment menu was positively associated with time-series variation in participant holdings of equity funds. Morrin et al. (2012) found that when a single retirement plan increased its menu size from 10 to 19 funds, new employees were more likely to accept the default investment option, but new employees who constructed their own portfolios invested in a larger number of funds when the fund menu was larger.
9. Similarly, Sialm et al. (2015) documented that flows between investment options in retirement plans were driven primarily by menu changes initiated by plan sponsors.
10. McDonald's Corporation pioneered the use of automatic enrollment in its 401(k) plan in 1984, and the feature was officially endorsed by the Internal Revenue Service in 1998 (Crowney 2002). Interestingly, McDonald's switched back to voluntary enrollment in 2002, as part of an integrated review of its plan (Crowney 2002). McDonald's introduced a generous employer match in 2004, but the firm continues to rely on voluntary enrollment for most employees (Probasco 2014).
11. While we cite statistics from Vanguard (2024) throughout this chapter, it is important to recognize that the statistics on participation rates and contribution rates are drawn from the recordkeeping clients for whom Vanguard performs nondiscrimination testing. Consequently, these statistics need not represent the broader industry. For example, in a sample of approximately 5,000 employer-sponsored DC retirement plans, Arnoud et al. (2021) reported that 80% of employer-sponsored plans offered an employer match in 2017, whereas Vanguard (2024) reported that 96% of employer-sponsored plans offered an employer match in 2019 and in 2023.
12. As Choi et al. (2024: 181) stated, 'the important property of these [hyperbolic] preferences is simply that they are characterized by more discounting in the short run than in the long run,' giving rise to time inconsistency.
13. In a calibration exercise involving four firms, Choi et al. (2003) estimated mean actual savings rates between 2.4%–8.2% but mean optimal default savings rates between 0%–15%. They concluded that 'firms whose employees have a high motive to save turn out to have higher optimal defaults than firms whose employees have a low motive to save' (p. 184).
14. Choukhmane and de Silva (2023: 2) estimated 'a coefficient of relative risk aversion of approximately 2.03, an elasticity of intertemporal substitution of approximately 0.38, and a portfolio adjustment cost of $201.'
15. Choi et al. (2003) emphasized that the choice of an optimal default savings rate requires knowledge of the underlying distribution of optimal savings rates and that extreme defaults are more likely to spur active choice. The choice of an optimal TDF is complicated, since on the one hand, it is conceivable that there is greater dispersion in optimal asset allocations than in optimal savings rates,

especially as employees get older. On the other hand, given low levels of financial literacy, it is unclear whether active choice in the absence of financial advice is likely to improve participant welfare (Carroll et al. 2009). As discussed in this section, defaulting employees into TDFs may also reduce demand for financial advice (Reuter and Richardson 2022).

16. Vanguard (2024) reported that 59% of plans featured AE in 2023, and 41% of plans combined AE with automatic escalation. The statistics were 50% and 34%, respectively, in 2019. By way of comparison, Arnoud et al. (2021) reported that 59% of plans featured AE in 2017, but only 18% combined AE with automatic escalation.
17. Zhong (2021) used participant reactions to automatic escalation in OregonSaves to estimate that the optimal contribution rate for that population was 7%.
18. To prevent manipulation of enrollment dates, size was determined by the number of employees in 2012.
19. From 2017 to late 2021, the first $1,000 in contributions were invested in a money market fund, with any additional contributions defaulted into an age-specific TDF. In other words, the program effectively combined safe liquid savings with risky retirement savings. (MarylandSaves, for example, still has this structure.) OregonSaves now transfers all money market assets to an age-specific TDF after an initial waiting period. While employees can still withdrawal their contribution without tax penalties, their account balances are exposed to market risk.
20. Crowney (2002) argued that turnover, a chronic problem in the fast-food business, was the reason McDonald's gave up on automatic enrollment.
21. A search for 'CalSavers' on SSRN.com returned four articles related to the legality of automatic IRAs, and no articles on participation rates or asset accumulation.
22. Specifically, Choukhmane and Palmer (2024) found that a £1 increase in total (employee plus employer) pension contributions was associated with a £0.67 decrease in monthly take-home pay and a £0.23 decrease in total spending, where £0.23 is approximately one-third of £0.67.
23. NEST was created as a public option with a mandate to serve all eligible firms, but it has several private sector competitors (Ladimeji 2024).
24. When Laibson considered the nudge literature more broadly, the only example he cited of a nudge having a large short-term effect and plausibly large welfare effect was Bettinger et al. (2012), who showed that simplifying college financial aid applications increased applications to and enrollment in college. More generally, one can expect the largest welfare effects when nudges involve choices that are difficult to undo.
25. Gropper (2024) argued that plan sponsors responded to growing litigation risk by excluding riskier options from 401(k) plan investment menus and, provocatively, that the reduced availability of riskier options was associated with lower plan portfolio returns and account balances.
26. Exceptions can arise when the share class with the higher expense ratio also pays higher revenue sharing.
27. Both papers use newly available retirement plan-level data provided by BrightScope Beacon.
28. SECURE is short for Setting Every Community Up for Retirement Enhancement.
29. It will also be necessary to take into account other capital market assets that participants hold, so as to present a fuller picture of the extent of saving, portfolio diversification, and decumulation of household wealth over the life cycle.

## References


Agnew, J., P. Balduzzi, and A. Sundén (2003). 'Portfolio Choice and Trading in a Large 401(k) Plan.' *American Economic Review*, 93(1): 193–215.

Arnoud, A., T. Choukhmane, J. Colmenares, C. O'Dea, and A. Parvathaneni (2021). 'The Evolution of U.S. Firms' Retirement Plan Offerings: Evidence from a New Panel Data Set.' NBER Working Paper No. NB20-14.

Balduzzi, P. and J. Reuter (2019). 'Heterogeneity in Target Date Funds: Strategic Risk-Taking or Risk Matching?' *Review of Financial Studies*, 32(1): 300–337.

Benartzi, S. (2001). 'Excessive Extrapolation and the Allocation of 401(k) Accounts to Company Stock.' *Journal of Finance*, 56(5): 1747–1764.

Benartzi, S. and R. H. Thaler (2001). 'Naive Diversification Strategies in Defined Contribution Saving Plans.' *American Economic Review*, 91(1): 79–98.

Berk, S. H., J. Beshears, J. Garg, J. J. Choi, and D. Laibson (2023a). 'Employer-Based Short-Term Savings Accounts.' NBER Working Paper No. 32074.

Berk, S. H., J. J. Choi, J. Garg, J. Beshears, and D. Laibson (2023b). 'Automating Short-Term Payroll Savings: Evidence from Two Large U.K. Experiments.' NBER Working Paper No. 32581.

Beshears, J., M. Blakstad, J.J. Choi, C. Firth, J. Gathergood, D. Laibson, R. Notley, J. D. Sheth, W. Sandbrook, and N. Stewart (2024). 'Does Pension Automatic Enrollment Increase Debt? Evidence from a Large-Scale Natural Experiment.' NBER Working Paper No. 32100.

Beshears, J., J. J. Choi, D. Laibson, B. C. Madrian, and W. L. Skimmyhorn (2022). 'Borrowing to Save? The Impact of Automatic Enrollment on Debt.' *Journal of Finance*, 77(1): 402–447.

Beshears, J., F. Guo, D. Laibson, B. C. Madrian, and J. J. Choi. (2023). 'Automatic Enrollment with a 12% Default Contribution Rate.' NBER Working Paper No. 31601.

Bettinger, E., B. T. Long, P. Oreopoulos, L. Sanbonmatsu (2012). 'The Role of Application Assistance and Information in College Decisions: Results from the H&R Block FAFSA Experiment.' *Quarterly Journal of Economics*, 127(3): 1205–1242.

Bhattacharya, V. and G. Illanes (2022). 'The Design of Defined Contribution Plans.' NBER Working Paper No. 29881.

Blanchett, D., M. Finke, and J. Reuter (2020). 'Portfolio Delegation And 401(K) Plan Participant Responses to COVID-19.' NBER Working Paper No. 27438.

Brown, J. R., N. Liang, and S. Weisbenner (2007). 'Individual Account Investment Options and Portfolio Choice: Behavioral Lessons from 401(k) Plans.' *Journal of Public Economics*, 91(10): 1992–2013.

CalSavers Retirement Savings Program (2024). 'Frequently Asked Questions.' www.calsavers.com/home/frequently-asked-questions.html.

Canilang, S., C. Duchan, K. Kreiss, J. Larrimore, E. Merry, E. Troland, and M. Zabek (2020). *Report on the Economic Well-Being of U.S. Households in 2019, Featuring Supplemental Data from April 2020.* Washington, DC: Board of Governors of the Federal Reserve System.

Carroll, G. D., J. J. Choi, D. Laibson, B. C. Madrian, and A. Metrick (2009). 'Optimal Defaults and Active Decisions.' *Quarterly Journal of Economics*, 124(4): 1639–1674.

Center for Retirement Initiatives (2024). 'State Programs 2024: Optimism More Programs Enacted While Several Newer Programs Will Partner with Existing Programs to Launch in 2024.' cri.georgetown.edu/states/

Chalmers, J., O. S. Mitchell, J. Reuter, and M. Zhong (2022). 'Do State-Sponsored Retirement Plans Boost Retirement Saving?' *AEA Papers and Proceedings*, 112: 142–146.

Chalmers, J, O. S. Mitchell, J. Reuter, and M. Zhong (2025). 'Evidence on Auto-Enrollment Retirement Plan Efficacy from OregonSaves.' *Journal of Public Economics*, 246: 105379.

Chalmers, J. and J. Reuter (2020). 'Is Conflicted Investment Advice Better Than No Advice?' *Journal of Financial Economics*, 138(2): 366–387.

Choi, J. J., D. Laibson, J. Cammarota, R. Lombardo, and J. Beshears. (2024). 'Smaller than We Thought? The Effect of Automatic Savings Policies.' NBER Working Paper No. 32828.

Choi, J. J., D. Laibson, and B. C. Madrian (2009). 'Mental Accounting in Portfolio Choice: Evidence from a Flypaper Effect.' *American Economic Review*, 99(5): 2085–2095.

Choi, J. J., D. Laibson, B. C. Madrian, and A. Metrick (2003). 'Optimal Defaults.' *American Economic Review*, 93(2): 180–185.

Choi, J. J., D. Laibson, B. C. Madrian, and A. Metrick (2004). 'For Better or for Worse: Default Effects and 401(k) Savings Behavior.' In D. A. Wise, ed., *Perspectives on the Economics of Aging*. Chicago: University of Chicago Press, pp. 81–125.

Choukhmane, T. (2024). 'Default Options and Retirement Saving Dynamics.' Unpublished manuscript.

Choukhmane, T. and T. de Silva (2023). 'What Drives Investors' Portfolio Choices? Separating Risk Preferences from Frictions.' NBER Working Paper No. 32476.

Choukhmane, T. and C. Palmer (2024). 'How Do Consumers Finance Increased Retirement Savings?' Unpublished manuscript.

Clark, R. L., A. Lusardi, and O. S. Mitchell (2017). 'Employee Financial Literacy and Retirement Plan Behavior: A Case Study.' *Economic Inquiry*, 55(1): 248–259.

Cribb, J. and C. Emmerson (2020). 'What Happens to Workplace Pension Saving When Employers are Obliged to Enroll Employees Automatically?' *International Tax and Public Finance*, 27: 664–693.

Cribb, J. and C. Emmerson (2021). 'What Can We Learn about Automatic Enrollment into Pensions from Small Employers?' *National Tax Journal*, 74(2): 377–404.

Crowney, P. (2002). 'Backing Off.' *Institutional Investors*. www.institutionalinvestor.com/article/2btghxk28lv1wj5wdwoao/culture/backing-off

Dao, N. (2024). 'Does a Requirement to Offer Retirement Plans Help Low-Income Workers Save for Retirement? Early Evidence from the OregonSaves Program.' *Contemporary Economic Policy*, 42(3): 524–543.

Degen, C. (2024). 'National Auto-IRA Legislation Garners Support, Faces Unclear Path.' *Pensions & Investments*. www.pionline.com/washington/national-auto-ira-bill-garners-support-faces-unclear-path

Derby, E., K. Mackie, and J. Mortenson (2023). 'Worker and Spousal Responses to Automatic Enrollment.' *Journal of Public Economics*, 223: 104910.

Duarte, V., J. Fonseca, A. S. Goodman, and J. A. Parker (2022). 'Simple Allocation Rules and Optimal Portfolio Choice Over the Lifecycle.' NBER Working Paper No. 29559

Goda, G. S., M. R. Levy, C. F. Manchester, A. J. Sojourner, and J. Tasoff (2019). 'Do Defaults Have Spillover Effects? The Effect of the Default Asset on Retirement Plan Contributions.' NBER Working Paper No. RRC NB18–12.

Goda, G. S., M. R. Levy, C. F. Manchester, A. Sojourner, and J. Tasoff (2020). 'Who is a Passive Saver Under Opt-In and Auto-Enrollment?' *Journal of Economic Behavior & Organization*, 173: 301–321.

Goda, G. S. and C. F. Manchester (2013). 'Incorporating Employee Heterogeneity into Default Rules for Retirement Plan Selection.' *Journal of Human Resources*, 48(1): 198–235.

Goda, G. S., C. F. Manchester, and A. J. Sojourner (2014). 'What Will My Account Really Be Worth? Experimental Evidence on How Retirement Income Projections Affect Saving.' *Journal of Public Economics*, 119: 80–92.

Goldin, J. and D. Reck (2020). 'Revealed-Preference Analysis with Framing Effects.' *Journal of Political Economy*, 128(7): 2759–2795.

Gomes, F., M. Haliassos, and T. Ramadorai (2021). 'Household Finance.' *Journal of Economic Literature*, 59(3): 919–1000.

Gropper, M. (2024). 'Lawyers Setting the Menu: The Effects of Litigation Risk on Employer-Sponsored Retirement Plans.' dx.doi.org/10.2139/ssrn.4393420

Horneff, V., R. Maurer, and O. S. Mitchell (2023). 'Fixed and Variable Longevity Annuities in Defined Contributions Plans: Optimal Retirement Portfolios Taking Social Security into Account.' *Journal of Risk and Insurance*, 90(4): 831–860.

Horneff, V., R. Maurer, and O. S. Mitchell (2024). 'Employer 401(k) Matches for Student Debt Repayment: Killing Two Birds with One Stone?' NBER Working Paper No. 32443.

Huberman, G. and W. Jiang (2006). 'Offering versus Choice in 401(k) Plans: Equity Exposure and Number of Funds.' *Journal of Finance*, 61(2): 763–801.

Investment Company Institute (2023). *Investment Company Fact Book.* Washington, DC: Investment Company Institute.

Keim, D. B. and O. S. Mitchell (2018). 'Simplifying Choices in Defined Contribution Retirement Plan Design: A Case Study.' *Journal of Pension Economics & Finance*, 17(Special Issue 3): 363–384.

Kronlund, M., V. K. Pool, C. Sialm, and I. Stefanescu (2021). 'Out of Sight No More? The Effect of Fee Disclosures on 401(k) Investment Allocations.' *Journal of Financial Economics*, 141(2): 644–668.

Ladimeji, K. (2024). '3 Alternative Providers to NEST Workplace Pensions – Autoenrolment.' *The Career Cafe Blog.* thecareercafe.co.uk/blog/3-alternative-providers-to-nest-workplace-pensions-autoenrolment/

Laibson, D. (1997). 'Golden Eggs and Hyperbolic Discounting.' *Quarterly Journal of Economics*, 112(2), 443–478.

Laibson, D. (2020). 'Nudges are Not Enough.' Presentation for the American Economic Association and American Finance Association.

Loseto, M. (2023). 'Plan Menus, Retirement Portfolios, and Investors' Welfare.' dx.doi.org/10.2139/ssrn.4623276

Lusardi, A. and O. S. Mitchell (2023). 'The Importance of Financial Literacy: Opening a New Field.' *Journal of Economic Perspectives*, 37(4): 137–154.

Madrian, B. C. and D. F. Shea (2001). 'The Power of Suggestion: Inertia in 401(k) Participation and Saving Behavior.' *Quarterly Journal of Economics*, 116(4): 1149–1187.

Mitchell, O. S. and S. P. Utkus (2022). 'Target-Date Funds and Portfolio Selection in 401(k) Plans.' *Journal of Pension Economics & Finance*, 21(4): 519–536.

Morrin, M., J. J. Inman, S. M. Broniarczyk, G. Nenkov, and J. Reuter (2012). 'Investing for Retirement: The Moderating Effect of Fund Assortment Size on the 1/N Heuristic.' *Journal of Marketing Research*, 49(4): 537–550.

OregonSaves (2024). *OregonSaves Program Monthly Dashboard as of March 31, 2024.* OregonSaves Report.

Parker, J. A., A. Schoar, A. Cole, and D. Simester (2023). 'Household Portfolios and Retirement Saving Over the Lifecycle.' NBER Working Paper No. 29881.

Pool, V. K., C. Sialm, and I. Stefanescu (2016). 'It Pays to Set the Menu: Mutual Fund Investment Options in 401(k) Plans.' *Journal of Finance*, 71(4): 1779–1812.

Pool, V. K., C. Sialm, and I. Stefanescu (2022). 'Mutual Fund Revenue Sharing in 401(k) Plans.' NBER Working Paper No. 30721.

Poterba, J. M. (2003). 'Employer Stock and 401(k) Plans.' *American Economic Review*, 93(2): 398–404.

Probasco, J. (2014). 'McDonald's 401(k) Plan is Supersized Compared to Many.' *Yahoo Finance.* finance.yahoo.com/news/mcdonalds–401–k–plan–supersized–185924799.html

Quinby, L. D., A. H. Munnell, W. Hou, A. Belbase, and G. T. Sanzenbacher (2020). 'Participation and Pre-Retirement Withdrawals in Oregon's Auto-IRA.' *Journal of Retirement*, (Summer): 1–14.

Ramnath, S. (2013). 'Taxpayers' Responses to Tax-Based Incentives for Retirement Savings: Evidence from the Saver's Credit Notch.' *Journal of Public Economics*, 101: 77–93.

Reuter, J. and D. Richardson (2022). 'New Evidence on the Demand for Advice Within Retirement Plans.' NBER Working Paper No. 30261.

Reuter, J. and A. Schoar (2024). 'Demand-Side and Supply-Side Constraints in the Market for Financial Advice.' NBER Working Paper No. 32452.

Samuelson, W. and R. J. Zeckhauser (1988). 'Status Quo Bias in Decision Making.' *Journal of Risk and Uncertainty*, 1(1): 7–59.

Sialm, C., L. T. Starks, and H. Zhang (2015). 'Defined Contribution Pension Plans: Sticky or Discerning Money?' *Journal of Finance*, 70(2): 805–838.

Tang, N., O. S. Mitchell, G. Mottola, and S. Utkus (2010). 'The Efficiency of Sponsor and Participant Portfolio Choices in 401(k) Plans.' *Journal of Public Economics*, 94(11–12): 1073–1085.

Thaler, R. and S. Benartzi (2004). 'Save More Tomorrow™: Using Behavioral Economics to Increase Employee Saving.' *Journal of Political Economy*, 112(S1): S164–S187.

US Bureau of Labor Statistics (BLS) (2021). *Employee Benefits in the United States News Release.* USDL-20-1792. Washington, DC: US BLS.

US Department of Labor (BLS) (2006). 'Default Investment Alternatives Under Participant-Directed Individual Account Plans.' *Federal Register*, 72(205): 60452–60480.

US Department of Labor (DOL) (2020). 'Pension Benefit Statements – Lifetime Income Illustrations.' www.dol.gov/agencies/ebsa/about-ebsa/our-activities/resource-center/fact-sheets/pension-benefit-statements-lifetime-income-illust rations

Vanguard (2024). *How America Saves.* Malvern, PA: The Vanguard Group.

Yang, H. (2025). 'What Determines 401(k) Plan Fees? A Dynamic Model of Transaction Costs and Markups.' dx.doi.org/10.2139/ssrn.5185177

Zhong, M. (2021). 'Optimal Default Retirement Saving Policies: Theory and Evidence from OregonSaves.' Pension Research Council Working Paper No. 2020-01.

Chapter 7

# The Implications of Gender Differences in Retirement Plan Investment Patterns

*Vickie Bajtelsmit*

Much academic and policy research has identified concerns about the adequacy of retirement savings in the US (Bajtelsmit and Rappaport 2018). As the human lifespan has increased without a corresponding increase in years of employment, the average number of years spent in retirement has risen. To meet their growing post-retirement needs, individuals must save regularly throughout their working years and invest in growth assets or alternatively plan to work much longer. Certain subgroups are particularly at risk of retirement wealth shortfalls, including those without employer-sponsored retirement plans and those in financially vulnerable situations, such as widows and divorcees (Enda and Gale 2021). On average, women spend more years in retirement, and more of those years being single or widowed. Using the EBRI Retirement Security Projection Model®, VanDerhei (2019) projected retirement saving shortfalls (additional savings required to meet basic needs in retirement) to be larger for widows and single women as well as those in the lowest income quartiles. Evidence from many sources suggests that women have lower retirement wealth, lower Social Security benefits,[1] and are more likely to end life in poverty than their male counterparts. Furthermore, this so-called gender wealth gap has widened over time.[2]

One explanation offered for women's lower retirement wealth is that they tend to be more conservative investors, leading to lower wealth accumulation even at similar levels of saving. Indeed, many now take for granted what has become the 'common wisdom' of gender differences in risk-taking and investing. Although gender differences in income and wealth are well-documented, the evidence of gender differences in investing is not as strong. Three decades ago, Bajtelsmit and Bernasek (1996) summarized the limited available evidence at that time and suggested potential explanations for the observed differences in investing. Since then, experts from a variety of fields (including finance, economics, sociology, psychology, and genetics) have contributed to a growing body of research. There

Vickie Bajtelsmit, *The Implications of Gender Differences in Retirement Plan Investment Patterns.* In: *Retirement Saving, Investment, and Spending.* Edited by: Olivia S. Mitchell and Nikolai Roussanov, Oxford University Press.

DOI: 10.1093/oso/9780197845752.003.0007

has also been great progress on gender equality in education, opportunities, and economic roles, but differences remain in terms of women's labor market participation, earnings, and representation among the top pay levels (Cortés and Pan 2023). In addition to the often-cited gender pay gap, there is also a persistent gender retirement gap: women tend to have lower retirement wealth and income (Bajtelsmit and Rappaport 2018).

Conservative investing over long periods of time can result in low wealth accumulation compared with investing in riskier assets. Investment choices can have substantial consequences for women, in particular, who often have low retirement account balances and face longer lifetimes than men. For example, assuming a typical woman is expected fewer years in the workforce, lower income, and lower average lifetime salary increases, Garnick (2016) estimated that her savings rate would need to be nearly double that of a similar-income man. If she also invested more conservatively, the necessary contribution would be even higher.

In what follows, we review recent evidence on gender differences in investing and retirement adequacy in order to identify potential causes, consequences, and policy solutions.

## Evidence of Gender Differences in Investing

Gender differences in investing can be manifested in several different ways, all of which could result in lower accumulations of retirement wealth. These include the following:

- Women may be less likely than men to have access to employer retirement plans, be less likely to participate in plans when offered, and/or receive less generous employer matches.
- Women may invest less than men, in dollars or as a proportion of income.
- Women may choose lower-risk investments than men, resulting in lower returns.

Previous research on each of these issues is summarized in the sections below.

### Women and Employer-Provided Retirement Plans

Tax-deferred savings vehicles such as traditional Individual Retirement Accounts (IRAs) and qualified retirement plans help workers save money for retirement. Based on the 2020 Survey of Income and Program Participation (SIPP) data, Hoffman et al. (2022) reported that 43.5%

of women and 47.8% of men owned some type of retirement account. Sabelhaus (2022) integrated findings from the SIPP data with other data sources and concluded that ownership rates were 53.7% for men and 50.8% for women, including plans provided by both current and former employers. In today's business environment, full-time workers' access to retirement plans within a company is gender neutral. Nevertheless, disparities in career paths, occupations, size of employers, part-time versus full-time work, contribution rates, years in the workforce, and investment choices still result in a gender gap in retirement plan participation.

In the US, defined contribution (DC) retirement plan saving rates are typically based on workers' salaries. Accordingly, to achieve comparable accumulations, lower-earning women then would need to contribute a higher percentage of pay than men. Vanguard (2024) analyzed 2.6 million participant accounts and found that with the exception of those earning less than $30,000 per year, women's plan participation rates and elective deferral rates were slightly higher than men's. Yet the median account balance for men was 40% higher than women's median balances, as the men earned more on average. When compared to similar-income men, women's account balances proved to be comparable to men's. Two contributors to the differences were women's lower likelihood of contributing the maximum allowed (9% versus 13%), and their lower likelihood of taking advantage of catch-up contribution opportunities (12% versus 17%).

Gropper (2023) used a large database covering over 2.5 million public employees to document that men in public sector DC plans contributed more than women to their retirement accounts, both in terms of dollar contributions and as a percentage of pay. Mean dollar contributions were about 50% higher for men across all age groups. For all but the youngest age group (20–29), the median contribution rate (dollar contributions divided by employee salary) was 0.5 to 1.3 percentage points higher for men. Not surprisingly, this pattern resulted in significant differences in account accumulations, with women's account balances averaging 70% of men's. For those in their 60s, women's median (mean) balance was $33,090 ($103,460), compared with men's at $51,734 ($147,319). In a nationally representative study of 401(k) participants, Banerjee (2023) showed that the median balance for women was 65% below that of men.

All of these studies concluded that the gender differences in accumulation were primarily driven by women's lower salaries and fewer years of investing. Women also tended to have more student loan debt than did their male counterparts, making it more difficult for them to save in their early years of employment (Banerjee 2023).

## Women and Investment Risk

The literature on risk preferences tends to claim that women are more risk averse than men, which could also explain their smaller retirement nest eggs. Yet Nelson (2015) analyzed the results of 28 risk aversion studies and concluded that widespread acceptance of gender differences in risk-taking was more likely the result of confirmation bias than reality. In fact, her analysis showed that prior research had overemphasized small differences and ignored similarities. A review of 15 experimental studies found consistent experimental evidence of gender differences in risk-taking over a hypothetical gamble (Charness and Gneezy 2012).

Although researchers have found statistically significant gender differences in subjective measures of survey respondents' self-assessed risk attitudes (Bajtelsmit et al. 1999), there is less evidence on gender differences in risk aversion driving actual financial decisions. Some focus on risky choices in experimental settings (Bajtelsmit and Coats 2023; Charness and Gneezy 2012; Holt and Laury 2002), while others assess portfolio choice patterns (Bajtelsmit and Bernasek 1996; Hinz et al. 1997; Neelakantan and Chang 2010).

Three methods are commonly used for studies of actual financial decisions: individual or household surveys, laboratory experiments, and retirement plan data from brokerage firms or employer plans. Survey research is usually based on large-scale national household surveys, such as the Survey of Consumer Finances (SCF), the Health and Retirement Survey (HRS), or similar surveys in many other countries.[3] Surveys offer the advantage of including substantial information on household-level assets and debts, as well as individual retirement plan balances, but they contain only limited information about asset allocation. Researchers sometimes estimate actual investment risk-taking from survey data by calculating the participant's risky asset share (risky assets/total assets) for either the whole portfolio or for certain assets (such as IRAs). Retirement account information does not usually include detailed asset allocation, so it is common to classify all such accounts as part of the risky asset share. An alternative method of classifying a person's investment risk investigates whether they have any stock investments (e.g., Bucher-Koenen et al. 2021). Although a simpler measure than asset share, there is also evidence that willingness to invest in the stock market is positively associated with other measures of risk aversion. An additional concern with household-level surveys is that it is often difficult to isolate male versus female decisions for married couples. If couples pool assets, observed asset allocation is not necessarily indicative of individual choices. Limiting analysis to allocation in IRAs, as in Mandal and Brady (2020), does not necessarily solve the problem if couples make joint decisions for these accounts as well.

Several surveys commonly ask participants to subjectively assess their own risk attitudes and risk-taking related to overall investments. Both the SCF and HRS include a question that asks whether the respondent invests mostly in stocks, mostly in bonds, or mixed, and another that asks about the level of risk the respondent is willing to take relative to return. Women prove somewhat less likely to report that they invest mostly in stocks and more likely to answer that they unwilling to take any level of risk; however, what people say is not always consistent with observed asset holdings. From their analysis of SCF data, Fisher and Yao (2017) concluded that gender differences in risk tolerance were explained by differences in the determinants of risk tolerance, primarily income uncertainty and net worth, rather than gender itself.

In experimental settings researchers can do a better job of eliciting reliable risk preferences, particularly if the experiments include economically meaningful incentives (Bajtelsmit and Coats 2023). The disadvantages of experiments include small sample sizes, nonrepresentative populations, minimal incentives, and limited information about participants' household finances. In contrast to experiments and research based on national surveys, financial services firms have detailed information on investment decisions and accumulations for their participant accounts, but they often lack information on their participants' other assets or demographics (beyond gender, marital status, and income at their primary employer). This can lead to incorrect conclusions about risk-taking if, for example, plan participants invest conservatively in their 401(k)s while holding risky assets outside these accounts. Nevertheless, given that most people do not have substantial savings outside of home equity and retirement plans, risk findings based on retirement plan account data are likely to be a good proxy for overall financial risk-taking.

In the Vanguard study discussed above (2024), men and women had similar average equity allocations, but women traded about 50% less frequently than men. Unlike the earlier study by Barber and Odean (2001) of discount brokerage account holders, which found similar gender differences in trading propensity, the Vanguard report attributed these results to the fact that women were more likely than men to hold target date funds. Using public employee plan data, VanDerhei (2021) analyzed asset allocation across fund categories and found that for those with at least some target date fund allocation, there were no gender differences in equity shares for any age group. This suggests that the increasing popularity of target date funds is resulting in riskier portfolios for women as compared with earlier studies (Bajtelsmit and VanDerhei 1997; Bajtelsmit et al. 1999).

Accordingly, the research implies that observed gender differences in wealth accumulation are not as likely to be due to differences in risk aversion, contrary to common wisdom. We next turn to some alternative explanations.

## Factors that Influence Investment Risk-Taking

Research over the last several decades and across a wide variety of disciplines has identified several other potential explanations for gender differences in investing decisions and wealth outcomes: these include gender differences in employment, biology, psychology, socialization, and decision making. Figure 7.1 summarizes the potential factors and their interactions. Inherent differences in risk preferences by gender are only one possible explanation, and indeed women's lower lifetime earnings compared to men is likely to be a large part of the cause. Moreover, while the gender wage gap is often attributed to discrimination,[4] it is more likely the result of a complex set of factors detailed in the diagram. For example, despite the rising prevalence of college-educated women, women are still relatively more likely to be in lower-paying and part-time employment and more likely to be the stay-at-home parent. These factors result in fewer years of paid employment (Blau and Kahn 2017).

Next, we summarize research related to each of the factors that are relevant to gender differences in investing.

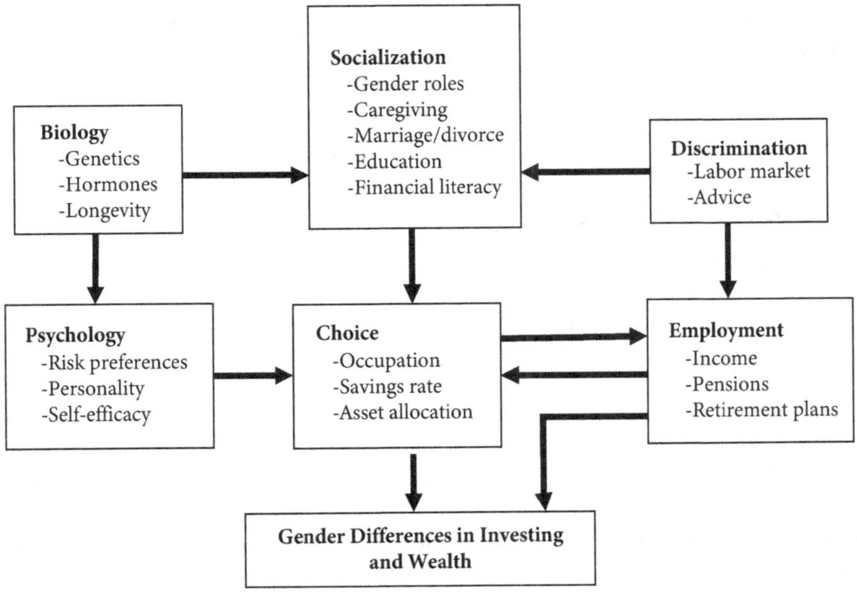


**Figure 7.1** Factors influencing gender differences in investing and wealth
*Source*: Author's rendition of the evidence reported in this chapter.

## Differences in Biology

Gender differences in biology include longevity, genetics, and hormones, all of which may impact financial decisions. With an additional three years of life expectancy compared to men, women must finance a longer period of retirement. Moreover, most married women are younger than their husbands, and hence they are likely to outlive their spouses by a decade or more. This can result in asset depletion for the surviving spouse's final years. Both factors should, in principle, allow them to take more investment risk compared to their male counterparts.

Scientists have also made connections between biology and behavior, with improvements in science and the mapping of the human genome. Higher levels of testosterone and cortisol in men are linked to risk-taking and the desire for immediate gratification (Herbert 2018), most likely a holdover from primitive times in which risk-taking was biologically necessary to male roles as hunters and protectors. Much genetic research initially studied the impact of single genes, but now genome-wide association studies can scan large numbers of genetic variants across millions of people looking for correlations with certain traits or diseases (Benjamin et al. 2024). For example, Linner et al. (2019) linked a polygenic score for risk tolerance to various financial behaviors. Coats and Bajtelsmit (2024) showed that the genetic propensity for the personality trait of neuroticism was associated with a lower likelihood of stock investing and a lower stock asset allocation, whereas the genetic propensity for the personality trait of openness increased the likelihood of stock investing. The genetic propensity for educational attainment is also positively associated with labor income and household wealth, along with the likelihood of stock ownership and allocations (Barth et al. 2020).

## Differences in Psychology

In addition to risk preferences discussed above, there are also psychological and behavioral differences between the genders. Personality types, financial self-efficacy, financial literacy, and gender roles have been shown to influence career paths, confidence, and financial decisions.

**Personality.** Psychologists have developed a set of five personality traits, called the Big Five, which include neuroticism, extroversion, openness, agreeableness, and conscientiousness.[5] Neuroticism describes the tendency to experience negative emotion and anxiety, which can also translate to being more careful and attentive to detail. Extraversion reflects sociability, assertiveness, and reward-motivation. Openness refers to creativity and how open one is to new experiences. Agreeableness is characterized by being trusting and cooperative. Higher scores for conscientiousness are associated with self-discipline and organization.

Studies have found that women score higher on all traits except openness and conscientiousness, although men score higher on certain trait aspects such as assertiveness, self-confidence, and sensation-seeking (Weisberg et al. 2011). Jiang et al. (2024) reported that people with high levels of neuroticism were pessimistic about future stock returns and expected higher inflation; in contrast, people with higher openness were more willing to take risks. Additionally, people who scored high on both neuroticism and extraversion were more likely to engage in herd behavior, such as following the latest investment trends. Parise and Peijnenburg (this volume) documented that conscientiousness had a positive impact on savings and retirement planning.

**Self-efficacy.** There are also significant gender differences in financial self-efficacy (FSE), defined as having confidence in one's own ability to make financial decisions. Farrell et al. (2016) reported that FSE was the strongest predictor of the type and number of financial products that a woman held (controlling for education, risk preferences, age and income). Those with high FSE were more likely to hold investment and saving products and less likely to hold debt. Asebedo et al. (2019) found that personality traits and FSE both indirectly supported saving behavior. While FSE differs from general overconfidence (i.e., overestimation of abilities relative to objective measures), both measures have been found to be correlated. Thus Adamecz-Völgyi and Shure (2022) documented that overconfidence was a strong predictor of the gender gap in top job employment. Gender differences in confidence levels have also been linked to the gender wage gap in that women have been less likely to negotiate starting salaries, request pay raises, and switch jobs for higher pay (Babcock and Laschever 2021). These, in turn, generate differences in retirement preparation (Dietz et al. 2003).

## Differences in Employment Patterns

Despite long-term increases in women's market work, their employment patterns continue to diverge from those of men's. Lower earnings, fewer years in the paid workforce, and lower coverage by retirement plans are all issues that affect their retirement preparation. On average, women earn 73 cents for every dollar earned by men, due in part to their greater prevalence of part-time and low-wage work.[6] Yet even among full-time workers, women earn only 84% of what men earn, with larger wage gaps for older workers[7] and women of color.[8] Since retirement plan contributions are usually set as a percentage of pay, lower average wages imply lower average dollar contributions.

Relatedly, while women have made progress in educational attainment and are more represented in previously male-dominated professions, white men are still more likely to be found in the highest-paying occupations, while women are over-represented in the lowest-paying occupations and in the lower ranks of other occupations.[9] There is also evidence of growing income inequality among women, worsening the relative situation of the lowest-income women (Hoffmann et al. 2020).

Labor force participation rates for women in the US have trended upward over time, while men's have been relatively flat or declining (Copeland 2023). Women are also remaining in the paid workforce longer over time (Brown et al. 2016), yet women still spend fewer total years in the workforce than men, on average, mostly due to caregiving. Cortés and Pan (2023) noted that the labor market trajectories of men and women tend to diverge sharply after the arrival of children. Fathers do not experience the same reduction in employment: men without children are 5 percentage points more likely to be employed than women but, for those with a child under age five, fathers are 39 percentage points more likely to be employed than mothers (Almeida and Salas-Betsch 2023). This 'motherhood penalty' results from both reduced years of work and a decline in wage rates resulting from shifts to more family-friendly occupations and employers. In addition to childcare responsibilities that affect early career employment, many women also experience a reduction in labor force participation in their later working years due to caregiving responsibilities for aging parents. Ten percent of working caregivers in a recent survey reported having to give up work entirely or retire early to accommodate their caregiver responsibilities, and 61% said they had experienced at least one work-related impact, including going in late, leaving early, or taking time off to accommodate care (AARP 2020). When women reduce work hours for caregiving, they may lose eligibility for employer-paid insurance benefits and thereby reduce what they are able to save for retirement.

## Differences in Socialization

The differences in labor market experiences of men and women discussed above have been linked to gender roles (e.g., child-rearing expectations), household economics (e.g., mother earns less than father), and gendered professional paths (e.g., education and nursing). In addition, societal changes, including declining marriage rates and rising late life divorces, are worsening older women's financial situations.

**Caregiving.** Caregiving roles can have a significant negative financial impact on women, since their reduced employment affects their wage growth, seniority, savings, retirement income, and Social Security benefits.

Using the 2018 American Time Use Survey, Hess et al. (2020) showed that women spend 37% more time on unpaid household and care work than men and twice as much time during child-rearing years, resulting in reduced earnings.[10] Johnson et al. (2023) used microsimulation methodology to estimate the average lifetime costs of family care to be nearly $300,000. Rutledge et al. (2017) estimated that the lifetime earnings of mothers with one child were 28% less than the earnings of childless women, and each additional child reduced lifetime earnings by another 3%. For women ineligible for spousal benefits, Social Security benefits were 17% less for mothers than for non-mothers due to their lower lifetime earnings.

**Marital status.** Women's retirement security has been affected by social changes producing lower marriage and higher divorce rates, particularly at older ages. Marriage is beneficial in that it allows pooling of resources (including survivor pensions and spousal Social Security benefits), sharing of financial skills and knowledge, and reduced variability of household income. The US Government Accountability Office (2020) reported that between 1980 and 2016, the unmarried proportion of the adult population (including never married, divorced, and widowed) rose from 39% to 48%, a trend more common among the lower-income and less-educated. For individuals age 65+ in 2021, 5.8% of married women were living in poverty, compared to 15.5% for widows, 17% for divorced women, and 19.5% for never married women (Congressional Research Service 2022). Using several waves of the HRS, Streeter (2020) documented that in the first two years after the death of a spouse, women lost 12% of their income and 10% of their wealth, whereas men's financial situations were unaffected by the death of a spouse.

**Divorce.** Although the overall divorce rate has declined in recent years, partly the result of fewer marriages among younger people, the rate of 'gray divorces' (after age 50) has increased, now representing about one-third of all divorces. Lin and Brown (2021) showed that women in the HRS who divorced after age 50 experienced a 45% decline in their standard of living versus divorced men's decline of 21%. Social roles can also negatively impact women's finances in divorce, since women in child-rearing years often negotiate away pension and retirement assets in favor of maintaining primary custody rights and keeping the family home (Joseph and Rowlingson 2012).

**Financial Literacy.** Financial literacy has also been shown to be important for financial well-being and retirement preparation. With the shift to participant-directed 401(k) plans, individuals are increasingly responsible for their own retirement planning and investment decisions. Significant gender differences in financial literacy (Lusardi and Mitchell 2008), and particularly for less educated and single women (Behrman et al. 2012), therefore have important implications for financial decisions. Higher financial literacy is associated with higher net worth (van Rooij et al. 2012), greater financial wealth (Bannier and Schwartz 2018), retirement readiness (Yakoboski et al. 2023), better investment outcomes (Fisch et al. 2016), stock market participation (Bucher-Koenen et al. 2021; Yeh and Ling 2022), and planning for retirement (Lusardi and Mitchell 2011; Yeh 2020). Higher financial literacy and financial knowledge can also temper poor financial decisions driven by risk and time preferences (Bajtelsmit and Coats 2023).

## Conclusions

Despite the common wisdom that women are more conservative investors than men, we have shown that the actual reasons for women's lower retirement wealth are heavily driven by different labor market experiences and household responsibilities. Women exhibit greater risk aversion than men, as measured by self-assessment and hypothetical survey questions. Yet their investment choices do not differ substantially by gender, given similar age and income. Instead, observed differences in retirement wealth result from women having fewer years in the workforce, lower earnings trajectories, and a higher incidence of part-time work, all of which result in fewer years of saving. Women's lower than average financial literacy, confidence in their financial knowledge, and ability to make important financial decisions also play a role. Despite Social Security spousal protections, benefits are still lower for women, and, with declining marriage rates, this differential could increase in the future.

It follows from these findings that solutions for reducing the gender retirement gap must focus on women's income and savings. In addition to continued efforts to ensure equal pay for equal work, reducing income and career penalties for time out of the workforce would improve both lifetime earnings and Social Security benefits. Family-friendly work policies, common in other OECD countries, can make it easier for caregivers to stay in the workforce. These include extended paid family and medical leave, scheduling flexibility, options for remote work, workplace solutions for quality childcare, and improved public investment in eldercare alternatives. Equal treatment of part-time and full-time workers with respect to prorated paid time off and other employee benefits could also reduce out-of-pocket costs (e.g., for health insurance), freeing up funds for savings. Continued investment in financial tools and services that employees can use for budgeting, retirement planning, and investing can help empower all employees, but particularly women, to make better long-term decisions (Fisch et al. 2020).

Federal policy could also help women's retirement finances by recognizing the value of unpaid caregiving in Social Security benefit calculation. Social Security is a major income component for elderly women and, as more women have entered the workforce, a growing percentage of retired women claim Social Security benefits based on their own earnings histories. Still, however, women's average benefits are much lower than men's and are insufficient to cover basic expenses. Many other countries recognize unpaid caregiving in their benefit formula by giving a caregiver credit so that women are not penalized for years spent out of the workforce for childcare (Jankowski 2011). A caregiving credit would especially benefit lower-income single mothers who are not eligible for spousal benefits.

## Notes

1. In 2023, average monthly Social Security benefits were $2106 for men and $1714 for women (SSA 2024). For women, Social Security also represented a larger share of retirement income (Bond et al. 2020).
2. For example, analyzing the Survey of Income and Program Participation for households age 65+, Brown et al. (2016) found that women had 26% less household income than men and were 80% more likely than men to be living in poverty. Lee (2022) found that although the gender income gap narrowed from the mid-1990s to the mid-2010s, the gender wealth gap widened during that period. Women's median wealth as a percentage of men's dropped from 90% to 60% over that time period.
3. International evidence of gender differences in investing is also based on either household survey data or experiments. For example, women have been shown to invest more conservatively than men in Australia (Watson and McNaughton 2007), Germany (Oehler and Horn 2023), Sweden (Almenberg and Dreber 2015), Finland (Halko et al. 2012), and Norway (Bucher-Koenen et al. 2021), among others. Kaustia et al. (2023) analyzed stock market participation data in 19 European countries and found that men were more likely to participate in the stock market, but conditional on holding stocks, there was no gender difference in equity share.
4. Although some experimental research has identified discrimination in hiring, it is more difficult to clearly identify pay discrimination. In an interesting study, Charles et al. (2022) used a survey to identify regional sexism against women working outside the home. It concluded that in areas with greater sexism, the gender pay gap was larger.
5. Factor scores for each of the Big Five are developed from questionnaires on up to 33 self-rated behaviors or tendencies (McCrae and Costa 2003).
6. Although women make up nearly half of the overall workforce, the lower paid the job, the greater the overrepresentation of women. Women comprise nearly 70% of those earning minimum wage (Tucker and Patrick 2017). Women also represent about 43% of full-time workers and 63% of part-time workers (US Department of Labor 2020).
7. Based on data for full-time workers in the Current Population Survey, women's median weekly earnings were 8% lower than men's for those ages 16–24, 16%

less at ages 25–54, 22% less at ages 55–64, and 27% less at ages 65+ (Almeida and Salas-Betsch 2023).

8. Patten (2016) reported that Black and Hispanic women in the 2015 CPS earned 65% and 58% as much as white men, respectively.
9. Based on 2019 Census data, Zhavoronkova et al. (2022) reported that white men were 40% of the total workforce, but were 65% of CEOs, 81% of engineering managers, 86% of pilots, 86% of financial advisors, 56% of physicians, and 61% of computer and information systems managers. Although women were 47% of the total workforce, they represented 95% of secretaries and administrative assistants, 94% of childcare workers, and 90% of receptionists and information clerks. The five most common occupations for women (schoolteachers, nurses, secretaries, customer service, and cashiers) had an average annual wage of $38,304, whereas the average wage for the five most common male occupations (construction, truck driving, management, retail sales, and management) was $59,670.
10. Hess et al. (2020) found that a 1% increase in time spent on unpaid work was associated with a 0.062% decrease in women's weekly earnings after controlling for age, education, race/ethnicity, marital status, and family income. Unpaid work had no effect on men's earnings.

## References

AARP (2020). *Caregiving in the U.S. 2020.* Washington, DC: AARP. doi.org/10.26419/ppi.00103.001

Adamecz-Völgyi, A. and N. Shure (2022). 'The Gender Gap in Top Jobs: The Role of Overconfidence.' *Labour Economics,* 79: 102283.

Almeida, B. and I. Salas-Betsch (2023). 'Fact Sheet: The State of Women in the Labor Market in 2023.' Center for American Progress. www.americanprogress.org/article/fact-sheet-the-state-of-women-in-the-labor-market-in-2023/

Almenberg, J. and A. Dreber (2015). 'Gender, Stock Market Participation and Financial Literacy.' *Economics Letters,* 137: 140–142.

Asebedo, S., M. Wilmarth, M. Seay, K. Archuleta, G. Brase, and M. MacDonald (2019). 'Personality and Saving Behavior Among Older Adults.' *Journal of Consumer Affairs,* 53(2): 488–519.

Babcock, L. and S. Laschever (2021). *Women Don't Ask: Negotiation and the Gender Divide.* Princeton, NJ: Princeton University Press.

Bajtelsmit, V. and A. Bernasek (1996). 'Why Do Women Invest Differently from Men?' *Financial Counseling and Planning,* 7(1): 1–10.

Bajtelsmit, B., A. Bernasek, and N. Jianakoplos (1999). 'Gender Differences in Defined Contribution Pension Decisions.' *Financial Services Review,* 8(1): 1–10.

Bajtelsmit, V. and J. Coats (2023). 'Designing Behavioral Prompts to Improve Saving and Investment Decisions: Implications for Retirement Plans.' *Financial Planning Review,* 6(2): e1163.

Bajtelsmit, V. and A. Rappaport (2018). *Retirement Adequacy in the United States: Should We Be Concerned?* Chicago: Society of Actuaries. soa.org/research-reports/2018/retire-adequacy-us-concern

Bajtelsmit, V. and J. Vanderhei (1997). 'Risk Aversion and Pension Investment Choices.' In M.S. Gordon, O. S. Mitchell, and M. M. Twinney, eds., *Positioning*

*Pensions for the Twenty-First Century*. Philadelphia: University of Pennsylvania Press, pp. 45–66.

Banerjee, S. (2023). *Closing the Gender Gap in Retirement Savings*. T. Rowe Price Insights on Retirement No. RTL-1 B2C.

Bannier, C. and M. Schwartz (2018). 'Gender- and Education-Related Effects of Financial Literacy and Confidence on Financial Wealth.' *Journal of Economic Psychology*. 67: 66–86.

Barber, B. and T. Odean (2001). 'Boys Will Be Boys: Gender, Overconfidence, and Common Stock Investment.' *Quarterly Journal of Economics*, 116(1): 261–292.

Barth, D., N. Papageorge, and K. Thom (2020). 'Genetic Endowments and Wealth Inequality.' *Journal of Political Economy*, 128(4): 1474–1522.

Behrman, J., O. S. Mitchell, C. K. Soo, and D. Bravo (2012). 'How Financial Literacy Affects Household Wealth Accumulation.' *American Economic Review*, 102: 300–304.

Benjamin, D. J., D. Cesarini, P. Turley, and A. S. Young (2024). 'Social Science Genomics: Progress, Challenges and Future Directions.' NBER Working Paper No. 32404.

Blau, F. and L. Kahn (2017). 'The Gender Wage Gap: Extent, Trends, and Explanations,' *Journal of Economic Literature*, 55(3): 789–865.

Bond, T., J. Saad-Lessler, and C. E. Weller (2020). *Still Shortchanged: An Update on Women's Retirement Preparedness*. Washington, DC: National Institute on Retirement Security. www.nirsonline.org/wp-content/uploads/2020/04/Still-Shortchanged-Final.pdf

Brown, J., N. Rhee, J. Saad-Lessler, and D. Oakley (2016). 'Short-Changed in Retirement: Continuing Challenges to Women's Financial Future.' dx.doi.org/10.2139/ssrn.2779813

Bucher-Koenen, T., R. Alessie, A. Lusardi, and M. van Rooij (2021). *Fearless Woman: Financial Literacy and Stock Market Participation*. NBER Working Paper No. 28723.

Charles, K., J. Guryan, and J. Pan (2022). 'The Effects of Sexism on American Women: The Role of Norms vs. Discrimination.' *Journal of Human Resources*. 60(3): 693–742.

Charness, G. and U. Gneezy (2012). 'Strong Evidence for Gender Differences in Risk Taking.' *Journal of Economic Behavior and Organization*, 83(1): 50–58.

Coats, J. and V. Bajtelsmit (2024). *Measures and Drivers of Financial Well-Being*. New York: TIAA Institute. www.tiaa.org/content/dam/tiaa/institute/pdf/insights-report/2024-05/tiaa-institute-measures-and-drivers-of-financial-wellbeing.pdf

Congressional Research Service (2022). 'Poverty Among the Population Aged 65 and Older.' Washington, DC: Congressional Research Service. sgp.fas.org/crs/misc/R45791.pdf.

Copeland, C. (2023). *Trends in Labor Force Participation and Employment*. EBRI Issue Brief 584. Washington, DC: Employee Benefit Research Institute.

Cortés, P. and J. Pan (2023). 'Children and the Remaining Gender Gaps in the Labor Market.' *Journal of Economic Literature*, 61(4): 1359–1409.

Dietz, B. E., M. Carrozza and P. N. Ritchey (2003). 'Does Financial Self-Efficacy Explain Gender Differences in Retirement Saving Strategies?' *Journal of Women & Aging*, 15(4): 83–96.

Enda, G. and W. G. Gale (2021) 'How Does Gender Equality Affect Women in Retirement?' In W. G. Gale, J. M. Iwry, and D. C. John, eds., *Wealth After Work: Innovative Reforms to Expand Retirement Security*. Washington, DC: Brookings Institution Press, pp. 73–81.

Farrell, L., T. Fry, and L. Risse (2016). 'The Significance of Financial Self-Efficacy in Explaining Women's Personal Finance Behaviour.' *Journal of Economic Psychology*, 54: 85–99.

Fisch, J., A. Lusardi, and A. Hasler (2020). 'Defined Contribution Plans and the Challenge of Financial Illiteracy.' *Cornell Law Review*, 105: 741–796.

Fisch, J.E., T. Wilkinson-Ryan, and K. Irvine (2016). 'The Knowledge Gap in Workplace Retirement Investing and the Role of Professional Advisors.' *Duke Law Journal*, 66: 633–672.

Fisher, P. and R. Yao (2017). 'Gender Differences in Financial Risk Tolerance.' *Journal of Economic Psychology*, 61: 191–202.

Garnick, D. (2016). *Gender Retirement Gap*. New York: TIAA Institute. conferences.pionline.com/uploads/conference_admin/income_gender.pdf

Gropper, M. (2023). *A Gender Lens on Public-Sector DC Savings Behaviors*. Public Retirement Research Lab Study September 28. Lexington, KY: PRRL.

Halko, M., M. Kaustia, and E. Alanko (2012). 'The Gender Effect in Risky Asset Holdings.' *Journal of Economic Behavior and Organization*, 83(1): 66–81.

Herbert, J. (2018). Testosterone, Cortisol, and Financial Risk-Taking.' *Frontiers in Behavioral Neuroscience*, 12: 101.

Hess, C., T. Ahmed, and J. Hayes (2020). *Providing Unpaid Household and Care Work in the United States: Uncovering Inequality*. Washington, DC: Institute for Women's Policy Research. www.jstor.org/stable/pdf/resrep34503.pdf

Hinz, R. P., D. D. McCarthy, and J. A. Turner (1997). 'Are Women Conservative Investors? Gender Differences in Participant-Directed Pension Investments.' In M. S. Gordon, O. S. Mitchell, and M. M. Twinney, eds., *Positioning Pensions for the 21st Century*. Philadelphia: University of Pennsylvania Press, pp. 91–103.

Hoffman, M. G., M. A. Klee, and B. Sullivan (2022). 'Who Has Retirement Accounts?' *US Census Bureau*. www.census.gov/library/stories/2022/08/who-has-retirement-accounts.html

Hoffmann, F., D. S. Lee, and T. Lemieux (2020). 'Growing Income Inequality in the United States and Other Advanced Economies.' *Journal of Economic Perspectives*, 34(4): 52–78.

Holt, C. and S. Laury (2002). 'Risk Aversion and Incentive Effects.' *American Economic Review*, 92(5): 1644–1655.

Jankowski, J. (2011). 'Caregiver Credits in France, Germany and Sweden: Lessons for the United States.' *Social Security Bulletin*, 71(4): 61–76.

Jiang, Z., C. Peng, and H. Yan (2024). 'Personality Differences and Investment Decision-Making.' *Journal of Financial Economics*, 153: 103776.

Johnson, R. W., K. Smith, and B. Butrica (2023). *Lifetime Employment-Related Costs to Women of Providing Family Care*. Washington, DC: Urban Institute. www.urban.org/sites/default/files/2025-02/Lifetime-caregiving-costs.pdf

Joseph, R. and K. Rowlingson (2012). 'Her House, His Pension? The Division of Assets Among (Ex-) Couples and the Role of Policy.' *Social Policy and Society*, 11(1): 69–80.

Kaustia, M., A. Conlin, and N. Luotenen (2023). 'What Drives the Heterogeneity in Portfolio Choice: The Role of Institutional, Traditional, and Behavioral Factors.' *Journal of Banking and Finance*, 148: 106743

Lee, A. W. (2022). 'The Gender Wealth Gap in the United States: Trends and Explanations,' *Social Science Research*, 107: 102745.

Lin, I. and S. Brown (2021). 'The Economic Consequences of Gray Divorce for Women and Men.' *Journals of Gerontology: Series B*, 10: 2073–2085.

Linnér, R., P. Biroli, E. Kong, S. Meddens, R. Wedow, M. Fontana, ... and J. Beauchamp (2019). 'Genome-Wide Association Analyses of Risk Tolerance and Risky Behaviors in Over 1 Million Individuals Identify Hundreds of Loci and Shared Genetic Influences.' *Nature Genetics*, 51: 245–257.

Lusardi, A. and O. S. Mitchell (2008). 'Planning and Financial Literacy: How Do Women Fare?' *The American Economic Review*, 98(2): 413–417.

Lusardi, A. and O. S. Mitchell (2011). 'Financial Literacy and Retirement Planning in the United States.' *Journal of Pension Economics and Finance*, 10(4): 509–525.

Mandal, B. and M. Brady (2020). 'The Roles of Gender and Marital Status on Risky Asset Allocation Decisions.' *Journal of Consumer Affairs*, 54 (1): 177–197.

McCrae, R. R. and P. T. Costa (2003). *Personality in Adulthood: A Five-Factor Theory Perspective*. New York: Guilford Press.

Neelakantan, U. and Y. Chang (2010). 'Gender Differences in Wealth at Retirement.' *American Economic Review*, 100(2): 362–367.

Nelson, J. (2015). 'Are Women Really More Risk Averse Than Men? A Re-Analysis of the Literature Using Expanded Methods.' *Journal of Economic Surveys*, 29(3): 566–585.

Oehler, A. and M. Horn (2023). 'Households' Decision on Capital Market Participation—What Are the Drivers? A Multi-Factor Contribution to the Participation Puzzle.' *Financial Services Review*, 31(4): 283–305.

Patten, E. (2016). *Racial, Gender Wage Gaps Persist in U.S. Despite Some Progress*. Pew Research Center Short Reads July 1. Washington, DC: Pew Research Center.

Rutledge, M., A. Zulkarnain, and S. E. King (2017). 'How Much Does Motherhood Cost Women in Social Security Benefits?' CRR Working Paper 2017-14.

Sabelhaus, J. (2022). 'The Current State of US Workplace Retirement Plan Coverage.' Pension Research Council Working Paper WP2022-07.

Social Security Administration (SSA) (2024). 'Fast Facts About Social Security, 2023.' www.ssa.gov/policy/docs/chartbooks/fast_facts/2024/fast_facts24.html

Streeter, J. L. (2020). 'Gender Differences in Widowhood in the Short-Run and Long-Run: Financial, Emotional, and Mental Wellbeing.' *Journal of the Economics of Ageing*, 17: 100258.

Tucker, J. and K. Patrick (2017). *Low-Wage Jobs are Women's Jobs: The Overrepresentation of Women in Low-Wage Work*. National Women's Law Center Chartbook August 2017. Washington, DC: NWLC.

US Government Accountability Office (2020). *Older Women Report Facing a Financially Uncertain Future.* Report to the Special Committee on Aging No. 20–435. Washington, DC: US Government Accountability Office.

van Rooij, M. C., A. Lusardi, and R. J. Alessie (2012). 'Financial Literacy, Retirement Planning and Household Wealth.' *Economic Journal,* 122(560): 449–478

VanDerhei, J. (2019). 'How Retirement Readiness Varies by Gender and Family Status: A Retirement Savings Shortfall Assessment of Gen Xers.' dx.doi.org/10.2139/ssrn.3318534

VanDerhei, J. (2021). *A Deeper Look at Asset Allocation: Plan Structure and Demography the Key to Effective Plan Design.* Public Retirement Research Lab Research Study No 3. Washington, DC: PRRL.

Vanguard (2024). *How America Saves.* Malvern, PA: Vanguard. institutional.vanguard.com/content/dam/inst/iig-transformation/insights/pdf/2024/has/how_america_saves_report_2024.pdf

Watson, J. and M. McNaughton (2007). 'Gender Differences in Risk Aversion and Expected Retirement Benefits.' *Financial Analysts Journal,* 63(4): 52–62.

Weisberg, Y, C. DeYoung, and J. Hirsh (2011). 'Gender Differences in Personality Across the Ten Aspects of the Big Five.' *Frontiers in Psychology,* 2: 11757.

Yakoboski, P., A. Lusardi, and A. Hasler (2023). *Financial Literacy, Longevity Literacy, and Retirement Readiness.* TIAA Institute-GFLEC Personal Finance Index, 2022. New York: TIAA Institute.

Yeh, T. (2020). 'An Empirical Study on How Financial Literacy Contributes to Preparation for Retirement.' *Journal of Pension Economics and Finance,* 21(2): 237–259.

Yeh, T. and Y. Ling (2022). 'Confidence in Financial Literacy, Stock Market Participation, and Retirement Planning.' *Journal of Family and Economic Issues,* 43: 169–186.

Zhavoronkova, M, R. Khattar, and M. Brady (2022). *Occupational Segregation in America.* Washington, DC: Center for American Progress. www.americanprogress.org/article/occupational-segregation-in-america/

Chapter 8

# Wealth Accumulation

## The Role of Others

*Michael Haliassos*

The importance of peer effects on individual behavior has been extensively studied and scrutinized, following the pioneering work of Manski (1993). Peer effects have recently been part of an active research agenda in the rapidly expanding area of household finance (Gomes et al. 2021). This chapter summarizes findings from four projects on how family members, neighbors, other peers, professional advisors, and external stressors influence the financial behavior of household wealth accumulation and retirement preparedness.

The first project focused on what Manski (1993) called 'exogenous peer effects' attributable to peers' characteristics rather than their behavior. The characteristic under study was financial literacy of neighbors with whom individuals interacted, a phenomenon we call 'financial literacy externalities' (Haliassos et al. 2020). The second project turned to an analysis of the effects of being exposed to different levels of local wealth inequality at the start of one's career, on subsequent risk-taking, wealth accumulation, and achievement of a higher rank in the cohort-specific wealth distribution (Haliassos et al. 2023). The third project used a German sample of professional financial advisors and lay persons for which we compared the advice provided by each group to exogenously given 'vignettes' of potential investors (Rumpf et al. 2024). The idea was to compare the advice given by the professionals versus various peers, taking into account observable and unobservable advisor heterogeneity. While these three projects examined information, knowledge, and inspiration likely to be provided by peers, the fourth project focused on the cognitive load imposed by others (exogenous stressors), and on whether and how this interfered with important household financial decisions (Assenza et al. 2023). This load, which burdens and distracts households trying to make important choices, can arise in the context of aggregate crises, such as the COVID-19 pandemic or war,

Michael Haliassos, *Wealth Accumulation*. In: *Retirement Saving, Investment, and Spending*. Edited by: Olivia S. Mitchell and Nikolai Roussanov, Oxford University Press. © Pension Research Council, The Wharton School, The University of Pennsylvania (2026). DOI: 10.1093/oso/9780197845752.003.0008

or from personal factors, such as life events, stressful occupational environments, or persistent health issues. The study involved an online experiment, conducted with a sample representative of the French population.

## The Financial Literacy of Neighbors

Unlike most other research on financial literacy which examines the effects of people's financial literacy on financial behavior, Haliassos et al. (2020) showed that financially literate neighbors promoted individuals' participation in retirement accounts and stockholding. This occurred when neighbors conveyed their knowledge of economics and business matters, provided that the recipient of the information could understand it.

Yet not surprisingly, confirming such results requires confronting many econometric and conceptual challenges. First, it tends to be difficult to secure household financial data indicating the precise location of a given household, as well as the relevant characteristics of its neighbors. In fact, in view of confidentiality concerns, a variable typically dropped from household finance datasets is the household's address, to protect the respondent's disclosure. Second, even if one can obtain such information, locational proximity does not establish an exogenous influence of neighbors on a household's behavior. The household may have chosen to live in that neighborhood because it shares common preferences or occupation with those neighbors. Even if the neighbors observably participated in retirement accounts or in stockholding, similar portfolio behavior could reflect common preferences or common shocks to which neighboring households were exposed.

Further, existing research documents that people tend to talk to very few about their personal financial matters, even if they have a large social circle.[1] Confidentiality concerns do not allow researchers to eavesdrop on conversations and interactions between households and their neighbors, even when the most advanced data on networks of friends are provided from digital social networks. Therefore, an outstanding question is whether the interactions involve learning or merely imitating neighbors' portfolios. Fourth, since better-educated people are more able to collect and process information, it is unclear whether a business or economics education is what is needed versus more education in general. Finally, it is of interest whether being located near educated neighbors suffices to generate financial literacy externalities or if it also requires the recipient households to be educated so they can process and apply the information obtained.

Our project solved many of these problems by drawing on an unusual natural experiment implemented in Sweden over the period 1987–1991. This was facilitated by the high quality of Swedish administrative data collected for purposes of taxing wealth during 1999–2007 and the high level of detail and tracking that Swedish data policies allow. The natural experiment originated when the Swedish government allocated destitute refugees to Sweden to specific apartments in the 277 participating municipalities that randomly became available. This policy was introduced to counter the typical tendency of refugees to settle in big cities, contributing to congestion and associated problems. This is as close as one can probably get to a random exogenous assignment of people to areas where they are confronted with different configurations of peers.

There is good reason to believe that the process of placing refugees was random. The narratives of the allocation process indicate that when placing refugees, the authorities were considering their education level, marital status, and the presence of neighbors speaking their language in the broader area. Importantly, as no interviews were conducted, researchers can control for these refugee characteristics as well as for any other information available to the authorities. The narratives do indicate that refugees were asked to express preferences over areas. Yet there is no indication that the authorities were allocating refugees according to their preferences. First, the self-allocation of refugees prior to implementation of the policy resulted in the problem that the policy was designed to focus on resolving excessive concentration in big cities. Second, the data allowed researchers to track the location of refugees over the following 20 years and to observe how they voted with their feet. By 1999, about three-quarters of the refugees had been relocated from their original sites. Yet such relocation took time, as destitute refugees had to set themselves up, get jobs, and accumulate the means to relocate. Refugees spent an average 5.4 years in their initially assigned parishes and an average 8.7 years in the broader area of the initial municipality.

Focusing on destitute refugees helped us avoid endogenous sorting of refugees into areas with specific characteristics, but it left no hope of finding interesting household portfolio behavior at the time of the placement. If researchers are to understand any longer-term effects of such initial placement on the tendency to save for retirement or to take financial risk, they need access to detailed portfolio data 10 to 20 years later, as well as the ability to link refugee placement data to portfolio holdings. Detailed portfolio data became available in Sweden between 1999 and 2007 due to the wealth tax in place during this period.[2] Sources of these data were not the individuals but rather the financial and other relevant institutions. All taxable assets were covered but so were debts written off for tax purposes. Data accuracy was carefully monitored by the tax authorities, and there were heavy penalties for misrepresentation and tax evasion. The availability and timing of such data allowed us to study the long shadow of initial placement features on subsequent financial behavior.

Our central finding was that those placed in areas with higher shares of neighbors having college education in business and economics were more likely to not only participate in private retirement accounts but also hold stocks 10–15 years later. Moreover, they continued to hold stocks 15–20 years later. Strikingly, the effects were evident only for those with at least a high school certificate, what we would expect if such participation were not an act of pure imitation but rather required the processing of information and knowledge received from neighbors.

It is important to examine whether the observed effects arose from exposure to the neighbors themselves or to other neighborhood characteristics. After all, one would expect financially knowledgeable educated people to live in areas with financial infrastructure such as banks, insurance companies, and financial advisors catering to their interests and preferences.[3] Accordingly, we also included controls for the electoral district in which each refugee's apartment was located to incorporate the location-specific fixed factors that might be relevant for the asset participation outcomes. Results support the hypothesis that neighbors' business and economics education levels were important. Specifically, the share of neighbors with quantitative education had a smaller effect on refugees' portfolios compared to those of business/economics-educated neighbors. In other words, our findings indicate that neighbors who conveyed relevant content were the most effective in influencing immigrants' financial behavior. Furthermore, the share of neighbors having business and economics education who did not hold the financial asset in question still had a significant effect on the refugees' behavior—even when the share of asset holders was included in the regression. This implies that if imitation were the main mechanism driving the participation effect in private retirement accounts and stockholding, refugees would not need to understand and process information, and neighbors would not need to convey their approaches to retirement and financial risk-taking.

Lacking direct observations on social network interactions, it remained to be determined whether the evidence was consistent with refugees interacting with their neighbors. When we varied the factors affecting the probability of interaction with neighbors to look for significant changes in the estimated magnitude of peer effects, we discovered that peer effects were operative in areas where Swedish neighbors were more positively predisposed to immigrants and where there was a critical mass of knowledgeable neighbors. Effects were also stronger for refugees who had children at the time of entry and thus greater incentives and opportunities to interact with other parents. All these findings are consistent with interactions producing these effects on retirement and financial risk-taking.

While the consistency across these results is encouraging, it also raises concern regarding the distributional implications of peer effects. This is because financial literacy externalities can generate a social multiplier when providing financial education to some, yet we cannot rely on such externalities to improve the financial behavior of all socioeconomic groups. The tendency of people to associate with others like them, termed 'homophily,' means that members of low socioeconomic groups are less likely to interact with knowledgeable peers, and when they do, they are unlikely to correctly interpret the information received.

## Wealth Inequality Propagates Financial Risk-Taking

Differential participation in stocks, both in taxable and in retirement accounts, tends to produce divergence in wealth outcomes, as it gives people access to different returns on wealth, and ultimately to wealth concentration at the top of the distribution where stockholding is significantly more prevalent. Research has shown that the key to understanding the level and volatility of top wealth shares is the pattern of historical wealth returns. The wealthy not only have higher amounts to invest, but they also tend to have higher expected returns (Bach et al. 2020) and earn higher actual investment returns (Fagereng et al. 2020). This propagates wealth inequality by linking the current wealth level to the potential for higher future wealth. Haliassos et al. (2023) investigated whether people who were exposed to greater wealth inequality at the start of their career were also more likely to engage in financial risk-taking and end up with higher wealth levels later in life. They also investigated whether this applied to everyone or only the more educated among the sample.

In principle, exposure to greater wealth inequality can provide the better-educated an encouraging signal about potential paths to upward mobility. To others, it can be a deterrent. As a result, the wealth and risk-taking gaps between the two groups widen, suggesting that a further propagation mechanism for wealth inequality may be at work.

To design a field experiment that isolates the role of early exposure to wealth inequality in shaping later household risk-taking and wealth outcomes, one would like to randomly allocate people early in their economic lives to areas with different levels of wealth inequality and observe their behavior and outcomes over several years. This poses several obvious problems, and it suggests that the refugee sample from Sweden used in the previous study could also be of interest here.

Rather than challenging external validity, a refugee sample could be informative for this project, not solely for circumventing locational endogeneity. The refugees were, by definition, just starting their economic lives in Sweden. The data allowed us to focus on those refugees who were starting off destitute, avoiding initial wealth heterogeneity. Unlike young people growing up in the country, who could be forming impressions about wealth inequality and the world around them at any point in their formative years, these refugees were faced with a novel environment and had a clear incentive to form an impression of that environment at the time of arrival. Although the refugees came from different countries, we knew their country of origin and could control for cultural predispositions through home-country fixed effects, which were shown to be relevant for financial behavior by various authors (see, for example, the references on culture in the survey by Gomes et al. 2021). The data also included the refugees' education levels at entry and later, and the Swedish statistics are careful to correct for educational level equivalence in origin countries. Moreover, the Swedish LINDA wealth tax dataset contains a long list of household characteristics relevant for wealth and portfolio behavior at the time this behavior is observed. And finally, researchers can control for common geographic factors in the form of fixed attributes of the area of initial allocation and of key time-varying characteristics.

Our research concluded that college-educated people who were exposed to greater wealth inequality at their initial locations, measured as the share of total local household wealth owned by the top 10% of the local wealth distribution, were more likely to be successful 10–20 years later in terms of having greater wealth, higher positions in the wealth distribution among people in their age cohort, and higher ratios of wealth to income. Importantly, these effects of initial wealth inequality at the time of entry were significant only for the college-educated placed in municipalities with above-median wealth mobility.[4] Strikingly, no significant effects of greater initial local wealth inequality were observed for the less educated, even when upward wealth mobility among less-educated locals was considered.

The broad trends we discerned were visible in raw data as well as in the econometric results. Figure 8.1 focuses on refugees in municipalities exhibiting above-median wealth mobility around the time of the refugees' arrival (1986–1992). It splits each of the two education subsamples by the level of local wealth concentration at the top 10% to which they were exposed upon arrival (above or below median), and it computes average wealth of these refugees for each year covered by the wealth tax data (1999–2007). The left panel shows a widening wealth gap, even among the college-educated, with those exposed to greater local wealth inequality amassing more wealth than the rest, on average. More striking for social polarization is the comparison to the wealth trajectories of the less educated in the right panel, regardless of initial exposure to local wealth inequality.

A question arises as to how the college-educated ended up being even when they were exposed to greater wealth inequality at the start of their economic lives. Our evidence indicates that the college-educated assigned to

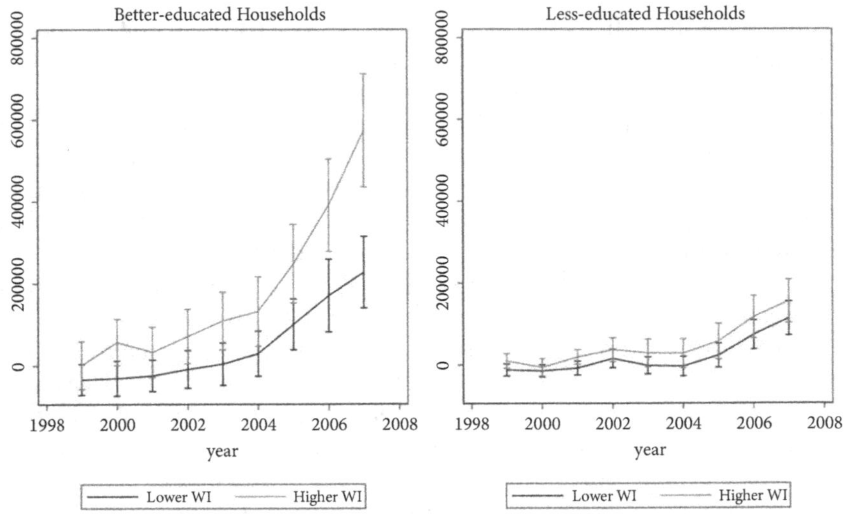


**Figure 8.1** Exposure to wealth inequality in high-mobility regions

*Notes:* The figure plots the evolution of mean household wealth of households in the respective education category who were exposed to above-median local wealth inequality ('higher WI') at the time of immigration (1987–1991) and of households exposed to below-median local wealth inequality ('lower WI'). Municipalities with above-median wealth mobility are considered. Wealth mobility is measured by the share of households in the municipality who moved from the bottom 90% of the wealth distribution to the top 10% of the wealth distribution between 1986 and 1992.

*Source:* Adapted from Haliassos et al. (2023).

areas with greater local wealth inequality were systematically more likely to take risks in the form of stockholding and homeownership, compared to similarly educated refugees facing less wealth inequality. One might expect that those in areas with greater local wealth inequality would be more likely to direct their efforts toward getting a better-paying and more secure job. Nevertheless, we found no evidence that being faced with greater wealth inequality generated higher labor income or lower risk of being unemployed 10–15 years later. Initial local wealth inequality also had no significant impact on the choices of refugees regarding whether and how much to invest in human capital following their migration.

We interpret these findings to mean that educated people perceived higher wealth inequality as an opportunity in environments that allowed upward mobility, and they were more likely to be successful with their risky financial and housing investments. In further support of this hypothesis, we found that educated refugees were more likely to react if they were placed in a small area within which more of their neighbors successfully moved upward in the local wealth distribution around the time of immigration.

Even though the refugees might not have perceived their higher income and higher education natives as a natural peer group, their nearby presence could raise refugees' aspiration levels, prompting them to take more risk to satisfy that aspiration. Higher inequality makes it more likely that one would observe peers of high enough wealth to raise their aspiration level, and higher wealth mobility is a signal that such an aspiration level might be attainable, in part, through greater risk-taking. This mechanism would be consistent with status models (e.g., Roussanov 2010).[5]

One may wonder whether local wealth inequality simply proxied for some other aspect of the local environment, which in turn was responsible for the observed outcomes. Yet our study controlled for municipalities' fixed characteristics across which wealth inequality was measured, as well as time-varying characteristics such as mean wealth, mean income, and income inequality by municipality. Recall too that significant effects of initial wealth inequality on future portfolio behavior and wealth outcomes were observed only in areas of high wealth mobility. Nevertheless, these opportunities failed to mobilize the less-educated households, and instead only propelled the college-educated to higher levels of risk-taking and ultimately wealth. One might wonder whether mobility opportunities were tailored to the more educated, explaining why the less educated did not respond. Yet the less educated were not significantly influenced by initial wealth inequality, even in areas that provided them with high wealth mobility opportunities, as measured by the probability of transitioning to higher wealth strata. Finally, when we partitioned the sample, we found that the effects were prominent not in the richer, but in the poorer regions. This suggests that they are likely not the result of automatic career advancement mechanisms, but rather to the high visibility of successes of others in those deprived regions.

These findings suggest that the institutional environment is unlikely to account for observed differences in mobilization and responses to initial wealth inequality. People's perceptions of wealth inequality influence their expectations regarding their ability to earn portfolio returns and become wealthier, as well as their optimism regarding expected asset returns; in all of these cases, the nature of social interactions is more likely to be important.

Recent research on perception, cognition, and developmental and social psychology, focusing mostly on income (rather than wealth) inequality, has concluded that people receive and process inequality cues from their environments (Phillips et al. 2025; Suss 2023). These can include social class cues from their peers, information gleaned from newspapers, and observation of the built environment. Sweden is a very transparent society where local newspapers often report on the wealth of the richest locals. Nevertheless, the less-educated immigrants may have had greater difficulty accessing cues, as their peers were less likely to be informed and to have direct access to the Swedish language press. We also showed, using cross-municipality regressions, that variation in wealth inequality around the time of entry was explained by a small number of factors more likely observed by the better-educated.

Perhaps more fundamental than perceiving wealth inequality, though, may be the question of whether less-educated people can make effective use of risky assets to improve their position in the wealth distribution. For one thing, research has shown that people of low socioeconomic status (i.e., the less educated and lower-income) tend to be more pessimistic about asset returns (Das et al. 2019; Kuhnen and Miu 2017). It has also been found that lower education is associated with earning lower returns on assets (e.g., Girshina 2019). Haliassos et al. (2020) also suggested that better-educated people benefit from their peers' financial knowledge since they take more financial risks than the less educated. These distinct responses may well be traceable to the different types of peers with which the two groups came in contact and the expectations they fostered, as well as the ability of the two groups to generate good wealth outcomes.

Although the first two research projects cited above documented an education split with respect to outcomes, it does not necessarily follow that propagation of wealth inequality, differential use of retirement products and premium assets, and social polarization could be reduced simply by raising the minimum number of required school years. A growing body of research suggests that educational attainment and returns on wealth are joint outcomes of innate information-processing ability as well as ability to manage one's finances (Barth et al. 2020; Fagereng et al. 2020).

For this reason, it may be more promising to explore a multi-pronged, AID approach. This program involves *alerting* the less educated about return opportunities and wealth mobility prospects; *informing* them on how to take advantage of higher-return assets without taking on excessive risk; and *designing* simpler financial products with desirable properties for less able investors. Empowering the less educated to make better financial decisions can contribute to democratizing finance, and it is less likely to be distortionary or raise political opposition compared to other options, such as wealth taxation. Instead of taking resources away from those who succeed, empowerment measures provide means to improve outcomes for those left behind.

## Peers as Advisors

While the research above emphasized interactions with peers, the data used contained no record of the content of these interactions. Accordingly another project, Rumpf et al. (2024), sought to shed light on what peers recommended to others, and how this compared to what professional advisors would recommend in the absence of reward structures potentially generating conflicts of interest. The research was conducted in Germany, a high-income country with a direct stock market participation rate of 15.4% and 20.6% participation in mutual funds.[6]

In this setting, professional advisors were presented with randomly assigned vignettes of investors and asked to make recommendations on people's share of risky assets in their retirement accounts. It was made clear to these advisors that they would receive no monetary compensation for their recommendations, let alone one that was linked to the recommended portfolio strategy. Instead, the advisors anticipated receiving information that would be of interest to them in their practice, conditional on responding to the questions. The objective was to incentivize them to take the exercise seriously but not to bias their advice. The provision of vignettes to advisors is attractive in that it overcomes the chance of endogenous client matching with financial advisors. Further, it avoids the pressures imposed on financial advisors of having to cater to clients' biases and prior experiences in their effort to win their business, as would be observed at first meetings and even when the clients were actually 'mystery shoppers' employed by researchers.[7]

This study also employed a similar elicitation procedure for lay people, subject to the requirements that they have basic knowledge and understanding of financial matters. This sample restriction was intended to capture the type of advice that people might get by approaching family or friends, peers who might have something useful to say on the subject.

The setup allowed a study of whether and how the elicited advice of professional and lay advisors differed systematically in relation to the investors' characteristics and to the advisors' own characteristics. In all cases, the advice elicited referred to the recommended risky portfolio share in a retirement account. Beyond standard Tobit estimation incorporating the (0, 1) limit in portfolio shares, the study also employed Bayesian methods that allowed for observed and unobserved advisor heterogeneity to illustrate the (estimated) distribution of advice that different investors received from unconflicted financial advisors and from suitably chosen peers. The study illustrated what is possible to estimate, by considering heterogeneous advice provided by one's age and education peers, as would be implied by homophily in peer group formation.

Controlling for advisor characteristics but initially not for recipient characteristics, we found that professional advisors tended to recommend a lower allocation to risky assets for retirement than did lay advisors. Older and more risk-tolerant advisors, as well as those expecting higher returns over a 10-year horizon, tended to recommend bigger risky exposures. Interestingly, controlling for their own characteristics, advisors' own portfolios positively influenced the advice they gave to others, encouraging their hypothetical clients to tilt portfolios in the same direction of riskiness.[8] In the initial set of regressions, there was still no way to compare the extent of this bias across professionals and lay advisors—a key focus and novelty of the project.

We also learned that both lay and professional advisors tailored their advice to investor characteristics included in the vignettes, despite the absence of incentives to cater to specific investor preferences. They tended to recommend higher risk exposures for investors with higher income, wealth, or lower debt, and they moderated their recommendations when the amount invested was larger. Advisors also recommended less risk for the more risk averse clients, for older individuals, and for people with little previous experience in the stock market. Overall, this study concluded that professionals and lay advisors both adjusted their recommendations in the direction implied by portfolio theory, even though their knowledge of such theory could not be presumed.

Including some interaction terms in the vignettes between the professional advisor and investor characteristics allows us to trace the moderating effect of professional advice on the risky portfolio share to differences in how professional advisors responded to investor characteristics as well as their own, relative to the lay advisors. One might expect that professionals would be less responsive to their own characteristics when giving unbiased financial advice. Nonetheless, we showed that professional advisors were more responsive to their own risk tolerance levels and incomes when recommending risky portfolio shares for others. Taking characteristics of advisees into account, professional advisors moderated their recommendations more with respect to investors' age and risk tolerance, compared to lay persons. This contrasted with their willingness to recommend higher risky shares for people with greater stock market experience, and it differed from lay advisors who did not adjust their recommendations for those with considerable investor experience. While professional investors responded to several investor characteristics more strongly than did lay advisors, this was not true of all characteristics. For example, professionals did not moderate their risk recommendations when faced with larger potential investment amounts.

Our study also sought to describe the heterogeneity in advice that specific potential investors might receive, since advisors, both professional and lay, might differ in ways not fully captured by the advisor characteristics we observed in the survey. Using Bayesian methods to allow for unobserved advisor heterogeneity, we estimated the range and distribution of advice given using posterior distributions characterizing recommendations provided by the different advisor types, conditional on investor characteristics presented in the vignette.[9] This exercise allowed us to choose investor types of most interest, as well as advisors that individuals might approach. Of course, this exercise can be conducted for any investor and advisor groupings of interest to the researcher or policymaker, if these are defined in terms of the respective characteristics collected in the survey.

Specifically, we considered a young low earner without a college education, a college-educated wealthy retiree, and a wealthy person in the latter half of their working life. The potential advisor types included a professional advisor, a peer with the same education and labor income, and other advisor traits that depended on the investor's age: a more senior family member or peer (in the case of young investors); a somewhat younger peer who still worked; and a considerably younger family member or friend who could be thought of as an offspring (in the case of older, retired investors).

What we found was that young low earners with little education were likely to get more conservative portfolio advice if they discussed financial matters with their peers versus with older people. They were also likely to get the largest risky portfolio share recommendations if they elected to speak to financial advisors. This predicted tendency of financial advisors to exceed the risky portfolio share recommended by the two other peer groups was reversed for the case of a college-educated wealthy retiree. Professional advisors were likely to be the most conservative toward wealthy retirees, and such retirees were also likely to be getting more conservative advice from high-income young people than from own age and education peers. Finally, a wealthy person age 50–65 could expect to get more conservative advice from a randomly chosen professional acting without conflict of interest than from a randomly chosen peer in the same age-education group. Differences in the distribution of advice were small, though, for investors declaring they had a high tolerance for risk.

The pattern of these results is intriguing, especially in the face of prior research on who tends to use professional financial advice. Starting with Hackethal et al. (2012) who considered clients of independent financial advisors and of a major bank in Germany, several subsequent studies concluded that the people more likely to be matched with a professional financial advisor are older, wealthier, and more experienced investors. When we combine the lessons from that literature with Rumpf et al.'s (2024) finding that professionals not facing conflicts of interest recommended more limited risk exposure to college-educated groups age 50+ (versus their peers or their children). The implication is that the current pattern of financial advice, if anything, tends to discourage stockholding exposures. This idea is reinforced by the further finding that professional advisors not subject to conflicts of interest would tend to encourage young, lower-educated individuals to include stocks in their financial portfolio more than their peers and elders would advise.

Among other things, this evidence provides a novel argument for promoting access to financial advice for the young and those lacking experience with financial markets: the sources they would normally approach, namely family and friends, are less likely to encourage them to use stocks and take advantage of the wealth creation potential of the equity premium when investing for retirement. An important challenge in this context would be to persuade the young that talking with professional advisors would be worthwhile, even if they had only a small amount of savings and made small contributions to retirement plans. It would also be necessary to convince professionals that young investors' long-term horizons would compensate for the small initial size of these accounts.

## Others as a Source of Stress

While the projects highlighted above focused on the role of others as sources of information, inspiration, or advice, the final study we review here turned to an analysis of the background stress imposed by others, which proves difficult to ignore or shake. Such stress can arise not only from a general crisis (e.g., a pandemic, fiscal or financial crisis, war) but also from aspects of daily life (e.g., stressful work environments, problematic relationships, children, health concerns). The common element of such stressors is that they tax peoples' ability to concentrate and perform other important tasks.

To this end, we conducted an online experiment using a representative sample of 1,881 French respondents. The specific tasks examined were consumption and saving choices in the presence of labor income risk, and, in some treatments, with additional uncertainty regarding the occurrence and duration of a significant drop in income such as what might arise from a furlough or from an unemployment spell. Specifically, the research question we posed was: Does cognitive load, either alone or in conjunction with adverse labor market shocks, affect individuals' consumption and saving decisions, and if so, how?

There are good a priori reasons to think that interfering with people's ability to concentrate and pay attention to making sound financial decisions could result in overspending and limited wealth accumulation. For instance, some individuals may seek to satisfy their current needs, while underestimating the future consequences of their actions. Also, certain population subgroups may be particularly prone to such types of behavior, calling for special attention from policymakers. Nevertheless, and surprisingly, findings turned out to be the opposite. Assenza et al. (2023) found that when people are confronted with cognitive load interfering with their consumption and saving decision making, they became more cautious, leading them to reduce consumption and boost savings more than they would have undertaken without cognitive load (all else equal). Moreover, this pattern was not confined to a few demographic groups but was present more generally, with only minor exceptions.

The study involved a 20-period consumption-saving problem in the presence of labor income risk. A control (Group 1) was asked to make 19 choices (in the 20th, subjects consumed all remaining wealth), and there were also three treatment groups. Group 2 faced an additional probability of a 30% reduction in period income, imposed with unknown duration; this could be thought of as furlough or unemployment risk. As expected, members of this group moderated their consumption and raised their accumulated wealth given the rise in background income risk. The remaining two groups also faced a cognitive load when trying to make their consumption/saving decisions. Group 3 faced the same labor income process as the control group and an additional cognitive load, while Group 4 faced the labor income process of Group 2, incorporating a furlough or unemployment probability with unknown duration, as well as the additional cognitive load.

The cognitive load was incorporated in the form of randomly appearing numbers to which the subjects had to respond within a short time, by pressing or not pressing the space bar. To make sure that subjects could not ignore this annoying task, they were told that they would be rewarded for correct answers, and their reward would be multiplicative across the cognitive load and the main (consumption/saving) task. Performance on the main task was also incentivized by instructing participants to closely track the optimal consumption behavior implied by an expected utility maximization model, reset every period to consider the realized level of available savings, and by providing frequent feedback on how they were performing relative to a rational optimizer. Their payoff in the consumption task was linked to the maximized expected utility resulting from their consumption decision that period, assuming optimal behavior in the future. In other words, participants were told that they would be rewarded based on the best that could be achieved from that period on because of their consumption/saving choice that period. This performance measure was illustrated diagrammatically before they were able to make their next choice. To maintain undiminished attention throughout the experiment, subjects were told that at the end of the task, two periods would be drawn at random, and they would be rewarded based on their performance in those two periods.[10]

Reassuringly, all groups' average behavior tended to get closer to optimal behavior predicted by the respective labor income model, as time elapsed and subjects became more familiar with the tasks at hand. Nevertheless, imposing the cognitive load did raise the deviation of average group consumption choices from optimal behavior, regardless of whether furlough or unemployment risk was present. The rational model's ability to describe heterogeneity in behavior within each group, as measured by the mean squared deviation of actual from optimal consumption, did not monotonically improve as the experiment progressed; however, the cognitive load shifted penalty functions upward. Whether we used the macro (group average) measure of model proximity or the micro (heterogenous behavior) measure, the cognitive load provoked substantial additional departures from optimal behavior implied by the model.

Our econometric analysis therefore sheds light on the effects of each treatment on average consumption and financial assets chosen by each subject over the life of the experiment, as well as on subjects' ability to approximate the optimal behavior implied by the model. Controlling for a range of subject characteristics elicited in the survey, the systematic impact of the cognitive load was to lower average consumption choices and raise subjects' average level of financial assets held. This meant that subjects' responses facing cognitive load compared to its absence were significantly farther from the rational model predictions. Moreover, the bulk of the effect came through a suboptimal level of consumption given the amount of available financial assets (a wrong policy rule for consumption, in dynamic programming jargon), rather than from subjects responding optimally to the level of financial assets resulting from previous decisions (a suboptimal evolution of the endogenous state).

The impact of cognitive load on those not facing increased furlough or unemployment risk was independent of observable subject characteristics, but measuring the combined effect both of furlough risk and cognitive load facing subjects proved to be a more challenging task. Results showed that college-educated subjects performed systematically better, in that they reduced their consumption less and exhibited smaller deviations from the model, compared to the less educated. Yet it was difficult to detect other characteristics moderating effects or departures from the model. In fact, one of the few factors that mattered, namely being patient, resulted in even greater drops in consumption in response to the cognitive load and in greater deviations from optimal behavior.

In sum, the findings suggest that people became more cautious in their spending and saving behavior when they were preoccupied, lowering their propensity to spend rather than creating significant household liquidity or solvency problems. Our results also imply that in the depths of a crisis, people become more cautious with their resources and deviate from long-term optimal behavior. Providing advice and support on how to better relate their consumption spending to their resources could therefore be part of an overall strategy to spur economic growth in times of economic downturn. Moreover, wide-reaching campaigns, rather than targeting specific disadvantaged groups, could be cost-effective. Analogously, if problems creating cognitive load are individual-specific (such as stressful life events or situations), people may benefit from coaching and advice to help them adopt a reasonable consumption plan given available resources.

## Conclusions

This chapter reviews findings from four recent research projects, with three of them ongoing at the time of writing. Key takeaways may be summarized as follows. First, interacting with a larger proportion of neighbors with college-level economics or business education tends to promote retirement saving. Yet people's tendency to associate with others like themselves means that members of low socioeconomic groups are unlikely to interact with knowledgeable others and unlikely to correctly interpret the information they receive when they do. Second, college-educated people exposed to more local wealth inequality, as well as more wealth mobility at the start of their economic lives, tend to take more asset risks later in life and thus accumulate greater wealth, leaving the less educated behind. Nevertheless, general education is likely to be insufficient to solve such problems, but programs to improve financial behavior among the less educated may be more useful.

Third, the current pattern of access to financial advice, where the young and less experienced are also less likely to receive financial advice, tends to discourage stock market participation and reduce equity in retirement portfolios. This is because the peers of the young tend to be more conservative in their recommendations than professionals would be. Finally, background stressors such as crises, wars, and personal problems burden people's minds as they make saving decisions. In our incentivized online experiment, background stress made people behave consistently more cautiously with respect to their finances, in the sense that they reduced their consumption and ended up with larger financial balances. Additionally, there was little evidence of heterogeneity across individual characteristics, so we conclude that aggregate crises may not require targeted policies to respond to these effects. Nevertheless, there is reason to support individuals who face person-specific circumstances preventing them from concentrating on important financial choices for their financial future.

## Acknowledgments

The author thanks his coauthors on the projects described including Tiziana Assenza, Alberto Cardaci, Thomas Jansson, Yigitcan Karabulut, Tetyana Kosyakova, Thomas Otter, and Matthias Rumpf. He also thanks participants in the 2024 Pension Research Council Symposium for their feedback, as well as his colleagues and students who contributed comments or research assistance on the many drafts of working papers associated with the four projects. He is also grateful to Macquarie University in Sydney, which hosted his visit during which part of this paper was written. He also acknowledges the funding institutions who supported the work on these projects including the European Savings Institute (OEE) through a research grant, the French National Research Agency (ANR) under the Investissements d'Avenir program grant ANR-17-EURE-0010, and the German Research Foundation (DFG) [HA 5167/2-1].

## Notes

1. Arrondel et al. (2022) reported that French households discussed such matters with three to five people on average, while their social circle exceeded 50 members, on average.
2. Unfortunately, Sweden stopped collecting such data following abolition of the wealth tax.
3. In fact, if the refugees were not influenced by their neighbors directly, but rather by features of their neighborhood, this would be an instance of what Manski (1993) called 'correlated effects' not necessarily attributable to interactions with peers.
4. We define municipalities with above-median wealth mobility as the municipalities where the locals not in the top 10% of the wealth distribution had an above-median probability of rising to that top wealth bracket over the five-year period for which the refugee allocation program lasted.
5. In status models this comes through a jump in utility at the 'aspiration' level (thanks to Nikolai Roussanov for this suggestion).
6. This is above average in the Eurozone (10.9% and 12.9%, respectively), but lower than in the US, where direct stockholding rose from 15% to 19% between 2019 and 2022 and combined direct and indirect stock market participation rose from 53% to 58% (Aladangady et al. 2023; ECB 2023).
7. Evidence of such catering was found by Mullainathan et al. (2012).
8. This finding on the stated beliefs of professional financial advisors is consistent with prior research (Linnainmaa et al. 2021) finding considerable similarities of professional advisors' portfolios to those of their respective clients. It also supports their interpretation that this similarity reflected beliefs of professional advisors.
9. Specifically, for a given client type, $h$, with household characteristics $x_h$, we compute predicted risky asset share recommendations, $y_{ah}$, for each adviser $a$ of a given peer type. Predicted risky asset share recommendations are computed at each draw of the reaction function of advisor $a$, defined as the vector of coefficients $\beta_a$. The results that are smaller than 0 and larger than 1 are censored to the respective portfolio share limits. All predicted values of risky share recommendations for a given peer type form the distribution of predicted risky asset share recommendations for client $h$ with client characteristics $x_h$ being discussed in the text.
10. The maximum payoff in each period of life was €2.50, and the maximum performance payoff a participant could get was €5.00, based on the two randomly chosen periods for reward purposes.

## References

Aladangady, A., J. Bricker, A. C. Chang, S. Goodman, J. Krimmel, K. B. Moore, S. Reber, A. H. Volz, and R. A. Windle (2023). *Changes in U.S. Family Finances from 2019 to 2022: Evidence from the Survey of Consumer Finances.* Washington, DC: Board of Governors of the Federal Reserve System. doi.org/10.17016/8799

Arrondel, L., H. Calvo-Pardo, C. Giannitsarou, and M. Haliassos (2022). 'Informative Social Interactions.' *Journal of Economic Behavior & Organization*, 203: 246–263.

Assenza, T., A. Cardaci, and M. Haliassos (2023). 'Consumption and Account Balances in Crises: Have we Neglected Cognitive Load?' IMFS Working Paper No. 197.

Bach, L., L. E. Calvet, and P. Sodini (2020). 'Rich Pickings? Risk, Return, and Skill in Household Wealth.' *American Economic Review*, 110(9): 2703–2747.

Barth, D., N. W. Papageorge, and K. Thom (2020). 'Genetic Endowments and Wealth Inequality.' *Journal of Political Economy*, 128(4): 1474–1522.

Das, S., C. M. Kuhnen, and S. Nagel (2019). 'Socioeconomic Status and Macroeconomic Expectations.' *Review of Financial Studies*, 33(1): 395–432.

European Central Bank (ECB 2023). *The Household Finance and Consumption Survey, Wave 2021 Statistical Tables.* European Central Bank Statistical Tables, July 2023. Frankfurt, Germany: European Central Bank.

Fagereng, A., L. Guiso, M. Holm, and L. Pistaferri (2020). *K-Returns to Education.* Einaudi Institute for Economics and Finance Working Paper No. 2002.

Fagereng, A., L. Guiso, D. Malacrino, and L. Pistaferri (2020). 'Heterogeneity and Persistence in Returns to Wealth.' *Econometrica*, 88(1): 115–170.

Girshina, A. (2019). 'Wealth, Savings, and Returns over the Life Cycle: The Role of Education.' Swedish House of Finance Research Paper No. 19-10.

Gomes, F., M. Haliassos, and T. Ramadorai (2021). 'Household Finance.' *Journal of Economic Literature*, 59(3): 919–1000.

Hackethal, A., M. Haliassos, and T. Jappelli (2012). 'Financial Advisors: A Case of Babysitters?' *Journal of Banking and Finance*, 36(2): 509–524.

Haliassos, M., T. Jansson, and Y. Karabulut (2020). 'Financial Literacy Externalities.' *Review of Financial Studies*, 33(2): 950–989.

Haliassos, M., T. Jansson, and Y. Karabulut (2023). 'Wealth Inequality: Opportunity or Unfairness?' CEPR Discussion Paper No. 17237.

Kuhnen, C. M. and A. C. Miu (2017). 'Socioeconomic Status and Learning from Financial Information.' *Journal of Financial Economics*, 124(2): 349–372.

Linnainmaa, J., B. Melzer, and A. Previtero (2021). 'The Misguided Beliefs of Financial Advisors.' *Journal of Finance*, 76(2): 587–621.

Manski, C. (1993). 'Identification of Endogenous Social Effects: The Reflection Problem.' *Review of Economic Studies*, 60(3): 531–542.

Mullainathan, S., M. Noeth, and A. Schoar (2012). 'The Market for Financial Advice: An Audit Study.' NBER Working Paper No. 17929.

Phillips, L. T., S. J. Tepper, D. Goya-Tocchetto, S. Davidai, N. Ordabayeva, M. U. Mirza, B. Szaszi, M. V. Day, O. P. Hauser, and J. Jachimowicz (2025). 'Inequality in People's Minds.' doi.org/10.31234/osf.io/vawh9_v2

Roussanov, N. (2010). 'Diversification and its Discontents: Idiosyncratic and Entrepreneurial Risk in the Quest for Social Status.' *Journal of Finance*, 65(5): 1755–1788.

Rumpf, M., M. Haliassos, T. Kosyakova, and T. Otter (2024). 'Do Financial Advisors Have Different Beliefs Than Lay People?' dx.doi.org/10.2139/ssrn.5035080

Suss, J. H. (2023). 'Measuring Local, Salient Economic Inequality in the UK.' *Environment and Planning A: Economy and Space*, 55(7): 1714–1737.

Chapter 9

# Aging in America

## An Examination of Financial and Health Decision Making Among Older Adults

*Gary R. Mottola, Lei Yu, and Patricia Boyle*

Aging is associated with cognitive, contextual, and psychosocial changes that can impact many aspects of life. Importantly, aging-related changes place older adults at risk of a host of adverse financial and health outcomes, including poor financial and health decision making, financial fraud victimization, loss of independence, dementia, and even early mortality. The impact of aging on decision making has garnered significant attention in recent years, as older adults face many significant financial and health decisions, and opportunities to recover from mistakes are limited. For example, in the financial domain, older individuals face decisions related to consumption, such as when to claim Social Security payments and whether to take a lump sum or annuity payments from a pension plan (Rohwedder and Hurd this volume). Further, suboptimal decision making can render older adults more vulnerable to fraud (Hall et al. 2022; Lichtenberg et al. 2018). This is especially troubling in view of the wide array of fraudulent offers targeting older adults (Senate Special Committee on Aging 2022).

In the health domain, older adults must navigate a complex health care system and make important and difficult decisions about health care insurance, prescription drug plans, medical treatments, and end-of-life care. These decisions are also often irreversible and can significantly impact older adults' physical, mental, and financial well-being. Hence, ineffective decision making in the health care realm is equally problematic.

In the last decade or so, considerable advances have been made in understanding how aging is related to decision making. This research strongly suggests that older adults are at risk for suboptimal decision making, drawing the attention of researchers, regulators, policymakers, and the public alike (National Academies of Sciences, Engineering, and Medicine 2021). Against that backdrop, researchers at the FINRA Foundation and Rush University Medical Center began a collaboration aimed to systematically

Gary R. Mottola, Lei Yu, and Patricia Boyle, *Aging in America*. In: *Retirement Saving, Investment, and Spending.* Edited by: Olivia S. Mitchell and Nikolai Roussanov, Oxford University Press. © Pension Research Council, The Wharton School, The University of Pennsylvania (2026). DOI: 10.1093/oso/9780197845752.003.0009

examine the relationship between aging and financial decision making, with a focus on scam susceptibility and financial fraud. This collaboration connected a diverse group of researchers and policymakers and brought together expertise on aging, cognition, decision making, financial fraud, and investor protection.

In our conceptual framework, decision making reflects a complex and dynamic interplay between diverse skills and resources, and aging-related changes can impair decision making in a variety of ways. For example, while the strong association between cognitive abilities and decision making is well-established (Stewart et al. 2019; Wilson et al. 2017), our collaborative work has demonstrated that a number of non-cognitive resources also play important roles. These include psychosocial factors, such as loneliness and well-being, as well as contextual factors, such as financial and health literacy and financial fragility. Interestingly, the nature of the associations of non-cognitive factors with decision making can differ in important and interesting ways that provide valuable clues for effective intervention and policy setting. That is, whereas some non-cognitive resources impact decision making directly (meaning relatively independent of cognition), others interact with cognition to impact decision making, and these interactions can vary depending on the specific resource and specific decisional outcome (Glover et al. 2021; Wilson et al. 2023). Figure 9.1 depicts the complex relationships and inter-relationships in our conceptual framework.

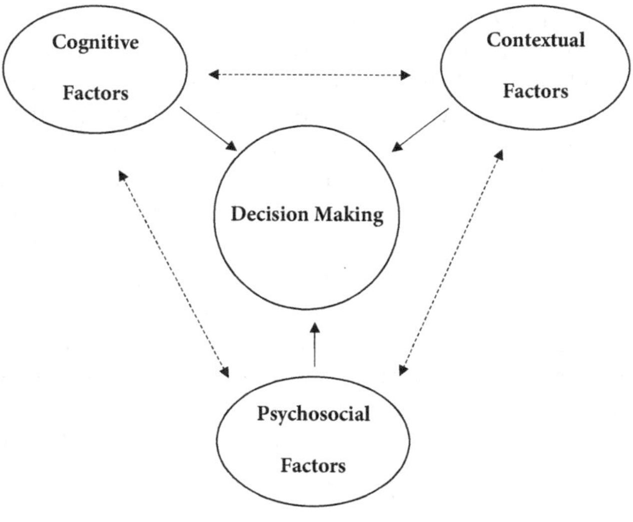


**Figure 9.1** Factors affecting decision-making
*Source:* Adapted with permission from Boyle et al. (2022).

To date, our research has generated numerous papers, issue briefs, and infographics that examine a variety of issues related to aging and decision making. Collectively, these studies provide a foundation for understanding how aging affects decision making, and the findings from several particularly relevant studies are discussed in this chapter.

## Data

We leverage data from the Rush Memory and Aging Project (MAP), a cohort study of common chronic conditions of aging and Alzheimer's disease focused on cognitive and functional decline and risk factors for Alzheimer's disease and related dementias. The study recruits older adults throughout the Chicago metropolitan area, and most participants are residents of continuous care retirement communities. The remainder are recruited from subsidized housing as well as through local churches and social service agencies that serve minorities and low-income older adults. Participants agreed to annual home visits for detailed clinical and cognitive evaluations and documentation of medical history, medication use, physical function, and experiential and psychosocial factors.

MAP started in September 1997 and is an ongoing study. A substudy of financial and health care decision making that conducts annual assessments of financial and health literacy, financial and health decision making, scam susceptibility, and related behaviors was initiated in 2010 and is also ongoing.[1] Importantly, because MAP started in 1997, longitudinal clinical and behavioral data for study participants are now available dating back over two decades. This detailed information combined with data from the financial and health care decision making substudy provide a rich platform for examining the relationship between aging and decision making.

The research discussed in this chapter focuses on two dependent variables: financial and health decision-making ability and scam susceptibility. Here we highlight important findings around the relationship between aging and decision making. Several independent variables are examined, including cognitive ability, loneliness, psychological well-being, financial and health literacy, memory misperception, and financial fragility. In what follows, we briefly describe these measures, and we provide detailed information on how these variables were measured in the Online Appendix.

## Cognitive Factors

### Cognitive Ability

Several of our studies provide evidence of the association between cognitive ability and decision-making ability. For example, one study (Yu et al. 2021) focused on the relationship between declining financial literacy and decision-making ability (described in more detail below), and it documented that lower levels of cognition were tied to lower levels of decision-making ability. In general, we have found that when looking at the associations of various non-cognitive factors with decision making and related outcomes (such as scam susceptibility), it is often important to account for the association between cognition and decision making in order to understand how non-cognitive factors work to affect decision making. Further, we have shown that declining cognitive abilities, even just the subtle changes that often occur with healthy aging, are associated with poorer decision making and greater scam susceptibility. This implies that there is an important role for cognition in understanding how aging impacts decision making.

## Memory Misperception

While cognitive ability is tied to decision-making ability, older adults are often unaware of their cognitive skills, and it is less clear how self-perceptions of cognitive ability play a role in decision making (Agarwal and Mazumder 2013; Samanez-Larkin 2013). Mazzonna and Peracchi (2024) showed that older adults who misperceive their memory skills are more likely to experience greater financial losses than those who are more attuned to the state of their memory. A possible reason could be that older adults who are unaware of their memory performance make poorer financial decisions, which leads to the aforementioned financial losses and other adverse outcomes (Yu et al. 2022).

We estimated memory skill misperception by comparing participants' subjective memory ratings with changes in their objectively assessed memory scores. To assess financial decision making, we asked participants six questions that mimic real-world tasks of choosing mutual funds (Boyle et al. 2012). More specifically, we showed participants tables with information about different mutual funds and asked three simple and three difficult questions. For example, one question asked participants to identify the account management fee of a mutual fund.[2]

We found that a greater misperception of memory skills was associated with poorer financial decision making among older adults. This effect remained even after controlling for age, sex, education, and financial literacy. To illustrate, we estimated how likely participants were to correctly answer financial decision-making questions with varying levels of memory skill misperception. As shown in Figure 9.2, the likelihood of answering only one mutual fund question correctly was higher when participants misperceived their own memory skills. These findings suggest that less accurate perceptions of memory performance are tied to poorer financial decision-making performance.

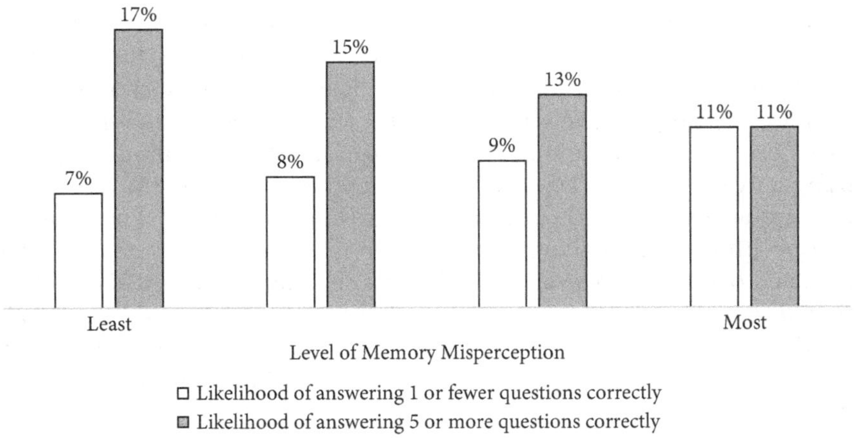


**Figure 9.2** Relationship between memory misperception and financial decision making

*Source:* Adapted from Yu et al. (2022).

Interestingly, although we found that misperceiving one's memory skills was related to poor financial decision making, the direction of the misperception did not seem to matter. That is, those who either overestimated or underestimated their memory skills both performed more poorly on decision making compared with those whose judgments were more accurate. This suggests that accurate awareness of one's cognitive abilities is important for good old-age decision making. It is also noteworthy that in addition to memory perception, financial literacy in this study was strongly tied to financial decision making—even more so than memory misperception. In fact, high levels of financial literacy somewhat buffered against the adverse effect of misperceived memory skills on financial decision making.

## Psychosocial Factors

### Loneliness

Although it is well-established that lower cognition is associated with poorer health care and financial decision making among older adults (Stewart et al. 2018), the relation of social vulnerabilities, such as loneliness, with decision making has received very little scientific attention until recently. This is true despite the strong correlation between loneliness, cognitive function, and poorer brain health. In particular, loneliness is associated with a reliance on intuition over analytic reasoning and diminished attentional abilities (Baumeister et al. 2005; Cacioppo and Hawkley 2009).

Accordingly, we hypothesized that loneliness would negatively influence decision making, especially in the context of low cognition. Stewart et al. (2020) examined the association of loneliness with financial and health decision making and whether the detrimental effect of loneliness was stronger among older adults with low cognition. We measured loneliness using a five-item scale (De Jong-Gierveld and Kamphuls 1985) and cognition was assessed via 19 cognitive tests (Wilson et al. 2015). The financial and health decision-making measure is an extended version of the financial decision-making measure described above. That is, it included questions similar to those in the financial domain but related to health decision making. Health care choices in this measure mimicked those on mutual funds but focused instead on HMO plan selection and included questions with varying levels of difficulty.

As expected, lower cognition was associated with poorer financial and health care decision making, but loneliness was not. Interestingly, however, loneliness was detrimental to decision making among older adults with low cognition, but not those with average or high cognition. For participants with average cognition, a one-point increase on the loneliness scale was associated with a 0.02-point decrease in the decision-making score; that is, there was essentially no relationship between loneliness and decision making. In comparison, for participants with low cognition, a one-point increase on the loneliness scale was associated with a 0.35-point decrease in the decision-making score. For context, subjects answered eight of 12 decision-making questions correctly, on average, and the mean score for loneliness, which was measured with 5-items that used a 5-point Likert scale, was 2.2.

To confirm the finding that loneliness is detrimental to decision making, especially among individuals with low cognition, we conducted subsequent analyses to account for a variety of potentially confounding factors, including depressive symptoms, social network size, medical conditions, and income. The main result persisted, even after accounting for these other factors, increasing our confidence that the findings are not driven by factors conceptually similar to loneliness or that might otherwise shape decision making.

## Psychological Well-Being

Another psychosocial factor of interest is psychological well-being, as this positive aspect of mental health has been shown to be protective against cognitive decline and a variety of health outcomes (Ryff et al. 2016). Based on those findings, we hypothesized that psychological well-being may slow declines in financial and health literacy and positively impact decision making (Stewart et al. 2023).

That study measured psychological well-being using an 18-item assessment (Ryff 2014). Financial literacy was assessed via a 23-item instrument including Lusardi and Mitchell's 'Big Three' financial literacy questions. Health literacy was assessed via nine items that measure knowledge of health information and concepts (e.g., Medicare and Medicare Part D coverage, following prescription instructions). The financial literacy score was the percentage of total financial literacy items answered correctly, and the health literacy score followed a similar calculation. We also generated a composite score for total literacy as the average of the domain-specific scores, with higher scores indicating higher financial and health literacy.

As predicted, higher well-being at baseline was associated with a higher level of financial and health literacy, as well as a slower decline in financial and health literacy over time. This is important because, as discussed in the next section, the rate at which financial and health literacy declines in old age is strongly tied to decreases in decision-making ability. The finding that well-being is related to a slower decline in literacy also provides new evidence that psychological well-being may protect against declines in decision-making ability and so could be a target for future interventions to help maintain decision making in old age. Further, the association between psychological well-being and financial and health literacy was relatively independent of other important factors, including depressive symptoms and cognition. This suggests that well-being helps stave off declining financial and health literacy and, by extension, promotes independence late in life.

## Contextual Factors

### Financial and Health Literacy

Financial and health literacy are important determinants of decision making, as good financial and health decision making require a basic knowledge of key concepts in these domains. Financial and health literacy involves the acquisition, processing, and utilization of pertinent information and concepts relevant to making sound financial and health decisions across the lifespan. Adequate financial and health literacy is especially critical in aging, as older adults are inundated with various financial and health care challenges. Unfortunately, however, as with decision making, many older adults struggle with basic financial concepts such as compound interest, inflation, and investments (Lusardi and Mitchell 2011), and many lack sophistication in areas such as risk diversification, asset valuation, portfolio choice and investment fees (Lusardi et al. 2014). In addition, inadequate health literacy is common, and its prevalence increases with age (Paasche-Orlow et al. 2005).

Lack of financial and health literacy in old age presents a formidable economic and public health problem. Older adults can suffer from unrecoverable financial loss and severe health consequences because of poor literacy and decision making (Braun et al. 2018; Lusardi and Mitchell 2007). We and others have shown that older adults with lower financial and health literacy make poorer financial and health decisions, are more susceptible to financial fraud and scams (Yu et al. 2021), are less likely to engage in health promoting activities (Bennett et al. 2012), and have poorer cognitive and mental health (Wolf et al. 2005). Nevertheless, most of the literature on the impacts of financial and health literacy has relied on cross-sectional data (i.e., data collected at a single point in time). These data have an inherent limitation since financial and health literacy are strongly influenced by experiential factors such as socioeconomic status, education, and occupation, as well as contextual factors like racism and sexism, and these can influence peoples' performance at a single point in time. Furthermore, along the aging process, older adults are vulnerable to a variety of diseases such as Alzheimer's disease and stroke, that degrade many functional abilities including financial and health literacy. Taken together, these findings raise an important question: are the adverse impacts of inadequate financial and health literacy in old age driven primarily by the level of literacy (e.g., that attained from earlier life experiences), age-related declines, or both?

We explored this question in a recent study using the cohort dataset described above (Yu et al. 2021). Financial and health literacy was assessed as above, as were financial and health decision making. Scam susceptibility was assessed based on participants' responses to five statements indicating vulnerability to scams according to Boyle et al. (2019). There we documented that 70% of financial and health literacy questions were answered correctly, on average, by participants at baseline, suggesting considerable room for improvement in older adults' financial literacy. In addition, we found an overall decline in financial and health literacy over time. There was also substantial person-to-person variation in the rate of decline. Most participants declined (83.5%), but some (16.5%) maintained their literacy performance over time. Being older, female, and less educated, and having lower income and impaired cognition were correlated with faster decline in financial and health literacy. In a series of regression analyses, we examined the relationship between changes in financial and health literacy and subsequent financial and health decision making and scam susceptibility, seeking to establish the temporal association between declining literacy, decision making, and scam susceptibility. This allowed us to better understand the consequences of declining literacy.

As expected, results indicated that those with a lower starting level of financial and health literacy made poorer decisions years later. Also, a faster decline was associated with poorer subsequent decision making, and the rate of decline in literacy was more strongly related to subsequent decision making than the starting level. We also examined the association of decline in financial and health literacy with susceptibility to scams. Again, older adults with a lower baseline level of financial and health literacy as well as a faster decline in literacy were more susceptible to scams. These findings strongly suggest that the adverse consequences of inadequate literacy among older adults are not merely the result of level differences but also due to age-related declines in literacy over time.

In separate research (Boyle et al. 2025), we examined whether there was heterogeneity in the likelihood and rate of decline in literacy and the potential basis of such heterogeneity—sex differences in particular. Our interest in sex differences stems from studies showing that women have significantly lower levels of financial literacy compared to men and that gender-based differences in financial literacy could have implications for financial decision making (Bajtelsmit this volume; Fonseca et al. 2012; Hasler and Lusardi 2017). This may impede their ability to accumulate, manage, and draw down retirement assets, and hence their economic well-being in later life. Moreover, since women typically live longer than men, low financial literacy coupled with age-related declines in financial literacy can be particularly problematic for women. In terms of health literacy, the findings are less clear, though some studies have found that women have higher health literacy levels than men (Clouston et al. 2017; Kutner et al. 2006). Nevertheless, if over the course of aging, women's financial and health literacy levels decline at rates that are different than men's, gender-based gaps in literacy could change, with implications for the financial and health outcomes men and women experience. Interestingly our longitudinal analyses showed no significant difference in the likelihood or rate of decline between men and women.

## Financial Fragility

Another contextual factor that could affect financial decision making is financial fragility, often measured as being unable to come up with an amount of money quickly (often $2000) if needed for an unexpected expense. Prior studies have suggested that financial fragility is an important risk factor for poor financial decisions, as well as financial fraud and scams among the general adult population. Anderson (2013) found that individuals who reported more debt than they could comfortably handle were twice as likely to be victimized by fraud compared with those reporting no debt. DeLiema et al. (2019) reported that financially fragile individuals also were more susceptible to scams. Nevertheless, it is unclear whether these findings extend to older adults. The proportion of financially fragile individuals is relatively low among Baby Boomers (Mitchell and Lusardi 2021; Society of

Actuaries 2019), and the relationship between financial fragility and scam susceptibility in older adults is not yet well understood.

In our recent work (Yu et al. 2022), we assessed financial fragility by measuring older adults' confidence in their ability to come up with $2,000 within one month to cover an unexpected expense. Participants rated their confidence on a four-level scale, from extremely confident to not at all confident. Those who reported being little or not at all confident were classified as financially fragile. Scam susceptibility was measured as noted above. Nearly 10% of participants were classified as financially fragile, reporting little or no confidence in their ability to access $2,000 in a month. This figure is smaller than what is typically reported for younger age cohorts. By comparison, Lusardi et al. (2011) reported that around half of 18- to 65-year-olds were unable to come up with $2,000 in a month, and younger adults ranked as the most financially fragile, which may explain the lower rate of financial fragility in our sample. That is, the lower rate likely stems from the fact that our sample is much older than the overall US adult population. Using data from the 2021 National Financial Capability Study, we calculated that 15% of US adults age 65+ are financially fragile, a rate close to that we found in our sample. Moreover, financially fragile older adults proved to be more than twice as likely to display high or very high levels of scam susceptibility (12% versus 28%), compared to non-fragile counterparts. Even after adjusting for key demographic factors (age, gender, income, and educational attainment), the average scam susceptibility score for financially fragile older adults exceeded that of their non-financially fragile counterparts. Notably, the difference in susceptibility to scams between older adults with and without financial fragility was equivalent to the difference of nearly a decade in age.

When we added controls for cognition, financial decision making, and financial literacy, we again found that both lower cognition and financial literacy were strongly associated with greater scam susceptibility. Nevertheless, financial fragility persisted as a significant factor, and the magnitude of the association remained essentially the same. This suggests that even in the presence of adequate cognition and financial literacy, financial fragility may still predispose older adults to fraud and scams.

## Scam Susceptibility Among Older Adults: A Behavioral Experiment

A key step toward protecting older adults from financial fraud and scams is to gain a better grasp of the scope of the problem. Nevertheless, this remains elusive, since data on fraud victimization come almost exclusively from complaints filed with government agencies or surveys (Deevy and Beals 2013).

Such data are widely used by the research community and provide valuable information on the prevalence, determinants, and consequences of financial fraud and scams (DeLiema et al. 2020; Lichtenberg et al. 2016; Shao et al. 2019). Yet because surveys rely on older adults' ability to recognize, acknowledge, and report fraud, survey data have significant intrinsic limitations. To name just some, these include recall bias, underreporting due to shame or lack of awareness that one has been victimized, and fear of loss of independence.

To address some of these challenges, we conducted a behavioral experiment designed to mimic a government impersonation scam (Yu et al. 2023). This experiment involved a fictitious government agency reaching out to community-living older adults about a potential compromise of personal information relevant to individuals' Social Security and Medicare benefits. The study focused on data collected via phone conversations, with a live agent posing as a representative from a government agency. Our primary aim was to assess the vulnerability of older adults to government impersonation scams.

Our results revealed that a sizable number of older adults (16.4%) engaged without skepticism (meaning readily answered the call and responded to questions), and of those, nearly three-quarters provided personal information. Some (15.1%) engaged but were potentially alert to the fraudulent nature of the outreach, and they did not confirm or share personal information. The majority (68.5%) did not engage in any capacity.

Examinations of the cognitive, functional, and psychosocial characteristics associated with engagement with the potential fraudster revealed that cognitive ability, financial literacy, and scam susceptibility (as measured above) proved to be important factors associated with vulnerability. Notably, subjects who engaged without skepticism were significantly less financially literate. They also had significantly higher levels of scam susceptibility.

## Conclusions

An aging population due to declining fertility rates and rising life expectancy is a global phenomenon with far-reaching economic and social consequences. By 2040, it is estimated that over 20% of Americans will be above the age of 64. In absolute terms, there will be 80 million Americans age 65+ by 2040, more than twice the number in 2000 (Administration for Community Living 2022). Given the aging population, it is imperative to better understand the impacts of aging on decision making.

This overview of our research based on cross-sectional and longitudinal data suggests that cognitive, contextual, and psychosocial variables are determinants of decision-making ability among older adults. We also report findings from a novel behavioral experiment that shows cognition, financial literacy, and scam awareness are related to the likelihood of responding to a fraudulent pitch. Our studies speak to the importance of informing policymakers and the public more broadly about the links between aging and impaired decision making. The research can also inform approaches to better protect older adults from suboptimal decision making, by identifying vulnerable populations (e.g., those with lower cognition but still in the normal range, lonely individuals) to whom interventions can be targeted and by using the research to inform the development of novel interventions that might prove effective (e.g., literacy interventions). In terms of the public more broadly, older adults (and their family members) who are aware of the potential for declining cognitive abilities and the consequences of decline can endeavor to make financial and health-related plans and decisions while their cognitive ability is unimpaired, for example, by creating a will or working with a trusted advisor or family member to make financial and health decisions.

In addition, having adequate financial literacy is an important component of good decision making among older adults who may benefit from educational programs addressing key knowledge gaps. Further, the research speaks to the need for additional efforts to improve decision making given how many older adults are vulnerable to suboptimal decision making as well as the financial repercussions flowing from suboptimal decisions, including losing money to financial fraud.

Regulators have already sought to address some of these challenges. For example, FINRA changes to Rule 4512 required investment firms to make reasonable efforts to identify a trusted contact for clients' accounts. These trusted contacts can serve as a resource for advisors working with older adults to help prevent financial exploitation (Boyle et al. 2022). Further, as noted by Boyle et al. (2022: 48), FINRA and several states are encouraging broker-dealers and investment advisers to 'temporarily pause suspicious transactions or disbursements so that investigators can investigate and, if needed, take action before a customer is harmed. Similarly, California has enacted a research-backed law that reformed the disclosures accompanying certain mortgage products.' Similar protections might be useful in the health care arena as well.

Our research also speaks to the importance of balancing consumer protection and consumer autonomy. There is clearly a link between aging and impaired financial decision making, yet our research also shows that many adults maintain their cognitive abilities well into their later years. This finding must be considered when developing educational initiatives related to aging and financial decision making as well as policy interventions. A heavy-handed approach to either could, potentially, do more harm than good if such an approach prevented older adults from seeking information and/or help for fear of losing autonomy over their financial lives. That is, many older adults are capable of making informed and effective financial decisions, but some are not. Therefore, it is critically important to consider how policy efforts can better protect those who need protection while not impinging upon the choices of older adults whose decision-making ability is still intact.

## Notes

1. More information on MAP can be found at the Rush Alzheimer's Disease Center's research and data sharing hub (https://www.radc.rush.edu/).
2. More information on how we assessed memory misperception and financial decision making as well as all measures discussed in this chapter can be found in the Online Appendix.

## References

Administration for Community Living (ACL) (2022). *2021 Profile of Older Americans.* ACL Report 2021.508. Washington, DC: ACL.

Agarwal, S. and B. Mazumder (2013). 'Cognitive Abilities and Household Financial Decision Making.' *American Economic Journal: Applied Economics*, 5(1): 193–207.

Anderson, K. B. (2013). *Consumer Fraud in the United States, 2011: The Third FTC Survey.* Federal Trade Commission Report No. 130419. Washington, DC: FTC.

Baumeister, R., C. DeWall, N. Ciarocco, and J. Twenge (2005). 'Social Exclusion Impairs Self-Regulation.' *Journal of Personality and Social Psychology*, 88(4): 589–604.

Bennett, J., P. Boyle, B. James, and D. Bennett (2012). 'Correlates of Health and Financial Literacy in Older Adults Without Dementia.' *BMC Geriatrics*, 12: 30.

Boyle, P., O. S. Mitchell, G. Mottola, and L. Yu (2025). 'Declining Financial and Health Literacy Among Older Men and Women.' *Journal of the Economics of Ageing*, 30: 100547.

Boyle, P., L. Yu, A. Buchman, and D. Bennett (2012). 'Risk Aversion is Associated with Decision Making Among Community-Based Older Persons.' *Frontiers in Psychology*, 3: 205.

Boyle, P., L. Yu, G. Mottola, K. Innes, and D. Bennett (2022). 'Degraded Rationality and Suboptimal Decision-Making in Old Age: A Silent Epidemic with Major Economic and Public Health Implications.' *Public Policy & Aging Report*, 32(2): 45–50.

Boyle, P., L. Yu, J. Schneider, R. Wilson, and D. Bennett (2019). 'Scam Awareness Related to Incident Alzheimer Dementia and Mild Cognitive Impairment: A Prospective Cohort Study.' *Annals of Internal Medicine*, 170(10): 702–709.

Braun, R., A. Barnes, Y. Hanoch, and A. Federman (2018). 'Health Literacy and Plan Choice: Implications for Medicare Managed Care.' *Health Literacy Research and Practice*, 2(1): 40–54.

Cacioppo, J. and L. Hawkley (2009). 'Perceived Social Isolation and Cognition.' *Trends in Cognitive Sciences*, 13(10): 447–454.

Clouston, S., J. Manganello, and M. Richards (2017). 'A Life Course Approach to Health Literacy: The Role of Gender, Educational Attainment and Lifetime Cognitive Capability.' *Age and Ageing*, 46(3): 493–499.

De Jong-Gierveld, J. and F. Kamphuls (1985). 'The Development of a Rasch-Type Loneliness Scale.' *Applied Psychological Measurement*, 9(3): 289–299.

Deevy, M. and M. Beals (2013). *The Scope of the Problem: An Overview of Fraud Prevalence Measurement.* Financial Fraud Research Center Report No. 201607. Stanford, CA: Stanford Center on Longevity.

DeLiema, M., M. Deevy, A. Lusardi, and O. S. Mitchell (2020). 'Financial Fraud Among Older Americans: Evidence and Implications.' *Journals of Gerontology: Series B*, 75(4): 861–868.

DeLiema, M., E. Fletcher, C. Kieffer, G. Mottola, R. Pessanha, and M. Trumpower (2019). *Exposed to Scams: What Separates Victims from Non-Victims?* Stanford, CA: Stanford Center on Longevity. longevity.stanford.edu/scamtracker/

Fonseca, R., K. Mullen, G. Zamarro, and J. Zissimopoulos (2012). 'What Explains the Gender Gap in Financial Literacy? The Role of Household Decision Making.' *Journal of Consumer Affairs*, 46(1): 90–106

Glover, C., L. Yu, C. Stewart, R. Wilson, D. Bennett, and P. Boyle (2021). 'The Association of Late Life Cognitive Activity with Healthcare and Financial Decision-Making in Community-Dwelling, Nondemented Older Adults.' *American Journal of Geriatric Psychiatry*, 29(2): 117–125.

Hall, L., J. Moray, E. Gross, and P. Lichtenberg (2022). 'The Relationship Between Financial Decision-Making and Financial Exploitation in Older Black Adults.' *Journal of Aging and Health*, 34(3): 472–481

Hasler, A. and A. Lusardi (2017). *The Gender Gap in Financial Literacy: A Global Perspective.* Stanford, CA: GFLEC. gflec.org/research/?type=reports

Kutner, M., E. Greenburg, Y. Jin, and C. Paulsen (2006). *The Health Literacy of America's Adults: Results from the 2003 National Assessment of Adult Literacy.* National Center for Education Statistics Report 2006-483.

Lichtenberg, P., K. Ocepek-Welikson, L. Ficker, E. Gross, A. Rahman-Filipiak, and J. Teresi (2018). 'Conceptual and Empirical Approaches to Financial Decision-Making by Older Adults: Results from a Financial Decision-Making Rating Scale.' *Clinical Gerontologist*, 41(1): 42–65.

Lichtenberg, P., M. Sugarman, D. Paulson, L. Ficker, and A. Rahman-Filipiak (2016). 'Psychological and Functional Vulnerability Predicts Fraud Cases in Older Adults: Results of a Longitudinal Study.' *Clinical Gerontologist*, 39(1): 48–63.

Lusardi, A. and O. S. Mitchell (2007). 'Baby Boomer Retirement Security: The Roles of Planning, Financial Literacy, and Housing Wealth.' *Journal of Monetary Economics*, 54(1): 205–224.

Lusardi, A. and O. S. Mitchell (2011). 'Financial Literacy and Planning: Implications for Retirement Well-being.' In O. S. Mitchell and A. Lusardi, eds., *Financial Literacy: Implications for Retirement Security and the Financial Marketplace.* Oxford: Oxford University Press, pp. 17–39.

Lusardi, A., O. S Mitchell, and V. Curto (2014). 'Financial Literacy and Financial Sophistication in the Older Population.' *Journal of Pension Economics & Finance*, 13(4): 347–366.

Lusardi, A., D. Schneider, and P. Tufano (2011). 'Financially Fragile Households: Evidence and Implications.' *Brookings Papers on Economic Activity*, Spring(2011): 83–150.

Mazzonna, F. and F. Peracchi (2024). 'Are Older People Aware of Their Cognitive Decline? Misperception and Financial Decision Making.' *Journal of Political Economy*, 132(6): 1793–1830.

Mitchell, O. S. and A. Lusardi (2021). 'Financial Literacy and Financial Behavior at Older Ages.' In D. Bloom, A. Sousa-Poza, and U. Sunde, eds., *The Routledge Handbook of the Economics of Ageing*. London: Routledge, pp. 553–561.

National Academies of Sciences, Engineering, and Medicine (NASCEM) (2021). *Implications for Behavioral and Social Research of Preclinical Markers of Alzheimer's Disease and Related Dementias: Proceedings of a Workshop in Brief*. Washington, DC: The National Academies Press. doi.org/10.17226/26295

Paasche-Orlow, M., R. Parker, J. Gazmararian, L. Nielsen–Bohlman, and R. Rudd (2005). 'The Prevalence of Limited Health Literacy.' *Journal of General Internal Medicine*, 20(2): 175–184.

Ryff, C. (2014). 'Psychological Well Being Revisited: Advances in the Science and Practice of Eudaimonia.' *Psychotherapy and Psychosomatics*, 83(1): 10–28.

Ryff, C., A. Heller, S. Schaefer, C van Reekum, and R. Davidson (2016). 'Purposeful Engagement, Healthy Aging, and the Brain.' *Current Behavorial Neuroscience Reports*, 3(4): 318–327.

Samanez-Larkin, G. (2013). 'Financial Decision Making and the Aging Brain.' *APS Observer*, 26(5): 30–33.

Special Committee on Aging (2022). *Fighting Fraud: Top Scams in 2021.* Washington, DC: US Senate Special Committee on Aging.

Shao, J., Q. Zhang, Y. Ren, X. Li, and T. Lin (2019). 'Why Are Older Adults Victims of Fraud? Current Knowledge and Prospects Regarding Older Adults' Vulnerability to Fraud.' *Journal of Elder Abuse Neglect*, 31(3): 225–243.

Society of Actuaries (2019). *Financial Fragility Across the Generations.* Society of Actuaries Aging and Retirement Series Report Issue 5.

Stewart, C., L. Yu, C. Glover, G. Mottola, D. Bennett, R. Wilson, and P. Boyle (2020). 'Loneliness Interacts with Cognition in Relation to Healthcare and Financial Decision Making Among Community-Dwelling Older Adults.' *Gerontologist*, 60(8): 1476–1484.

Stewart, C., L. Yu, C. Glover, G. Mottola, O. Valdes, R. Wilson, D. Bennett, and P. Boyle (2023). 'Well-Being and Aging-Related Decline in Financial and Health Literacy in Advanced Age.' *Journals of Gerontology: Series B*, 78(9): 526–1532.

Stewart, C., L. Yu, R. Wilson, D. Bennett, and P. Boyle (2018). 'Correlates of Healthcare and Financial Decision Making Among Older Adults Without Dementia.' *Health Psychology*, 37(7): 618–626.

Stewart, C., L. Yu, R. Wilson, D. Bennett, and P. Boyle (2019). 'Healthcare and Financial Decision Making and Incident Adverse Cognitive Outcomes Among Older Adults.' *Journal of the American Geriatrics Society*, 67(8): 1590–1595.

Wilson, R., P. Boyle, L. Yu, L. Barnes, J. Sytsma, A. Buchman, and J. Schneider (2015). 'Temporal Course and Pathologic Basis of Unawareness of Memory Loss in Dementia.' *Neurology*, 85(11): 984–991.

Wilson, R., L. Yu, B. James, D. Bennett, and P. Boyle (2017). 'Association of Financial and Health Literacy with Cognitive Health in Old Age.' *Neuropsychology, Development, and Cognition. Section B, Aging, Neuropsychology and Cognition Journal*, 24(2): 186–197.

Wilson, R., L. Yu, C. Stewart, D. Bennett, and P. Boyle (2023). 'Change in Decision-Making Analysis and Preferences in Old Age.' *Journals of Gerontology: Series B*, 78(10): 1659–1667.

Wolf, M., J. Gazmararian, and D. Baker (2005). 'Health Literacy and Functional Health Status Among Older Adults.' *Archives of Internal Medicine*, 165(17): 1946–1952.

Yu, L., G. Mottola, L. L. Barnes, O. Valdes, R. S. Wilson, D. A. Bennett, and P. A. Boyle (2022). 'Financial Fragility and Scam Susceptibility in Community Dwelling Older Adults.' *Journal of Elder Abuse & Neglect*, 34(2), 93–108.

Yu, L., G. Mottola, D. Bennett, and P. Boyle (2021). 'Adverse Impacts of Declining Financial and Health Literacy in Old Age.' *American Journal of Geriatric Psychiatry*, 29(11): 1129–1139.

Yu, L., G. Mottola, C. Kieffer, R. Mascio, O. Valdes, D. Bennett, and P. Boyle (2023). 'Vulnerability of Older Adults to Government Impersonation Scams.' *JAMA Network Open*, 6(9): e2335319.

# Part III

# Spending Challenges in Later Life

Chapter 10

# Insights on Economic Well-Being at Older Ages from Analyses of Household Spending

*Michael D. Hurd and Susann Rohwedder*

Consumption is considered by economists as the most direct measure of economic well-being. While a household's economic resources (income and net wealth) determine its spending possibilities, it is consumption that produces utility.[1] Despite this, it is difficult to study life-cycle consumption at the household level since information on household spending is rarely collected in general-purpose cross-section surveys that typically ask about only a few spending components, such as food, rent/housing, and utilities. Longitudinal collection of comprehensive spending information, which is vital in life-cycle studies, is even more scarce.

In the absence of detailed information on household spending, assessments of economic well-being often rely on household (pre-tax) income, which is a poor proxy for economic well-being for households whose consumption differs considerably from their income, either due to taxes, saving, or dissaving. This difference is especially a problem for the study of older adults' economic situations, as many of them have accumulated retirement savings in order to consume more than their incomes in later life.

The US Health and Retirement Study (2022) is a rare exception: it gathers biennial longitudinal data on detailed components of total spending of individuals over age 50 and their households. The dataset can be used to compute total household spending and consumption, and it can also be linked to the rich longitudinal information collected in the HRS core survey. The latter includes detailed information on the complete household budget constraint: income, assets and claims on pensions, Social Security, and other annuities.

In this chapter, we first review what economic theory suggests about how household spending should evolve at older ages assuming utility maximizing behavior so as to provide a frame of reference for the empirical patterns reported subsequently. We discuss how spending changes at retirement, and

Michael D. Hurd and Susann Rohwedder, *Insights on Economic Well-Being at Older Ages from Analyses of Household Spending*. In: *Retirement Saving, Investment, and Spending*. Edited by: Olivia S. Mitchell and Nikolai Roussanov, Oxford University Press. © Pension Research Council, The Wharton School, The University of Pennsylvania (2026). DOI: 10.1093/oso/9780197845752.003.0010

we quantify the composition of household spending and how it varies by age and marital status. We also document age profiles for total spending. Next, we turn to two applications that use spending data to provide insights regarding the well-being of older households: a consumption-based poverty assessment and assessments of the adequacy of economic resources for retirement.

## Theory: Implications from the Life-Cycle Model

Economic models hold that consumption is an important determinant of well-being. While income and wealth can be used to purchase consumption, they do not have independent value because they do not directly produce utility. For example, wealth is valuable because it can finance consumption, and it is particularly valuable when the environment changes adversely. Wealth is also valuable for bequests because it can finance consumption for inheritors. Yet because consumption produces utility, economists consider it the core argument of the utility function; income and wealth define households' budget constraint. In the context of the life-cycle model, the most widely used framework for analyzing individual and household decision making, agents choose consumption within and across periods to maximize their utility over their (remaining) lifetimes. The model solution produces the optimal, affordable consumption path. In this chapter, we focus on the implications of the model for the consumption trajectory at older ages, beginning around the time of retirement to the end of life.

### The Basic Life-Cycle Model

A simple version of the standard life-cycle economic model accounts for uncertainty about the age of death and assumes no bequest motive. The solution specifies that consumption declines with age; however, *when* that occurs will depend on the household's utility function and environmental parameters (Yaari 1965). The driving force causing spending to decline is that mortality risk increases with age. In the absence of a bequest motive, wealth not consumed prior to death is wasted. To reduce the risk of dying with high wealth, individuals can increase lifetime utility by consuming more earlier so as to carry over less wealth into advanced age where mortality risk is high. Yet those who survive will need to reduce consumption (and therefore their wealth depletion rate) to guard against having to reduce consumption precipitously if they live longer than expected. This leads to the prediction that consumption will decline at older ages. Accordingly, the wealth path will have a negative slope, which does not signal a lack of optimizing behavior. In the presence of annuities, such as Social Security benefits, consumption will decline until it reaches the level of income from annuities, after which the consumption path will follow the annuity income path.

## Extensions

Many extensions of the life-cycle model introduce additional sources of uncertainty (e.g., De Nardi et al. 2025). For example, extending the model from a single person to a coupled household introduces the need to account for the mortality risk of both partners. The chance that both die in the same period is low, and any wealth not yet consumed at the death of the first spouse is not wasted as it can still be consumed by the surviving spouse. Therefore, less consumption needs to be brought forward, flattening the consumption path. Further extensions account for additional uncertainties faced by older households, such as those associated with out-of-pocket medical expenses, long-term care costs, rate-of-return risk, and inflation. Increased uncertainty flattens the predicted consumption trajectory, but it is unlikely to eliminate the negative slope at old age because mortality risk increases exponentially, eventually dominating other considerations. Greater uncertainty leads to higher wealth holdings, to guard against bad stochastic outcomes. At the population level, less wealth is consumed and more will be accidentally bequeathed.

Several mechanisms help reduce the impact of uncertainty. Various government programs provide insurance against excessively low consumption (e.g., Social Security and Medicaid, as well as Supplemental Security Income and Disability programs). Some households may also receive payouts from employer-provided defined benefit and defined contribution pension plans, while others may rely on assistance from their extended families.

**Home Production.** Individuals can often achieve a given level of consumption by substituting time inputs for purchased goods. For example, they can use time to identify stores that sell items at a lower price, they can consume meals cooked at home instead of eating out, and they can perform their own home repairs and maintenance. In retirement, people have more time available for these activities and time becomes cheaper. An important implication of time use during retirement is that households may not need to spend as much to achieve a given level of consumption compared to when they were working (Aguiar and Hurst 2005; Hurd and Rohwedder 2003).

**The role of health.** There are several ways in which health interacts with spending, suggesting that utility production is health dependent. Some types of spending are substitutes for health, some are complements, and others are neutral. When in good health, people can derive utility from spending on goods and services that are complements (such as travel), but these may produce little utility when in bad health. Conversely, in bad health, people can derive utility from spending on health care. Because health declines with age, this health-spending interaction is reflected in the composition of household spending (budget shares). Health can also interact with spending via home production. People in bad health may be less able to use their time as an input to consumption, as working in the house or garden becomes physically more burdensome.

### Measurement

While the economic theory just described focuses on consumption, it is difficult in practice to ask respondents in a household survey about their consumption (such as the flow of owner-occupied housing services). Instead, household spending can be a close proxy used to obtain a measure of consumption. The main differences between consumption and spending are: (1) consumer durables are purchased in one period but consumed over multiple periods;[2] (2) spending by one person can be shared with or consumed by another person in the same household (e.g., housing); and (3) some consumption can use time as an additional input (e.g., home production) that can either replace or complement market-based spending. Since our main data source asks people about their spending, in what follows, we rely on empirical evidence on spending patterns. To learn about household well-being, we therefore adjust household spending to account for consumption flows from durables and owner-occupied housing, thus obtaining a close proxy measure of households' total consumption.

## Datasets

The analyses below rely on data taken from the HRS and its supplement: the Consumption and Activities Mail Survey (CAMS). The HRS is a biennial panel rolled out in 1992, covering the cohorts born 1931–1941 (Juster and Suzman 1995). Additional cohorts were added in 1993 and 1998, so that in 1998, the HRS represented the population from the cohorts of 1947 or earlier. In 2004 new cohorts were added, making the HRS representative of the population over age 50. The HRS is very rich in content and, importantly for this study, it stands out for its high-quality and detailed information on economic resources.

The CAMS is a supplemental survey to the HRS, administered via mail to a random subsample of HRS households.[3] One of its main objectives is to elicit total household spending over the preceding twelve months, which can be linked to the rich information collected in the HRS core survey on the same individuals and households. The first wave of CAMS was collected in 2001, and longitudinal follow-up surveys have been conducted every two years since. When HRS inducts a refresher cohort into the survey, a random subsample of households from the refresher cohort is also inducted into the CAMS. Initially, CAMS queried about spending in 32 and later 39 categories, to obtain a complete measure of annual spending.[4]

## Empirical Evidence: Spending Patterns at Older Ages

### Changes in Spending in Retirement

Standard economic theory states that the marginal utility of consumption evolves smoothly over the life cycle: were there to be a large change, a reallocation of consumption across the jump would increase total utility. This theoretical statement has sometimes been interpreted to mean that consumption should evolve smoothly, but this would be inaccurate if other inputs to utility interacted with consumption. Time is such an input: it can be combined with purchased goods to produce utility so that if more time suddenly became available, spending on purchased goods would also change. Thus, life events, such as retirement, would be expected to result in a change in household spending, and the direction and size would depend on individual circumstances.

Consider the simplest case of a one-person household where the individual retired from a full-time job. Several changes ensue: income from work and work-related expenses change, and the individual now has some 2,000 hours of time to reallocate from work to leisure, self-care, or home production. Because some time uses are complementary to spending and some are substitutes, the ultimate impact of increased time after retirement on spending will be the result of personal choice, strongly influenced by economic circumstances, health, and marital status.

There is a sizeable literature on how household spending changes right at retirement.[5] Using panel data from the HRS, our work found that spending declined by 4.4% at the median, a magnitude that would be consistent with increases in home production, smart shopping, and the cessation of work-related expenses. But perhaps more importantly, we also detected substantial heterogeneity by economic status in changes in spending upon retirement, consistent with the view that the extra time available in retirement is used to complement or to substitute for market purchased goods. Specifically, for those in the upper half of the wealth distribution, total spending increased at retirement, but in the low-wealth population, spending declined. The main explanation for the difference appears to be early retirement due to poor health. In addition, for a minority of the population, a short planning horizon may contribute to reduced spending at retirement because wealth is inadequate to maintain consumption when earnings and income drop (Hurd and Rohwedder 2003, 2005, 2013).

## Spending Trajectories

Overall, the simple economic life-cycle model predicts that spending will fall with age because of increasing mortality risk; the extended life-cycle model also incorporates declining health. In the case of married households, a substantial spending decline is expected to occur at widowing. For example, the returns-to-scale parameter embedded in the Social Security program implies that a widow(er) needs about two-thirds of a couple's consumption to achieve the same level of economic well-being. Large out-of-pocket medical and long-term care expenditures could result in spending increases for some households, but it is an empirical matter as to whether this effect is large enough to counteract the downward trend in other spending categories.

Because we seek to measure the population rate of change in spending at each age, it is important to control for mortality. If we were to use a balanced panel of those surviving to some advanced age, the rates of change observed at earlier ages would be conditioned on survival to that advanced age; nevertheless, the life-cycle model predicts that long-lived persons would choose a flatter consumption path earlier in life than would shorter-lived persons. The upshot is that the rates of change in consumption by long-lived persons would misstate the population rate of change of consumption at earlier ages. Accordingly, we estimate rates of change of consumption at each age using all households observed in two adjacent waves. In other words, we estimate rates of change over living persons at each age.

To implement this, we stack all adjacent CAMS wave pairs at times $t$ and $t+1$ and compute the rate of change by five-year age bands, stratifying by marital status and by initial (approximately age 65) wealth quartile. We find the quartile by comparing a household's wealth position to other households at a similar age and with the same marital status.[6] We then use the estimated rates of change to trace out a spending path from age 65 onward (see Figure 10.1).

Our central finding is that spending paths decline for all groups: single as well as married, and all wealth quartiles. These declines are consistent with life-cycle model predictions and confirm that spending decline per se is likely not the result of tightening budget constraints because those with high resources reduce spending as they age in a fashion similar to those households with fewer resources.

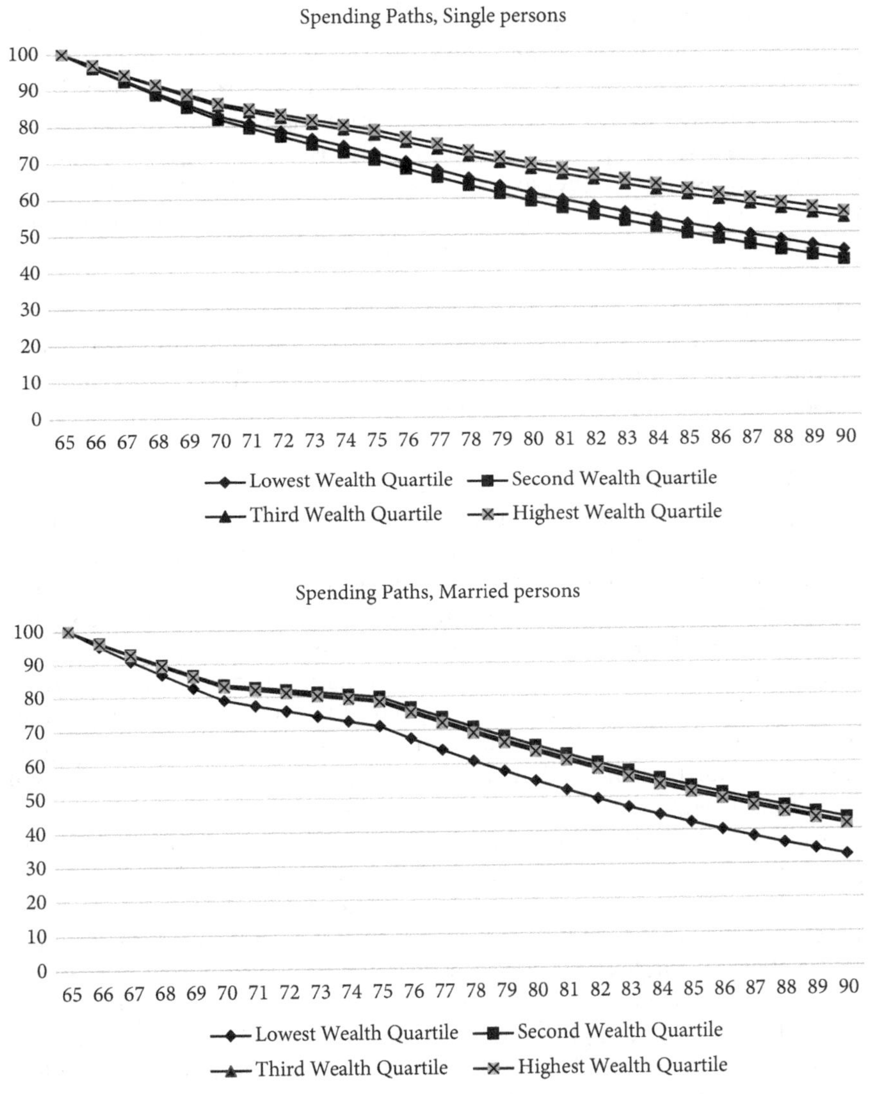


**Figure 10.1** Spending paths, single and married persons, by initial wealth quartile

*Notes:* The initial wealth quartile is determined using the long panel of the HRS data. For each CAMS observation used in estimating the spending paths we obtained the household's wealth position from the HRS wave nearest to when the individual was age 65, relative to other households of the same wave with the same marital status and part of the same five-year age band.

*Source:* Authors' calculations, CAMS waves 2005–2021; see also Hurd and Rohwedder (2023a).

Consumption paths of married persons do exhibit a larger rate of decline than the paths of single persons (average annual rate of change of −2.7 ppts compared to −2.0 ppts). If the couple survives to age 85, spending is about 50% of what it was at age 65 for those in the second through highest initial wealth quartile, and about 42% of what it was at age 65 among those in the lowest initial wealth quartile. An implication is that the spending path is flatter for those with higher average life expectancy (higher initial wealth), which is also consistent with predictions from economic theory: this group shifts less consumption to earlier ages because of their elevated chances of survival and the corresponding need to preserve resources for old age. Single people with relatively low initial wealth (bottom two quartiles) at age 85 spend about 50% of what they spent at age 65. The reductions are smaller for the two highest wealth quartiles (third and highest): spending at age 85 is about 62% of what it was at age 65.

## Budget Shares

A key policy question is whether the observed decline in spending with age is forced on people because of unexpected tightening budget constraints or whether it results from optimizing choice. In the Yaari (1965) framework, individuals choose to consume too much early in retirement with the knowledge that should they survive, they will reduce spending. Thus, the lifetime budget constraint is a determinant of the path, but a spending decline in later life is not evidence of inadequate preparation for retirement or of a mistake. In behavioral frameworks, by contrast, the spending decline may signal a lack of forward-looking behavior, indicating that people are surprised that economic resources are inadequate and must reduce spending.

Seeking evidence on these distinct hypotheses, we examined categories of spending or budget shares. Figure 10.2 shows the share of total spending devoted to six categories of spending, stratified by marital status. As anticipated, the share of health care spending increases with age. Further, the health share of single persons does not differ greatly from that of couples, indicating that in health care spending, there are very limited returns to scale. The moderately higher spending share of couples is the result of their higher economic status. The share spent on transportation (automobiles) peaks in the 50s and then declines thereafter; it accelerates when people are in their 70s. A plausible explanation for the later decline is that health conditions limit the desire for extended car travel, and they also increase the perceived risk of driving. The pattern observed for trips and vacations is likely the result of several factors. The relaxing of time constraints due to retirement permits increased travel in people's late 60s and early 70s, and the subsequent decline is likely due to worsening health, which makes travel more difficult. Single people spend much less than married people, likely due to a lack of companionship, in many cases.

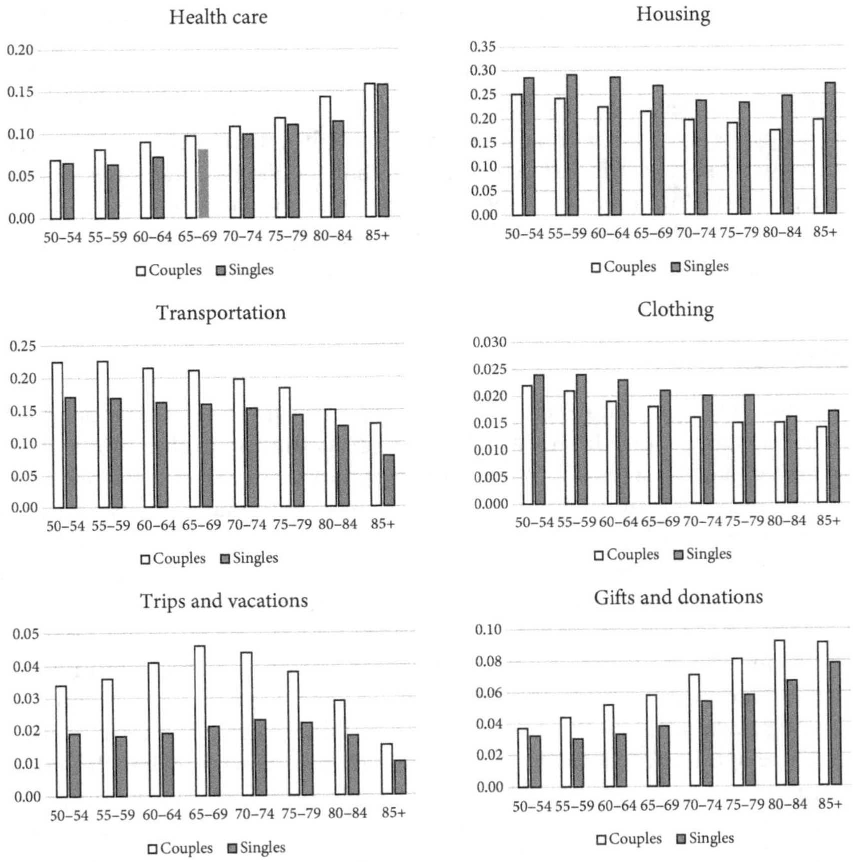


**Figure 10.2** Budget shares by age and marital status

*Notes:* The budget shares are calculated as spending on category [x] divided by total household spending. Observations with highly incomplete data dropped (i.e., those who reported fewer than 10 out of about 39 spending categories, about 1.5% of the sample)
*Source:* Authors' calculations based on pooled CAMS 2011–2021.

The evolution with age of budget shares for transportation, trips, and vacations suggests that health plays a role in later life spending. That is, some spending is complementary with health, such that when health is good people spend more, and some is substitutable with health, such as health care spending itself, which increases when health declines. Some is likely neutral, such as gifts and donations.

In terms of life-cycle spending behavior, individuals will tend to spend more on items that are complementary to health relatively early in the retirement period when health is good, with the anticipation that later, when health deteriorates, they will reduce spending on those items. In our data, these reductions outweigh increases in spending on health itself, producing a decline in total spending. This interpretation is strengthened by the evolution of the budget share for gifts and donations. Under the assumption that spending on these is neutral with respect to health, the fact that their budget share increases sharply with age suggests that the decline in total spending is largely not due to an unexpectedly tightening budget constraint; rather, it suggests a lack of desire to spend on a number of categories that require good health combined with *inter vivos* transfers, an alternative to bequests.

## Discussion

The fact that spending paths decline with age for all socioeconomic status groups including the most well-off suggests that the reductions in total spending at older ages are mostly not forced by unexpectedly tight budget constraints. A plausible explanation based on budget share data is that worsening health can lead to reduced spending across some categories. While spending on health does increase with age, it rises by less than the reduction in those categories, so that total spending declines.

To obtain additional evidence on this issue, we added to the CAMS 2019 survey questions on whether the individual's enjoyment from spending on certain categories increased, decreased, or stayed the same compared to six years earlier. Our objective was to determine whether marginal utility for these spending categories had changed, and, if so, in what direction. We found at advanced ages (75+), close to 50% said they got less enjoyment from traveling, and the fraction rose steeply, reaching 75% for those age 85+ (Figure 10.3, left panel). Similar patterns emerged for enjoyment from 'having a new car' or from 'having new appliances, TV, PC, etc.,' as well as several other spending-related activities. The right panel (Figure 10.3) averages across all seven age bands and shows that reductions in enjoyment increase with age. Our regression analyses of whether someone reported reduced enjoyment was also strongly related to being in poor health (Rohwedder et al. 2022).

## Insights into Older Households' Economic Well-Being

Next, we discuss examples of policy-relevant applications that use data on consumption to draw inferences about older households' economic well-being. Because consumption is more directly related to well-being than either income or wealth, it can provide a more accurate measure of retirement security. To obtain a measure of consumption from the CAMS

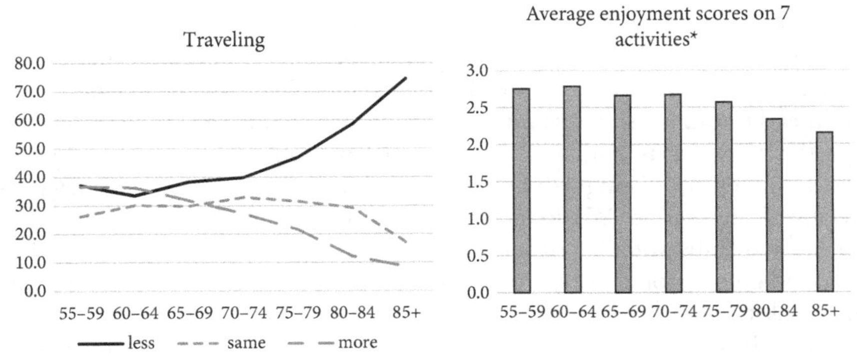


**Figure 10.3** Reported changes in enjoyment in traveling, and average enjoyment scores by age for seven activities

*Notes:* The seven activities were traveling, going out to eat, leisure activities, having a new car, having new appliances, providing financial support to family, and providing financial support to friends. The change in enjoyment was scaled from 1 (much less) to 5 (much more). A score of 3 corresponds to 'no change.' The average score (right panel) is less than 3 at all ages, meaning that enjoyment declines on average across all age bands, and the decline accelerates with age by 0.6 of an enjoyment category (2.8 at age 55–59 to 2.2 at age 85+).

*Source:* Authors' calculations based on CAMS 2019; see also Rohwedder et al. (2022) for further detail.

spending measures, we replace spending on durables and housing with estimated values of consumption services from durables and owner-occupied housing.

## Consumption-Based Poverty Assessment

Official US poverty rates are based on pre-tax incomes, yet there are several reasons that poverty in the older population should be assessed using consumption rather than income data. It is not controversial that particularly for the older population, consumption is more directly linked to well-being than income because wealth is widely held by older persons, and that wealth can be used to purchase additional consumption beyond what can be supported by income alone. A stylized simple model would be that prior to retirement, people consume less than their income, and after retirement, they consume more than their income. It would then be logical to base a poverty measure on consumption rather than income.

To this end, we compute both income-based poverty rates and consumption-based poverty rates in the HRS data. To estimate consumption-based poverty rates, we use HRS core data on the value of housing, automobiles, and durables, and spending data on nondurables from CAMS. We impute a service flow from five durables, automobiles, and housing (rather than spending on housing). We follow the method used in official poverty rate calculations, and we do not place a value on Medicare or Medicaid, even though we recognize that those programs have considerable value to the older population. Similarly, we do not include health care consumption financed by others, such as employers. Moreover, while the HRS core survey queries about gifts and money received from others outside the household, it does not distinguish between them, so we exclude non-money gifts received from others. We do include out-of-pocket spending for health care. Because of substantially noisier measurement of income and consumption in multi-generational households, we confine our analysis to single persons living alone and to couples living alone.

Our HRS income-based poverty measures are similar to CPS measures. More novel are our consumption-based poverty rates estimated from CAMS waves 2001–2013 and the adjacent HRS waves, which appear in Table 10.1. Overall, consumption-based poverty rates are substantially lower than those based on after-tax income, at slightly less than half the rate for singles (7.6 ppts versus 16.0 ppts) and for married persons (1.5 ppts versus 3.3 ppts). This is consistent with the older population's ability to use savings to finance consumption. Both measures show higher poverty rates at relatively younger ages. Among those who survive to advanced ages (75+), consumption-based poverty is 6.1% among single persons and 1.2% among married persons. Married persons have very low poverty rates, 1.5% by consumption and 3.3% by income.[7]

Since the difference between income-based and consumption-based poverty rates is expected to vary with age, this has implications for age-related welfare judgments. For example:

TABLE 10.1 Consumption and After-Tax Income-Based Poverty Rates for Single and Married Persons (in %)

| | Single persons | | Married persons | |
|---|---|---|---|---|
| | Consumption | Income | Consumption | Income |
| 55–59 | 9.0 | 22.4 | 2.3 | 4.8 |
| 60–64 | 9.5 | 19.1 | 1.6 | 3.7 |
| 65–74 | 7.8 | 14.6 | 1.2 | 2.8 |
| 75+ | 6.1 | 13.1 | 1.2 | 2.1 |
| All | 7.6 | 16.0 | 1.5 | 3.3 |

*Notes:* In Census Bureau Statistics, income-based poverty rates are traditionally computed on pre-tax income. Here, we report poverty rates based on after-tax income because that concept is closer to consumption than pre-tax income. As an empirical matter the difference is trivial: 0.32 ppts among couples and 0.19 ppts among single persons. See also Hurd and Rohwedder (2006).

*Source*: Authors' calculations based on CAMS waves 2001–2013 and HRS waves 2000–2012; after-tax income calculated using the NBER TAXSIM calculator.

- Tax rates decline with age.
- Many older households use retirement savings to finance a consumption level greater than after-tax income, where the difference is financed out of wealth.
- Consumption-in-kind is more important for older versus middle-aged households
  - because of Medicare and Medicaid;
  - because consumption of owner-occupied housing services peaks at 70–74, and ownership of housing declines with age, albeit slowly;
  - because of service flows from durables: older households may depreciate their durables more thoroughly so that they still receive a flow of consumption even though expenditures are nil.

## Economic Preparation for Retirement

To assess the financial security of the older population and how it varies across subgroups, we use a simulation model we have developed (Hurd and Rohwedder 2012, 2023a, 2023b, 2024). Broadly, we ask whether a household's economic resources can support a projected spending trajectory from retirement to the end of life. The main features of the simulation model are as follows. We estimate consumption paths using CAMS panel data on spending by marital status and education separately because theory suggests that the slopes of spending paths differ by mortality risk. The mortality risk of a two-person household depends on the mortality risk of each person so that the sample must be stratified by marital status and by education level. In the CAMS, we observe initial spending of individuals and couples in the 66–69 age range. The simulations assess whether the individual or couple can maintain a spending trajectory anchored at its initial level which follows the estimated spending trajectory (subject to stochastic shocks) without running out of wealth.

Specifically, we simulate spending paths until death and track changes in economic resources: if spending exceeds after-tax income, wealth is drawn down to cover the gap. Our estimations and simulations account for differential mortality risk and, for couples, the lifespan for each spouse and the loss of returns to scale in consumption at widowing. We permit the rate of change of consumption to vary by marital status, age, and education because of the different levels of mortality risk by education and because of the interactions between health (which varies with education) and consumption. We incorporate the risk of large out-of-pocket spending on health care by assigning spending shocks from the observed distribution of such spending. We also account for taxes, as these can substantially reduce resources available for consumption for households with large holdings of tax-advantaged

TABLE 10.2 Percentage Adequately Prepared, Defined as 95%–100% Chance of Dying with Positive Wealth

| | Single Persons | | | | Married Persons | | | |
|---|---|---|---|---|---|---|---|---|
| | N | All | Males | Females | N | All | Males | Females |
| *Education* | | | | | | | | |
| Less than high school | 274 | 27.0 | 45.6 | 22.1 | 221 | 69.2 | 72.1 | 67.4 |
| High school | 417 | 54.4 | 67.0 | 50.6 | 626 | 79.2 | 81.8 | 78.3 |
| Some college | 266 | 48.1 | 52.6 | 46.9 | 369 | 78.0 | 70.5 | 81.1 |
| College and above | 168 | 63.1 | 58.5 | 64.6 | 363 | 84.8 | 86.9 | 83.7 |
| All | 1125 | 47.6 | 57.5 | 44.7 | 1579 | 78.8 | 79.0 | 78.8 |
| *Race/Ethnicity* | | | | | | | | |
| Non-Hispanic white | 717 | 58.2 | 64.5 | 56.1 | 1265 | 81.9 | 82.8 | 81.5 |
| Non-Hispanic Black | 271 | 28.0 | 38.2 | 25.5 | 157 | 65.0 | 65.5 | 64.6 |
| Hispanic | 103 | 27.2 | 57.9 | 20.2 | 129 | 64.3 | 60.5 | 65.9 |
| All | 1125 | 47.6 | 57.5 | 44.7 | 1579 | 78.8 | 79.0 | 78.8 |

*Notes*: Includes 61 observations whose race/ethnicity is 'other'.
*Source*: Authors' calculations using the HRS 2002–2016 and CAMS 2003–2017, based on methodology in Hurd and Rohwedder (2012) and using more recent data; see also Hurd and Rohwedder (2006).

savings, but not for those with little tax liability. Rates of return vary by asset type and are applied to each household's remaining portfolio in each simulation period. Most of the model elements permit heterogeneous response as a function of age, sex, marital status, and education.

We perform repeated simulations of the spending paths of each individual or couple to estimate the probability that the individual or survivor dies with positive wealth (Hurd and Rohwedder 2012, 2023a, 2023b, 2024). We consider an individual to have adequate preparation for retirement if 95% of the simulations indicate positive wealth at death. Results show that 47.6% of persons initially single at ages 66–69 (N = 1,125) were adequately prepared for retirement, and 78.8% of married persons (N = 1,579) were adequately prepared. The overall weighted average was 65.9% (Table 10.2). Yet there was also considerable heterogeneity: only 22% of single females without a high school education were adequately prepared, and Blacks and Hispanics were less likely to be prepared than non-Hispanic whites. The shortfall was especially large among those initially single: 58.2% of non-Hispanic whites, 28.0% of Blacks, and 27.2% Hispanics were prepared.

Our consumption-based measure also produces considerably higher preparation levels than income-based measures. For example, the income-based Retirement Risk Index (RRI) stood at 51% in 2010 (Yin et al. 2024), about the middle of our sample period. That is, the RRI estimated that 49% were not at risk, while we found that 66% were adequately prepared. One reason for the difference is that the income-based measure does not account for a number of observed empirical regularities in actual spending that the longitudinally based spending paths incorporate. For example, according to our calculations, life expectancy conditional on reaching age 65 can vary by as much as 20 years across subpopulations, by marital status, sex, and education. Because longer life expectancy is positively correlated with economic resources, the well-to-do and the less well-to-do have different saving requirements. This differential is accounted for in our model but not in the income-based measures.

A second reason is that spending declines with age, and this decline is not driven mainly by lower economic resources, but rather, it is chosen (at least on average). This reduction is particularly important when most retirement spending is financed by Social Security. For example, if half of a household's spending were financed with Social Security benefits, the need for private wealth accumulation would vary 2:1 with the reduction in lifetime spending. Thus a 15% decline in spending would reduce required wealth accumulation by 30%. For many people, taxes also decline after retirement. We also track taxes in our simulation model. Single persons had an average total tax rate of 4.8% during their retirement years, and couples had an average rate of 7.3%. These rates are much lower than average tax rates during the working life.

## Conclusions and Directions for Future Research

Our empirical evidence on older households' spending is consistent with an augmented life-cycle model in which consumption is produced with spending and time inputs, and utility from consumption depends on health status. This framework predicts heterogenous changes in spending at retirement; that is, some households increase spending while others decrease spending. Spending paths do decline with age after retirement, and the composition of spending shifts as health declines, with reductions in spending complementary to good health (travel, leisure, etc.), and increases in spending that substitutes for good health (health care). As confirmed by respondents' own assessments, many older adults' enjoyment from certain types of spending declines as their health deteriorates with age, indicating that spending reductions are chosen and not the result of unexpectedly tight budget constraints. We also confirmed heterogeneity in spending paths by socioeconomic status: the wealthier have flatter spending paths (and longer life expectancies) than the lower wealth groups—in line with model predictions.

These findings have important implications for retirement planning. If decreasing spending paths are consistent with declines observed across all economic status groups and even among the well-to-do, then households will need to save less for retirement than they would under the assumption that spending will be flat or even increased in retirement. Our microsimulation model, which uses these declining spending paths to assess the fraction adequately prepared for retirement, comes to more favorable conclusions than other approaches.[8] We estimate that 65.9% of older adults age 65–69 in our data are adequately prepared for retirement; that is, the chances that they will have positive wealth at death is 95% or higher. Consumption-based poverty rates are about half of those based on (after-tax) income.

Still, some groups do fare substantially worse, and it will be important to better understand the causes of these disparities. The fraction adequately prepared is particularly low among single females with less than a high-school education and among non-Hispanic Black and Hispanic single older adults. Our overall conclusion from this research is that the use of consumption data to analyze the economic well-being of older households is essential to more accurately identify economically vulnerable populations, an important prerequisite for studying underlying causes and for designing effective solutions.

There is a wide range of opportunities for future research leveraging spending data more generally and the longitudinal CAMS spending data of the HRS in particular. For example, more work is needed on quantifying the importance of home production and its contribution to household consumption. We noted earlier that utility derived from consumption depends on health status and so does the ability to engage in home production. Future research should analyze these interdependencies further. Another important topic is how individuals' expectations about the future and perceived sources of uncertainty impact their spending decisions in later life. This has implications not only for the intertemporal allocation of resources of individual households but also for the macro economy. For example, with the long-term shift from defined benefit to defined contribution pension plans, households today must assume greater uncertainty with respect to investment returns and longevity risk. Additionally, more research is needed on the heterogeneity in preferences regarding spending composition and spending trajectories, for example, by cultural background, family structure, race and ethnicity.

A challenge to progress on these issues using CAMS data is the limited sample size of CAMS, which otherwise stands out for its longitudinal spending information linked to the rich core HRS data. Additional promising innovations from research studies are using spending data from financial transactions including scanner data or credit card records. While such data sources often lack detailed information beyond what is available in the administrative or transaction data, a powerful combination would link financial transactions data to household survey data.

## Acknowledgments

This chapter draws on several research studies conducted with financial support from several agencies over the years, including the National Institute on Aging (NIA), the Department of Labor (DOL), and the Social Security Administration (SSA) via the Michigan Retirement and Disability Research Center (MRDRC). The opinions and conclusions expressed are solely those of the authors and do not represent the opinions or policy of NIA, DOL, SSA, MRDRC, or any agency of the federal government. Joanna Carroll provided excellent programming support.

## Notes

1. This abstracts from bequests and the insurance value of wealth against financial risk.
2. Averaging spending on durables across the population or by subgroups yields an estimate of average consumption on durables.
3. For example, the 2020 HRS obtained interviews with 11,490 households. In the fall of 2021, HRS sent out 5166 CAMS household spending questionnaires, of which 2986 were completed and returned to HRS.
4. Total spending in CAMS aggregates closely to total spending from the Consumer Expenditure Survey (Hurd and Rohwedder 2015). For example, among those age 65–74 and 75+, CAMS spending in 2007 was $40,700 and $29,400, respectively. In the Consumer Expenditure Survey, such spending was $39,700 and $29,400. These cross-section figures should not be interpreted as life cycle variation in spending. Spending paths constructed from two-year panel changes in CAMS do decline with age as we show in our previous work, updated in results reported below.
5. The early literature was concerned with documenting and understanding the retirement-consumption puzzle, which refers to the large drop in spending on food at retirement (e.g., Banks et al. 1998; Bernheim et al. 2001). This was considered a puzzle because according to the simple life-cycle model, consumption should be smoothed over time. Subsequent studies noted that retiring households tend to increase home production or use time to shop more cheaply so they can achieve about the same level of consumption after retirement as before retirement (Aguiar and Hurst 2005; Hurd and Rohwedder 2003, 2005, 2013). Also, using longitudinal data on total spending, we found that spending declined only by 4.4% at the median, which could easily be explained by increases in home production (as well as smart shopping and the cessation of work-related expenses). Yet when poor health led to earlier than expected retirement, declines were larger.
6. Specifically, for each household in CAMS that contributed one or more spending transitions for estimating the spending trajectories, we used the long HRS panel to find the wave when the household was observed closest to age 65. Within that wave we compared that household's wealth position to that of other households of that same five-year age band and same marital status (Hurd and Rohwedder 2023a).

7. This chapter does not explicitly consider the survivor bias in poverty rates at older ages due to people in poverty being more likely to die young. Clark et al. (2024) showed that older people move into and out of poverty just as younger individuals do, and models that account for nonrandom sample attrition because of the competing risks of death and other loss to survey follow-up generate somewhat different results from hazard models that ignore those risks. Specifically, they reported that poverty exit was more likely for respondents who remained longer in the HRS panel than were those who attrited from the sample because of loss to follow-up or death.
8. The National Retirement Risk Index assumes a flat spending path while many financial advisors reference the 'retirement smile' (Blanchett 2014), which posits that spending increases at advanced ages.

## References

Aguiar, M. and E. Hurst (2005). 'Consumption versus Expenditure.' *Journal of Political Economy* 113(5): 919–948.

Banks, J., R. Blundell, and S. Tanner (1998). 'Is There a Retirement-Savings Puzzle?' *American Economic Review*, 88(4): 769–788.

Bernheim, B. D., J. Skinner, and S. Weinberg (2001). 'What Accounts for the Variation in Retirement Wealth Among U.S. Households?' *American Economic Review*, 91(4): 832–857.

Blanchett, D. M. (2014). 'Exploring the Retirement Consumption Puzzle.' *Journal of Financial Planning*, 27(5): 34–42.

Clark, R., A. Lusardi, and O. S. Mitchell (2024). 'A Competing Risk Analysis of Poverty Entry and Exit Patterns of Older Americans.' *Social Security Bulletin*, 84(3): 11–27.

De Nardi, M., E. French, J. Bailey Jones, and R. McGee (2025). 'Why Do Couples and Singles Save During Retirement? Household Heterogeneity and its Aggregate Implications.' *Journal of Political Economy*, 133(3): 713–1082.

Health and Retirement Study (2022). *RAND HRS Longitudinal File 2018 (V2) Documentation.* RAND Center for the Study of Aging. doi.org/10.7249/TLA2097-1

Hurd, M. D. and S. Rohwedder (2003). 'The Retirement-Consumption Puzzle: Anticipated and Actual Declines in Spending at Retirement.' NBER Working Paper No. w9586.

Hurd, M. D. and S. Rohwedder (2005). 'The Retirement-Consumption Puzzle: Anticipated and Actual Declines in Spending at Retirement.' MRDRC Paper No. 2004-069.

Hurd, M. D. and S. Rohwedder (2006). 'Consumption and Economic Well-Being at Older Ages: Income- and Consumption-Based Poverty Measures in the HRS.' NBER Working Paper No. 12680.

Hurd, M. D. and S. Rohwedder (2012). 'Economic Preparation for Retirement.' In D. A. Wise, ed., *Investigations in the Economics of Aging.* Chicago: University of Chicago Press, pp. 77–113.

Hurd, M. D. and S. Rohwedder (2013). 'Heterogeneity in Spending Change at Retirement.' *Journal of the Economics of Ageing*, 1: 60–71.

Hurd, M. D. and S. Rohwedder (2015). 'Wealth Dynamics and Active Saving at Older Ages.' In C. Carroll, T. Crossley and J. Sabelhaus, eds., *Improving the Measurement of Consumer Expenditures.* Chicago: University of Chicago Press, pp. 388–413.

Hurd, M. D. and S. Rohwedder (2023a). 'Economic Preparation for Retirement.' In D. E. Bloom, A. Sousa-Poza, and U. Sunde, eds., *The Routledge Handbook of the Economics of Ageing.* Abbington, UK: Routledge, pp. 217–233.

Hurd, M. D. and S. Rohwedder (2023b). 'Spending Trajectories After Age 65: Variation by Initial Wealth.' *Journal of the Economics of Ageing,* 26: 100468.

Hurd, M. D. and S. Rohwedder (2024). 'Inflation and Economic Security of the Older Population.' MRDRC Working Paper No. 2024-480.

Juster, F. T. and R. Suzman (1995). 'An Overview of the Health and Retirement Study,' *Journal of Human Resources,* 30: S7–S56.

Rohwedder, S., M. D. Hurd, and P. Hudomiet (2022). 'Explanations for the Decline in Spending at Older Ages.' NBER Working Paper No. 30460.

Yaari, M. E. (1965). 'Uncertain Lifetime, Life Insurance, and the Theory of the Consumer.' *Review of Economic Studies,* 32(2): 137–150.

Yin, Y., A. Chen, and A. H. Munnell. (2024). *The National Retirement Risk Index: An Update from the 2022 SCF.* Center for Retirement Research Issue in Brief 24–5. Chestnut Hill, MA: Center for Retirement Research.

Chapter 11

# Patterns of Consumption and Savings Around Retirement

*Arna Olafsson and Michaela Pagel*

Voluntary savings schemes have gained importance in many developed countries over time, shifting the responsibility of preparing for retirement onto individuals, making it more important than ever to ensure that people engage in sound personal financial behavior. Yet many have barely any savings and hold substantial amounts of consumer debt at the time of retirement (Anguelov and Tamborini 2009; Poterba et al. 2012; Skinner 2007). Understanding what happens to household spending and balance sheets around retirement is informative for helping to assess whether people plan properly and save enough for retirement.

There is a large economics literature regarding two so-called retirement puzzles: (1) the empirical observation that spending drops after retirement (the 'retirement-consumption' puzzle) and (2) the observation that wealth rises after retirement (the 'retirement-savings' puzzle). The retirement-consumption puzzle considers a central implication of standard life-cycle models of household consumption and savings: that the marginal utility of consumption should be smoothed across periods of predictably high and low income. Yet a number of empirical studies (e.g., Banks et al. 1998; Bernheim et al. 2001; Fe 2019; Haider and Stephens 2007; Schwerdt 2005) find a sharp decline in consumption during the first years of retirement.[1] A leading explanation for this puzzle was provided by Aguiar and Hurst (2005, 2013) and Hurst (2008), who argued that spending, rather than consumption, decreased because people reduced their work-related expenses and overall spending through bargain shopping and household production.[2]

The retirement-savings puzzle considers the prediction of the standard life-cycle model that individuals will decumulate assets over the course of retirement. Recent literature documents that mean and median cohort wealth for both singles or couples remains constant or rises for many years after retirement (Kieren and Weber 2022; Love et al. 2009; Poterba et al. 2011a, 2011b).[3] The leading explanations for this puzzle are longevity and

Arna Olafsson and Michaela Pagel, *Patterns of Consumption and Savings Around Retirement.* In: *Retirement Saving, Investment, and Spending.* Edited by: Olivia S. Mitchell and Nikolai Roussanov, Oxford University Press.

DOI: 10.1093/oso/9780197845752.003.0011

medical expense risks, as theorized by DeNardi et al. (2010) and Laitner et al. (2018), and empirically analyzed by Jones et al. (2018) and Ameriks et al. (2016).

Some prior studies have looked at how other elements of household balance sheets are affected by retirement. Using the University of Michigan's Panel Study of Income Dynamics (PSID) dataset, Addoum (2017) showed that household portfolios became less risky when men retired. Agarwal et al. (2009) documented that financial mistakes such as suboptimal use of credit card balance transfer offers followed a U-shaped pattern over the life cycle: financial mistakes increased among older adults. Agarwal et al. (2015) showed that credit card spending declined, while debit card spending increased in retirement, perhaps indicative of a change in consumer debt. Carlin et al. (2019) also discussed generational differences in managing personal finances.

This chapter uses transaction-level data from personal financial management software in Iceland to investigate how individuals' liquid savings and consumer debt positions changed in the 10-year window around retirement. We show that after they retired, individuals were 4% more likely to have liquid savings and saved 28% more. Additionally, they were 4% less likely to overdraw their checking accounts post-retirement. Such overdrafts were the predominant way of rolling over high-interest unsecured consumer debt in Iceland. New retirees also reduced their amounts of overdraft debt by 55%. We document these effects using several different specifications, from simple individual-level mean comparisons before versus after retirement to event study designs controlling for individual and month-by-year fixed effects as well as income.

If people anticipate that their incomes will fall in retirement, they would be expected to save more in anticipation of this decline. The income decline in retirement is particularly sizable in Iceland, and the pension system is transparent and comprehensive so that near-retirees can easily ascertain how much their annuitized pension income will be. Moreover, benefits are indexed to the consumer price level, protecting them from inflation risk. People could conceivably compensate for their lower retirement income by liquidating voluntary retirement accounts, investment accounts, or other illiquid assets, such as real estate, potentially explaining our findings. Yet because we observe all pension withdrawals as well as liquidations from investment accounts and other uncategorized inflows (from real estate transactions for instance), we can confirm that these are unaffected or fall around retirement for the average individual. Instead, spending drops by more than income upon retirement, which is why liquid savings rise and consumer debt falls.

Potential explanations could include drops in work-related expenses, increases in home production, or bargain shopping due to the lower cost of time. Yet if people knew in advance that they would do better by retiring, they should retire as early as possible, unless the additional pension benefit from working longer exceeded the additional money saved by retiring. In Iceland however, after age 67, the additional benefit in pension payments from working one more month are quite small: approximately 0.5% or $10 per month in additional pension income. These pension increases are much smaller than the average savings from retiring for our sample, which equal monthly reductions in overdrafts of approximately $102 and monthly increases in liquid savings balances of approximately $210.

Surprisingly, older individuals in Iceland continue to work for many months, and sometimes years, beyond reaching the retirement eligibility age. Therefore, we conclude that our findings cannot be fully explained by work-related expenses, bargain shopping, or other reasons that reduce consumption needs around retirement. Instead, a different explanation is required for why individuals still defer retirement.

One possibility is that health shocks could cause individuals to simultaneously retire and increase their needs for precautionary savings. Yet we argue that health shocks and increased medical expense risks cannot fully explain our findings for three reasons. First, Iceland is a Nordic welfare state: pension benefits are not subject to income risk due to either longevity or inflation. Moreover, the health care system is comprehensive, and individuals do not bear the large medical health care expense risks faced by many US households. Out-of-pocket expenses are capped, even for small items, such as copays for medical supplies. Second, we do not observe increases in pharmacy spending at retirement (and pharmacy expenditures are a very small share of individuals' budgets). Because copayments are mandatory in Iceland up to the cap, pharmacy spending is a proxy for health status. We find that the average individual does not appear to retire because of health shocks, and such shocks would not simultaneously increase medical expenditure risks.[4] Third, if individuals rationally expected rising medical expenses after retirement, then they should save more before retirement rather than only afterward.

To explain our findings, two ingredients are necessary: first, we must explain why consumption falls at retirement, and second, we must learn why people keep working even though they could save more by retiring. We propose several potential explanations. For instance, reductions in consumer debt might be driven by a decrease in borrowing capacity. Yet we do not find that individual borrowing capacity or liquidity decreases around retirement. We also discuss labor-leisure substitution, intra-household bargaining, consumption insurance, lump-sum pension payments, and inventory savings, but we still conclude that these cannot fully rationalize our findings.

We then turn to limited-rationality approaches and consider two classes of models: nonstandard planning behavior and nonstandard preferences.

Even with a limited planning horizon, workers would begin to smooth consumption once they near retirement. We thus need an additional change in information processing or planning behavior at the time of retirement. To model this, we turn to nonstandard preferences, first considering the most widely applied model with a time-inconsistent overconsumption problem due to hyperbolic discounting (Laibson et al. 1998). This model does not predict a fall in consumption and an increase in savings upon retirement per se, but if we assume that people correct their time-inconsistency problems and stop overconsuming after retirement, then the model can explain the joint findings. This assumed change in discount factors could be due to changes in information-processing capacity, more ability to plan, or other limited rationality.[5] We also show that changes in people's time inconsistency rather than just changes in patience is essential in generating an increase in savings after retiring. Such a correction of time-inconsistent overconsumption is present in a life-cycle model with expectations-based loss aversion (Koszegi and Rabin 2009; Pagel 2017). We can rationalize a simultaneous decrease in consumption and increase in savings upon retirement in a realistically calibrated, life-cycle model with two of the most widely applied nonstandard preference specifications in the literature.

Our analysis relies on Icelandic data due to their unusually high quality, yet we document similar findings using other sources including survey data from the US and bank account data from Germany. We first look at the most in-use US consumption survey data sets, the Consumer Expenditure Survey (CEX) and the Survey of Consumer Finances (SCF). We control for cohort, age, and year effects, although one must keep in mind that these results suffer from selection bias and measurement error. In the CEX data, we find that retirement results in an increase in saving (measured as income minus spending), checking account balances, and saving account balances. In the SCF data, we find that retirement results in reductions in leverage and debt, as well as increased checking, savings, and call account balances. We replicate our results in another set of individual- and transaction-level bank account data from Germany employing fixed-effects regressions. Finally, we use two US survey datasets to replicate our results: PSID and the Health and Retirement Study (HRS). Because these surveys poll the same households several times, we can also include household fixed effects in our regressions. In all cases, we find that consumption and debt holdings decrease on the onset of retirement, but savings and checking account balances increase, as do other measures of wealth.

In what follows, we first briefly review the Icelandic pension system, describe our data, and report summary statistics. Next, we present our empirical methodology and findings. Subsequently, we discuss how our findings can be theoretically rationalized. Finally, we offer some concluding remarks.

## The Icelandic Pension System: Background

The Icelandic pension system consists of three pillars: a tax-financed public pension (i.e., Social Security benefits); compulsory occupational pension funds (i.e., defined benefit/contribution plans), which are the dominant feature of the system; and voluntary private pensions with tax incentives (i.e., tax-deductible savings). The age thresholds at which individuals are no longer punished for retiring early are as follows: the needs-based public pension is paid from age 67, and private pension savings can be withdrawn from age 60.

The occupational pension system is transparent, and individuals can easily acquire all the necessary information about their annuitized and indexed retirement income using an online pension calculator. Furthermore, the Icelandic pension is paid as a monthly annuity, indexed to the consumer price level. The occupational pension is paid from age 67, but one can start withdrawing it as early as 65 with a reduced benefit or as late as 70 with additional benefits. The system is designed so that an individual with the average life expectancy is actuarially indifferent between working longer and retiring between the ages of 67 and 72. The monthly payment is approximately $2,525 if one retires at the age of 67, while it is $3,112 if one retires at the age of 72. Total payments forgone between the ages of 67 and 72 are $151,500 total ($2,525 per month over five years). It thus takes about 22 years of receiving the higher rate ($3,112) to make it worth forgoing those first five years of the lower rate (individuals would have to reach the age of 94).

This means that after age 67, the additional benefits in pension payments from working an additional month are small, worth approximately $10 ((3,112–2,525)/(5*12)) or around 0.5% of monthly pension income.[6]

## Empirical Approach

### Datasets

Our empirical analysis employs data generated by Meniga, a financial aggregation software provider in Iceland offering an account-aggregation platform that lets users view all of their accounts and credit cards across multiple banks. This provides us with a comprehensive picture of individuals' financial lives, as consumers in Iceland almost exclusively use electronic means of payments. We study a subsample of 12,143 individuals with complete records (they have passed an 'activity test' designed to verify that we capture all of their relevant financial information and described in the Online Appendix). We have data on spending by category, income by source, overdraft interest, and bank fees from 2011 to 2017, and data on balances and limits from 2014 to 2017. The analysis employs user-level data aggregated to the monthly level. Expenditure and income categories are very accurate and comprehensive. For instance, in the domain of restaurant spending, we observe very fine categories, such as bakeries, and we can distinguish individual trips from all daily spending.

Income is measured by adding all incoming transactions or inflows. Thus, when retirees receive monthly pension payments, this income is effectively drawing down their pension assets. That said, we call it pension income and look at liquid savings in bank accounts rather than considering the dissaving in pension assets. Furthermore, when individuals sell investment assets, we observe investment income. Other sale transactions are considered unclassified incoming transactions or other income.

All financial accounts are individual in Iceland, but household members can link their accounts in the app, so we can also observe total household income for robustness checks. In our data, individuals older than 60 are labeled as retired if all of the following three conditions hold: (1) they receive at least 1,000,000 ISK (approximately $10,000) in pension payments over the sample period, (2) the pension payment in the current month is at least 30,000 ISK (approximately $300), and (3) monthly pension payments in the following three months or the last three months amount to at least 30,000 ISK. As an alternative measure, we label individuals as retired only if these three conditions hold and (4) there is no labor income payment higher than 150,000 ISK ($1,466) in the current month or the three months before and after. Both retirement definitions are associated with a step down in total income. The two retirement definitions are interesting in our context because some individuals in Iceland continue to work part time after first claiming their annuitized pension payments. We thus have a first step down in income and then another step down for this subset of individuals. Our results are qualitatively and quantitatively similar for both measures.

Figure 11.1 displays the share of retired individuals at each age. The amount of savings and overdrafts that individuals hold can be inferred from information on balances, interest income from savings accounts, and interest paid on overdrafts. An overdraft occurs when withdrawals from a checking account exceed the available balance. This means that the balance is negative, and the bank is providing credit to the account holder with interest charged at the agreed upon rate. Virtually all checking accounts in Iceland offer an overdraft facility, and the limits are based on individual credit scores and histories. Moreover, individuals rarely roll over credit card debt. Instead, they repay their credit cards in full each month (in fact, the automatic payment is mandated for the vast majority of credit cards) and then roll over overdraft debt instead.

Figure 11.1 also shows the life-cycle profiles of indicators and amounts of overdraft interest payments and interest earnings from savings accounts.

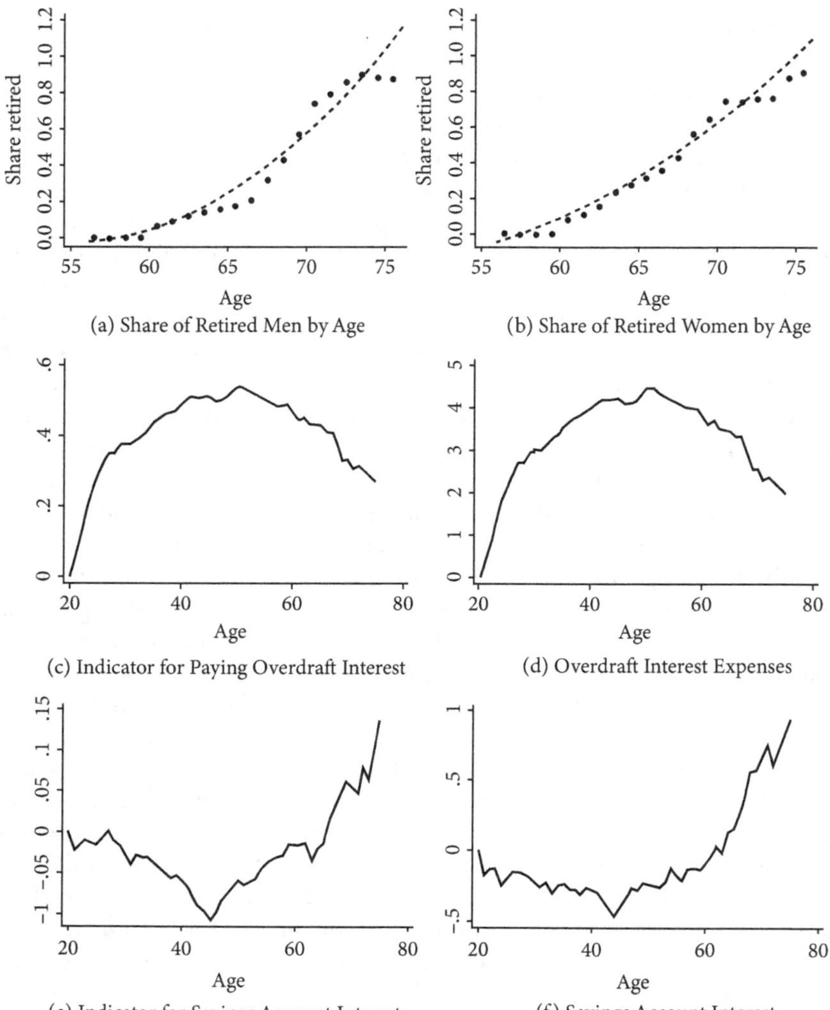


(a) Share of Retired Men by Age

(b) Share of Retired Women by Age

(c) Indicator for Paying Overdraft Interest

(d) Overdraft Interest Expenses

(e) Indicator for Savings Account Interest

(f) Savings Account Interest

**Figure 11.1** Share of retired individuals by age

*Notes:* Panels (a) and (b): Raw data using the inferred retirement date. Panel (c): Estimated coefficients from a regression of an indicator for overdraft interest expenses on a full set of age dummies, with age 20 being the reference age, regressions include month-by-year and individual fixed effects. Panel (d): Estimated coefficients from a regression of overdraft interest expenses on a full set of age controls (age 20 as reference age). Regressions include month-by year and individual fixed effects. Overdraft interest is measured in terms of its inverse hyperbolic sine to accommodate months when individuals have no overdraft interest expenses. Panel (e): Estimated coefficients from a regression of an indicator for interest earnings from savings account deposits on a full set of age controls (age 20 as the reference age). Regressions include month by-year fixed effects. (f): Estimated coefficients from a regression of interest earnings from savings account deposits on a full set of age controls (age 20 as the reference age). Regressions include month-by-year and individual fixed effects. Interest earnings are measured in terms of their inverse hyperbolic sine to accommodate months when individuals do not earn any interest from their bank deposits.

*Source:* Authors' calculations using financial aggregator transactions and balances data.

Consumer debt decreases and interest earnings increase around the time of retirement.

## Empirical Analyses and Results

### Summary Statistics

Next, we describe the spending, income, and demographic summary statistics of our user population and how they compare to those of the representative consumer survey of Statistics Iceland (Olafsson and Pagel 2018). Our sample of individuals is similar to the overall population, which is reassuring because when using app data, there might be concerns that the user population could be unrepresentative (i.e., younger, better-situated, more likely to be male, and more tech-savvy). Nevertheless, the app is marketed through online banking interfaces and used by 20% of the adult population.[7] Furthermore, even if individuals never use the software or app, the moment they sign up, we obtain their data.

Table 11.1 displays summary statistics for retired and non-retired individuals eligible for retirement (they attained age 60, observed as retired at some point during our sample period). For both definitions of retirement, the raw data indicate that on average, retired individuals have lower incomes, are more likely to hold liquid savings, are less likely to hold consumer debt, pay less interest on their overdrafts, and incur fewer late fees. Using the second definition of retirement is also consistent with a pronounced decrease in spending (note that spending reflects discretionary categories only and excludes recurring expenses such as rent and bill payments). As the first definition of retirement conditions are only on the presence of retirement income and not the absence of labor income, there is no drop in spending at retirement in the raw data mean averages. Since this cross-sectional mean comparison can be affected by outliers, time trends, and selection, our regression specifications handle this with month-by-year and individual fixed effects.

### The Effects of Retirement on Personal Finances and Expenditures

To examine the effects of retirement on personal finances and spending we run the following regression:

$$\log(C_{it}) = \beta * Retired_{it} + \phi_t + \eta_i + \gamma\Theta_{it} + \epsilon_{it}, \quad (1)$$

where $\phi_t$ is a time (month-by-year) fixed effect, and $\eta_i$ is an individual fixed effect. Controlling for individual fixed effects allows us to compare individuals to themselves before and after retirement. $Retired_{it}$ is an indicator equal

TABLE 11.1 Descriptive Statistics Before and After (Part-Time) Retirement

| | Eligible but not retired | | Retired receiving pensions | | Retired receiving pensions and low salary | |
|---|---|---|---|---|---|---|
| | Mean | St. dev. | Mean | St. dev. | Mean | St. dev. |
| ***Demographics*:** | | | | | | |
| Age (years) | 65.9 | 3 | 69.7 | 5.2 | 71.4 | 5.6 |
| Female (share) | 0.43 | 0.5 | 0.4 | 0.5 | 0.4 | 0.49 |
| ***Monthly income*:** | | | | | | |
| Labor income (USD) | 4,497 | 5,610 | 2,276 | 4,862 | 818 | 3,681 |
| Pensions (USD) | 74 | 1,063 | 1,899 | 1,869 | 2,147 | 1,699 |
| ***Personal finances*:** | | | | | | |
| Overdraft indicator | 0.46 | 0.5 | 0.38 | 0.49 | 0.31 | 0.46 |
| # Overdrafts | 0.52 | 0.65 | 0.46 | 0.67 | 0.36 | 0.59 |
| Overdraft interest (USD) | 24 | 66 | 17 | 56 | 11 | 48 |
| Late fees (USD) | 6 | 36 | 5 | 31 | 3.8 | 23.6 |
| Interest income indicator | 0.32 | 0.47 | 0.53 | 0.5 | 0.53 | 0.5 |
| Interest income (USD) | 45 | 724 | 79 | 609 | 472 | 6113 |
| Liquidity in days of average spending | 180 | 152 | 201 | 330 | 400 | 527 |
| ***Monthly spending (USD)*:** | | | | | | |
| Total discretionary | 1,809 | 1,987 | 1,887 | 2,480 | 1,706 | 1,958 |
| Groceries | 495 | 330 | 529 | 332 | 507 | 318 |
| Fuel | 291 | 270 | 230 | 222 | 201 | 207 |
| Alcohol | 94 | 156 | 96 | 169 | 87 | 158 |
| Ready-made food | 103 | 132 | 119 | 153 | 106 | 142 |
| Home improvements | 206 | 557 | 224 | 1,273 | 187 | 500 |
| Home security | 12 | 38 | 11 | 42 | 11 | 46 |
| Vehicles | 168 | 1,663 | 185 | 1,890 | 152 | 1,673 |
| Clothing and accessories | 96 | 186 | 97 | 191 | 83 | 167 |
| Sports and activities | 8 | 40 | 10 | 46 | 8 | 41 |
| Pharmacies | 70 | 88 | 80 | 94 | 78 | 94 |

*Notes:* All numbers are inflation adjusted and in US dollars. All income, spending, and interest statistics are at the individual-month level. We study a subsample 12,143 active users with complete records, that is, for whom we observe all balances, labor income arrivals, and transactions. The activity test that is designed to verify that we capture all relevant financial information (see the Online Appendix). Discretionary spending excludes recurring spending such as rents or utilities bills. Individuals older than 60 are labeled as retired if three conditions hold (1) they receive at least 1,000,000 ISK (approximately $10,000 USD) in pension payments over the sample period; (2) the pension payment in the current month is at least 30,000 ISK (approximately $300 USD); and (3) monthly pension payments in the following three months or the last tmee months amount to at least 30,000 ISK. Alternatively, we label individuals as retired if these three conditions hold and (4) there is no labor income over 150,000 ISK ($1,466 USD) in the current month, or the three months before and after. Pension payments are calculated for each individual and all bank accounts are individual level (there are no joint accounts in Iceland). Liquidity is defined as cash holdings plus overdraft limits and credit card limits minus overdrafts and credit card balances.
*Source:* Author's calculations.

to 1 if individual $i$ is retired at time $t$(else 0), and hence the $\beta$ coefficient measures the individual-specific conditional mean effect of retirement. The outcome variables, $C_{it}$, include consumer debt, liquid savings, and spending. We also provide results for additional specifications in which we include other control variables $\Theta_{it}$ for individual $i$ at time $t$ (for instance, log income is $\log(Y_{it})$).

Clearly, retirement status is endogenous, since individuals may be induced to retire by the pension benefits thresholds discussed above. Yet as Figure 11.1 shows, there are no discontinuities in the fraction of individuals retiring at ages 60, 65, 67, and 70. Furthermore, between ages 67 and 72, it is beneficial to work longer only if individuals expect to live until the age of 94. We thus cannot argue that the retirement coefficient $\beta$ has a causal interpretation. Below we discuss which omitted variables can explain our findings by driving the decision to retire and the effects of retirement on consumer debt, liquid savings, and spending.

## Results for Overdrafts, Liquid Savings, Bank Fees, and Credit Lines

Next, we investigate the effects of retirement on personal finances—in particular whether individuals use overdrafts and liquid savings as well as their credit limit sand bank fees. Table 11.2 displays the estimated effects of retirement on personal finances based on the individual fixed effects model, Equation (1), with and without controls for total individual income for both definitions of retirement.

At retirement, individuals reduce their consumer debt considerably. Focusing on consumer debt, interest expenses fell by 55% (56% after controlling for income).[8] Furthermore, the likelihood of borrowing, measured by the indicator of holding an overdraft at any point in a given month, also decreased by 4.4% (4.5% after controlling for income). The baseline probability is 46% (Table 11.1), which thus amounts to an approximately 10% decrease. Additionally, both the likelihood of receiving interest income as well as the amount of interest income increases after retirement. The increase in the likelihood equals 3.6% on a baseline probability of 32% (Table 11.1), which thus amounts to an approximately 10% increase, and the increase in interest income payments is 28%. Individuals also reduce their late fee payments, but their credit capacity does not change.

Initial positions in overdraft debt and liquid savings are large. In Table 11.1, the average overdraft interest paid per month equals \$24, which implies that at the 13% annualized interest over the period, the overdraft balance averaged 24*12/0.13 = \$2,215.[9] Average interest income is \$45, implying at a 6% annualized interest that average savings account balances were \$9,000. A 55% reduction in overdrafts and a 28% increase in

TABLE 11.2 The Effects of Retirement on Personal Finances

| | (1) Overdraft indicator | (2) Over-drafts | (3) Overdraft interest | (4) Late fees | (5) Interest income indicator | (6) Interest income | (7) Credit lines |
|---|---|---|---|---|---|---|---|
| *Without controlling for income:* | | | | | | | |
| Retired receiving | −0.044*** | −0.043** | −0.549*** | −0.249** | 0.036** | 0.281*** | −0.060 |
| pension | (0.016) | (0.021) | (0.133) | (0.081) | (0.016) | (0.098) | (0.080) |
| $R^2$ | 0.001 | 0.001 | 0.002 | 0.007 | 0.455 | 0.513 | 0.012 |
| Retired for (months), receiving pensions: | | | | | | | |
| <12 | −0.050*** | −0.049** | −0.577*** | −0.263*** | 0.042*** | 0.487*** | −0.048 |
| | (0.016) | (0.020) | (0.134) | (0.084) | (0.015) | (0.098) | (0.081) |
| 12><24 | −0.037** | −0.031 | −0.468*** | −0.149 | 0.029 | 0.296*** | −0.134 |
| | (0.018) | (0.024) | (0.155) | (0.099) | (0.019) | (0.108) | (0.108) |
| >24 | −0.039** | −0.043 | −0.574*** | −0.319*** | 0.033 | −0.047 | −0.020 |
| | (0.020) | (0.028) | (0.166) | (0.104) | (0.023) | (0.115) | (0.152) |
| $R^2$ | 0.001 | 0.001 | 0.002 | 0.007 | 0.455 | 0.513 | 0.012 |
| Retired for (months), receiving pensions and low salary: | | | | | | | |
| <12 | −0.052** | −0.059 | −0.585*** | −0.234* | −0.009 | −0.021 | −0.187 |
| | (0.021) | (0.033) | (0.195) | (0.130) | (0.024) | (0.022) | (0.123) |
| 12> <24 | −0.033 | −0.014 | −0.492** | −0.321* | −0.004 | 0.038 | −0.224 |
| | (0.025) | (0.038) | (0.216) | (0.167) | (0.035) | (0.023) | (0.189) |
| >24 | −0.052 | −0.068 | −0.675** | −0.432** | 0.074* | 0.061*** | −0.209 |
| | (0.031) | (0.057) | (0.270) | (0.176) | (0.044) | (0.022) | (0.194) |
| $R^2$ | 0.002 | 0.003 | 0.005 | 0.008 | 0.460 | 0.516 | 0.012 |
| *Controlling for income:* | | | | | | | |
| Retired receiving | −0.045*** | −0.045** | −0.561*** | −0.284*** | 0.021** | 0.281*** | −0.058 |
| pension | (0.016) | (0.021) | (0.133) | (0.081) | (0.016) | (0.098) | (0.080) |
| $R^2$ | 0.002 | 0.002 | 0.003 | 0.009 | 0.463 | 0.513 | 0.012 |

| | | | | | | | |
|---|---|---|---|---|---|---|---|
| Retired for (months), receiving pensions: | | | | | | | |
| <12 | $-0.051^{***}$ | $-0.051^{**}$ | $-0.590^{***}$ | $-0.300^{***}$ | 0.020 | $0.487^{***}$ | −0.047 |
| | (0.016) | (0.020) | (0.134) | (0.084) | (0.015) | (0.098) | (0.081) |
| 12> <24 | $-0.038^{**}$ | −0.032 | $-0.480^{***}$ | −0.182* | 0.013 | $0.296^{***}$ | −0.133 |
| | (0.018) | (0.024) | (0.155) | (0.099) | (0.018) | (0.108) | (0.109) |
| >24 | $-0.041^{**}$ | −0.044 | $-0.587^{***}$ | $-0.355^{***}$ | 0.029 | −0.047 | −0.018 |
| | (0.020) | (0.028) | (0.166) | (0.104) | (0.022) | (0.155) | (0.152) |
| $R^2$ | 0.002 | 0.002 | 0.003 | 0.009 | 0.463 | 0.513 | 0.012 |
| # obs | 746,669 | 746,669 | 746,669 | 746,669 | 746,669 | 746,669 | 331,487 |
| # individuals | 12,143 | 12,143 | 12,143 | 12,143 | 12,143 | 12,143 | 12,143 |
| Individual FE | ✓ | ✓ | ✓ | ✓ | ✓ | ✓ | ✓ |
| Month-by-year FE | ✓ | ✓ | ✓ | ✓ | ✓ | ✓ | ✓ |

*Notes*: This table shows OLS regression results of the effect of retirement on log interest payments, balances, and limits, using individual, fixed effects, with and without controlling for total income. All specifications include month-by-year fixed effects. All coefficients represent percentage changes. All continuous variables are measured in terms of their inverse hyperbolic sine to accommodate observations with zero values. Standard errors are clustered at the individual level and displayed in parentheses. We define credit lines as overdraft limits and credit card limits minus overdrafts and credit card balances normalized by monthly income. Late fees are fees assessed for paying bills after their due dates.

*p < 0.1; **p < 0.05; ***p < 0.01

*Source:* Authors' calculations.

savings equal monthly repayment of overdrafts in the neighborhood of 0.55*2,215/12 = $102 and increases in savings balances of approximately $210 per month. Individuals thus save much more than the additional $10 per month, or 7% of extra pension income per year, that they would receive more from working longer (pension payments average $1,899; Table 11.1). Because consumption falls by more than income, individuals should retire as soon as possible.

Table 11.2 also shows that the results depend on whether an individual is retired for under 12 months, between 12–24 months, and over 24 months. We can thus look at the dynamics of the reduction in overdraft interest expenses and interest earnings. For overdrafts, all three estimates are large and significant, around 50% reductions in overdraft expenses and 5% for the likelihood of overdrawing checking accounts. Again, we find no effect on borrowing capacity as measured by available credit. The effect on the amount of interest income received depends on the definition of retirement. When individuals retire for good, it takes a year for the effect to manifest, whereas the effect is larger in the first two years if individuals receive retirement income but work part time.

Additional robustness checks in Table 11.3 add individual, month-and-year, and month-by-year fixed effects. Our estimates remain robust to the different fixed effects regimes. When we control only for individual fixed effects, the coefficients are simple conditional means of within-individual comparison of overdraft debt levels before and after retirement. These show that the average individual decreases overdraft debt after retirement and increases liquid savings.

We find similar results when we control for total individual income since individuals could simply liquidate assets after entering retirement to repay their consumer debt. We also control for income at the household level, which does not affect our results materially, as shown in Table 11.3.[10]

When we employ the stricter definition of retirement that conditions not only on the presence of pension payments but also the absence of labor income, results are similar. Both retirement definitions are associated with a step down in total income. Conditioning only on the presence of pension income, the fall in income equals approximately 8%, whereas conditioning also on the absence of labor income yields a drop in income of approximately 22%, in line with US estimates (Ameriks and Zeldes 2011).

Overall, for a number of specifications, we find that households not only delever but also increase their liquid savings at retirement.

## Results for Spending by Category

In additional results reported in an Online Appendix, we also examine the estimated effect of retirement on spending based on the individual fixed-effects model with and without controlling for total income. Here

TABLE 11.3 The Effects of Retirement on an Indicator for Paying Overdraft Interest or Interest Earnings from Savings: Alternative Specifications

| FE type: | (1) None | (2) Individual | (3) Individual month, year | (4) Individual month-by-year |
|---|---|---|---|---|
| *Effects on Indicator for Paying Overdraft Interest (N = 746,669):* | | | | |
| Retired | −0.089*** | −0.047*** | −0.044*** | −0.044*** |
| | (0.017) | (0.015) | (0.016) | (0.016) |
| $R^2$ | 0.001 | 0.000 | 0.001 | 0.001 |
| *Effects on Indicator for Interest Earnings from Savings (N = 886,439):* | | | | |
| Retired | 0.196*** | 0.365*** | 0.035** | 0.036** |
| | (0.015) | (0.016) | (0.016) | (0.016) |
| $R^2$ | 0.005 | 0.006 | 0.419 | 0.455 |
| # individuals | 12,143 | 12,143 | 12,143 | 12,143 |

| Income control: | (1) Income | (2) Regular income | (3) Irregular income | (4) Pension |
|---|---|---|---|---|
| *Effects on Indicator for Paying Overdraft Interest (N = 746,669):* | | | | |
| Retired | −0.044*** | −0.044*** | −0.044*** | −0.047*** |
| | (0.016) | (0.016) | (0.016) | (0.016) |
| $R^2$ | 0.001 | 0.001 | 0.001 | 0.001 |
| *Effects on Indicator for Interest Earnings from Savings (N = 886,439):* | | | | |
| Retired | 0.036** | 0.036** | 0.036** | 0.032** |
| | (0.016) | (0.016) | (0.016) | (0.016) |
| $R^2$ | 0.455 | 0.455 | 0.455 | 0.455 |
| # individuals | 12,143 | 12,143 | 12,143 | 12,143 |
| Individual FE | ✓ | ✓ | ✓ | ✓ |
| Month-by-year FE | ✓ | ✓ | ✓ | ✓ |

*Notes*: This table shows the estimated effect of retirement on overdraft interest and interest earnings from savings accounts using different fixed effects regimes and control variables. Specifications (1–4) include fixed effects regimes as indicated in each column, Specifications (5–8) control for individual and month-by-year fixed effects. Standard errors are clustered at the individual level and are within parentheses.

* p<0.1

** p<0.05

*** p<0.01

*Source*: Authors' calculations.

we see that spending drops upon retirement by 21.6% (26.8% controlling for income). Drops in spending for categories, such as groceries, could be attributed to more efficient shopping and home production since retirees have more time at their disposal after retirement. Yet leisure-related expenses (e.g., sports and activities) also decrease substantially, suggesting that retirees are correcting overconsumption. Other spending that cannot be attributed to work, such as alcohol bought in stores and pharmacy spending, also falls at retirement, and the same is true when turning to a finer categorization of food. Analyzing spending on food in more detail than previous studies is important because food expenses have received the most attention in the retirement consumption literature (Aguiar and Hurst 2005). The observed drop in expenditures after retirement is not fully explained by work-related expenses or bargain shopping. Yet this does not paint a fully conclusive picture of whether the retirement puzzles remain puzzling. For instance, fine dining could be a work-related expense as well.

### Replicating the Analysis in Other Datasets

We have also replicated these results in the most commonly used US survey datasets, namely the CEX and SCF. Unfortunately, both suffer from selection bias and measurement error due to their survey designs and non-longitudinal structures (Pistaferri 2015). Therefore, we also repeat the analysis using two US survey datasets, the PSID and HRS, where we can run individual fixed effects regressions, and another transaction-level dataset from Germany. We document similar findings across all of these, so we conclude that our results are not specific to Iceland (full results are provided in the Online Appendix).

## Behavioral Explanations

Our findings are inconsistent with the two leading explanations for the retirement-consumption and retirement-savings puzzles. That is, if work-related expenses or savings due to bargain shopping are larger than the difference between pension and labor income, then workers should retire early unless the additional monthly pension benefits for an additional month of work exceed the savings from retiring. In Iceland, however, the additional pension benefit from one month of work is much smaller than the reduction in overdrafts and increase in liquid savings observed. We thus need some other explanation for why people continue to work.

If we seek to explain our results with health shocks or medical expenses, then individuals would need to systematically revise downward their health beliefs. A detailed discussion of work-related expenses, health shocks, and medical expense risk is provided in the Online Appendix, along with other potential explanations. In particular, we discuss wealth shocks, liquidation of assets, and returns of savings versus borrowing, credit constraints, consumption insurance, inventory considerations, or lump-sum pension withdrawals.

Additional explanations could turn to limited rationality and other behavioral factors, though even with limited planning horizons (Caliendo and Aadland 2007; Gabaix 2016; Huang and Caliendo 2011), rational individuals would still be anticipated to start smoothing consumption near retirement. Less standard preferences, such as time inconsistency and quasi-hyperbolic discounting preferences (DellaVigna 2009; Koszegi and Rabin 2006, 2007, 2009; Laibson et al. 1998, 2018), could also be explored to determine if their predictive power extends to this out-of-sample test. Nevertheless, hyperbolic discounting would not predict a fall in consumption and an increase in savings upon retirement. By contrast, if consumers were to correct their time-inconsistency and stop overconsuming after retirement, this could explain the findings. Similarly, if people corrected their time-inconsistent preferences upon retirement due to a drop in income uncertainty, this would also drive a reduction in future spending. Indeed, this formulation of nonstandard preferences would generate a simultaneous drop in consumption at retirement and an increase in savings, as we show using simulated consumption data (see the Online Appendix). One could also allow for a change in present bias at the time of retirement, generating a pattern of falling income and consumption with rising liquid savings (or lower borrowing).

Changing discount factors at retirement might result from alterations in information-processing capacity, planning ability, or other factors.[11] One could also consider models of salience, memory, focusing, or relative thinking (Bordalo et al. 2013, 2020; Bushong et al. 2021; Heimer et al. 2019; Koszegi and Szeidl 2013). For example, income and spending after retirement could become more salient, memorable, focused, or easier to compare in relative terms, all of which could imply changes in planning behavior around retirement. Insufficient planning models (Caliendo and Aadland 2007; Campbell and Mankiw 1989; Gabaix 2016; Huang and Caliendo 2011; Reis 2006) could also be combined with information or planning ability updates to generate an increase in savings on top of a drop in consumption at retirement. In sum, numerous additional behavioral factors might help explain the observed facts, and much remains to be done.

## Conclusions

Understanding whether people save enough and are adequately prepared for retirement is increasingly important in an aging world. Using a large transaction-level data set from a financial aggregator on income, spending, account balances, and credit limits in Iceland, we document substantial increases in liquid savings and substantial decreases in consumer debt around retirement.

These findings are difficult to explain using a conventional economic framework that assumes rational planning and foresight. If forward-looking optimizing individuals anticipate a fall in income, they should rationally save more before the anticipated decrease rather than afterward. Yet this is not what we find. For this reason, our results add to the literature on empirical household consumption and savings patterns by showing that consumption drops while savings and wealth rise after retirement. We test several additional hypotheses and conclude that they do not provide fully satisfactory explanations for our new findings; rather, we believe that the evidence is consistent with changes in peoples' effective discount rates at retirement.

## Acknowledgments

The authors are grateful for the financial support of the Pension Research Center (PeRCent) at Copenhagen Business School. For helpful comments they thank Doug Bernheim, Andrew Caplin, Emir Kamenica, Botond Koszegi, Rachel Kranton, David Laibson, Jennifer La'O, Olivia S. Mitchell, Chris Moser, Emi Nakamura, Jon Parker, Matthew Rabin, Alex Rees-Jones, Nick Roussanov, Steve Zeldes, Jon Zinman, and participants at workshops at CEPRA/NBER, Brown University, NYU Sloan-Nomis Conference on Attention and Applied Economics, Federal Reserve Bank of Richmond, Frankfurt School of Finance, CEPR European Conference on Household Finance, NBER Behavioral Macro Summer Institute, AFA, Stanford Institute for Theoretical Economics Psychology and Economics, University of Queensland, PerCent 2017 Conference, University of Minnesota, Columbia University, 8th conference of the CESifo network on Behavioral Economics, and the Western Finance Association. They are also indebted to Meniga and their data analysts for providing and helping with the Icelandic data and to Steffen Meyer for replicating results in German bank data. They also thank David Westerheide, Fedra De Angelis Effrem, Andrea Marogg, and Belinda Chen for outstanding research assistance.

## Notes

1. Following Davies (1981) and Hamermesh (1984), Banks et al. (1998) document a decline in consumption at retirement using a pseudo-panel from the Family Expenditure Survey (FES) in the UK. Bernheimt al. (2001) confirm this finding using longitudinal data from the Panel Study of Income Dynamics (PSID). The drop in consumption at retirement is theoretically rationalized by Huang and Caliendo (2011), Laitner and Silverman (2005), and Pagel (2017), among others. Moreover, Ameriks et al. (2007) and Haider and Stephens (2007) provide evidence that the drop is expected.

2. While some additional studies provide evidence supporting this explanation (e.g., Battistin et al. 2009; Hurd and Rohwedder 2003), others argue against it (Been et al. 2019; Hurd and Rohwedder this volume; Stephens Jr. and Toohey 2025).
3. Love et al. (2009) construct a measure of wealth beginning at age 65 and document that it rises with age. Poterba et al. (2011a, 2011b) show that individuals do not withdraw more funds from their personal retirement accounts relative to their rate of return, which causes wealth to effectively rise during retirement. Guo et al. (2020) shows, however, that individuals tend to claim Social Security benefits early.
4. The Icelandic healthcare system is financed by taxes as is common in the Nordic welfare state and provides the population with equal access to the healthcare and welfare system. Iceland does not operate its healthcare system based on financial need, but some disadvantaged groups, including disabled and elderly individuals, receive discounts on personal health expenses. Out-of-pocket payments are a source of funding for the universal healthcare system and amount to 9% of GDP. By comparison, in the US, out-of-pocket medical expenditures amount to 17.7% of GDP. Furthermore, in Iceland, there is no risk of personal costs for large health expenses because they are capped.
5. To this point, Carlin et al. (2023) show that individuals curtail their insufficient funds costs after a reduction in the costs of monitoring their finances. See also Bordalo et al. (2013, 2020); Bushong et al. (2021); Fulford and Schuh (2017); Heimer et al. (2019); Heimer this volume; Koszegi and Szeidl (2013); Malmendier and Shen (2024); Mitchell and Lusardi (2011).
6. The Online Appendix provides a more detailed review of the key features of the pension system in Iceland.
7. According to Elmeskov et al. (2023), 94% of Icelanders used internet banking in 2018.
8. Our estimates are not qualitatively or quantitatively affected by running the regressions in levels, winsorizing to address outliers, or taking the log of the variables instead of the sine transformation.
9. See the Online Appendix for interest rates over the sample period.
10. Additionally, the Online Appendix confirms that no other sources of income increase after retirement (e.g., from liquidations of real estate assets).
11. See, for instance, Ameriks et al. (2007); Carvalho et al. (2016); Fulford and Schuh (2017); Haider and Stephens (2007); Malmendier and Shen (2024); and Mitchell and Lusardi (2011). Carlin et al. (2023) show that individuals reduce their consumer debt after a reduction in the costs of monitoring one's finances.

## References

Addoum, J. M. (2017). 'Household Portfolio Choice and Retirement.' *Review of Economics and Statistics*, 99(5): 870–883.

Agarwal, S., J. C. Driscoll, X. Gabaix, and D. Laibson (2009). 'The Age of Reason: Financial Decisions over the Life Cycle and Implications for Regulation.' *Brookings Papers on Economic Activity*, 2009(2): 51–117.

Agarwal, S., J. Pan, and W. Qian (2015). 'The Composition Effect of Consumption around Retirement: Evidence from Singapore.' *American Economic Review Papers & Proceedings*, 105(5): 426–431.

Aguiar, M. and E. Hurst (2005). 'Consumption versus Expenditure.' *Journal of Political Economy*, 113(5): 919–948.

Aguiar, M. and E. Hurst (2013). 'Deconstructing Life Cycle Expenditure.' *Journal of Political Economy*, 121(3): 437–492.

Ameriks, J., J. Briggs, A. Caplin, M. D. Shapiro, and C. Tonetti (2016). 'Late-in-Life Risks and the Under-Insurance Puzzle.' NBER Working Paper No. 22726.

Ameriks, J., A. Caplin, and J. Leahy (2007). 'Retirement Consumption: Insights from a Survey.' *Review of Economics and Statistics*, 89(2): 265–274.

Ameriks, J. and S. P. Zeldes (2011). 'How Do Household Portfolio Shares Vary with Age?' Columbia University Working Paper.

Anguelov, C. E. and C. R. Tamborini (2009). 'Retiring in Debt-Differences Between the 1995 and 2004 Near-Retiree Cohorts.' *Social Security Bulletin*, 69(2): 13–34.

Banks, H., R. Blundell, and S. Tanner (1998). 'Is There a Retirement-Savings Puzzle?' *American Economic Review*, 88(4): 769–788.

Battistin, E., A. Brugiavini, E. Rettore, and G. Weber (2009). 'The Retirement Consumption Puzzle: Evidence from a Regression Discontinuity Approach.' *American Economic Review*, 99(5): 2209–2226.

Been, J., S. Rohwedder, and M. Hurd (2019). 'Household Consumption Spending and Home Production Responses to Retirement: Do Retirees Substitute Consumption Spending?' *Review of the Economics of the Household*, 19(4): 959–985.

Bernheim, B. D., J. Skinner, and S. Weinberg (2001). 'What Accounts for the Variation in Retirement Wealth Among U.S. Households?' *American Economic Review*, 91(4): 832–857.

Bordalo, P., N. Gennaioli, and A. Shleifer (2013). 'Salience and Consumer Choice.' *Journal of Political Economy*, 121(5): 803–843.

Bordalo, P., N. Gennaioli, and A. Shleifer (2020). 'Memory, Attention, and Choice.' *Quarterly Journal of Economics*, 135(3): 1399–1442.

Bushong, B., M. Rabin, and J. Schwartzstein (2021). 'A Model of Relative Thinking.' *Review of Economic Studies*, 88(1): 162–191.

Caliendo, F. and D. Aadland (2007). 'Short-Term Planning and the Life-Cycle Consumption Puzzle.' *Journal of Economic Dynamics and Control*, 31(4): 1392–1415.

Campbell, J. Y. and N. G. Mankiw (1989). 'Consumption, Income, and Interest Rates: Reinterpreting the Time Series Evidence.' *NBER Macroeconomics Annual*, 4: 185–216.

Carlin, B., A. Olafsson, and M. Pagel (2019). 'Generational Differences in Managing Personal Finances.' *AEA Papers and Proceedings*, 109: 54–59.

Carlin, B., A. Olafsson, and M. Pagel (2023). 'Mobile Apps and Financial Decision Making.' *Review of Finance*, 27(3): 977–996.

Carvalho, L. S., S. Meier, and S. W. Wang (2016). 'Poverty and Economic Decision-Making: Evidence from Changes in Financial Resources at Payday.' *American Economic Review*, 106(2): 260–284.

Davies, J. B. (1981). 'Uncertain Lifetime, Consumption, and Dissaving in Retirement.' *Journal of Political Economy*, 89(3): 561–577.

DellaVigna, S. (2009). 'Psychology and Economics: Evidence from the Field.' *Journal of Economic Literature*, 47(2): 315–372.

DeNardi, M., E. French, and J. B. Jones (2010). 'Why Do the Elderly Save? The Role of Medical Expenses.' *Journal of Political Economy*, 118: 39–75.

Elmeskov, J., H. Slegrova, D. Stefanescu, and F. Bernadic (2023). *Peer Review Report on Iceland.* Eurostat Peer Review Report Iceland. Luxembourg City, LUX: Eurostat.

Fe, E. (2019). 'What Can We Learn About the Average Treatment Effect of Retirement on Consumption?' dx.doi.org/10.2139/ssrn.3329588

Fulford, S. and S. D. Schuh (2017). 'Credit Card Utilization and Consumption over the Life Cycle and Business Cycle.' Consumer Financial Protection Bureau Office of Research Working Paper No. 2017–03.

Gabaix, X. (2016). 'Behavioral Macroeconomics via Sparse Dynamic Programming.' NBER Working Paper No. 21848.

Guo, R., J. Skinner, and S. Zeldes (2019). 'Inattentive Households and Consumption Declines During Retirement.' SSA Research Consortium 2019RDRC–P3. Ann Arbor, MI: MRDRC.

Guo, R., W. Sun, J. Wang, and G. Xiao (2020). 'Why Do Retired Workers Claim their Social Security Benefits So Early? A Potential Explanation Based on the Cumulative Prospect Theory.' *Applied Economics*, 52(5): 490–505.

Haider, S. J. and M. Stephens (2007). 'Is There a Retirement-Consumption Puzzle? Evidence Using Subjective Retirement Expectations.' *Review of Economics and Statistics*, 89(2): 247–264.

Hamermesh, D. S. (1984). 'Life-Cycle Effects on Consumption and Retirement.' *Journal of Labor Economics*, 2(3): 353–370.

Heimer, R. Z., K. O. R. Myrseth, and R. S. Schoenle (2019). 'YOLO: Mortality Beliefs and Household Finance Puzzles.' *Journal of Finance*, 74(6): 2957–2996.

Huang, K. X. and F. Caliendo (2011). 'Rationalizing Multiple Consumption-Saving Puzzles in a Unified Framework.' *Frontiers of Economics in China*, 6(3): 359–388.

Hurd, M. and S. Rohwedder (2003). 'The Retirement-Consumption Puzzle: Anticipated and Actual Declines in Spending at Retirement.' NBER Working Paper No. 9586.

Hurst, E. (2008). 'Understanding Consumption in Retirement: Recent Developments.' In J. Ameriks and O. S. Mitchell, eds., *Recalibrating Retirement Spending and Saving.* Oxford: Oxford University Press, pp. 29–45.

Jones, J. B., M. De Nardi, E. French, R. McGee, and J. Kirschner (2018). 'The Lifetime Medical Spending of Retirees.' NBER Working Paper No. 24599.

Kieren, P. and M. Weber (2022). 'When Saving Is Not Enough: The Wealth Decumulation Decision in Retirement.' *Journal of Pension Economics and Finance*, 21(3): 446–473.

Koszegi, B. and M. Rabin (2006). 'A Model of Reference-Dependent Preferences.' *Quarterly Journal of Economics*, 121(4): 1133–1165.

Koszegi, B. and M. Rabin (2007). 'Reference-Dependent Risk Attitudes.' *American Economic Review*, 97(4): 1047–1073.

Koszegi, B. and M. Rabin (2009). 'Reference-Dependent Consumption Plans.' *American Economic Review*, 99(3): 909–936.

Koszegi, B. and A. Szeidl (2013). 'A Model of Focusing in Economic Choice.' *Quarterly Journal of Economics*, 128(1): 53–104.

Laibson, D., P. Maxted, A. Repetto, and J. Tobacman (2018). 'Estimating Discount Functions with Consumption Choices over the Lifecycle.' NBER Working Paper No. 13314.

Laibson, D., A. Repetto, and J. Tobacman (1998). 'Self-Control and Saving for Retirement.' *Brookings Papers on Economic Activity* 1: 91–196.

Laitner, J. and D. Silverman (2005). 'Estimating Life-Cycle Parameters from Consumption Behavior at Retirement.' NBER Working Paper No. 11163.

Laitner, J., D. Silverman, and D. Stolyarov (2018). 'The Role of Annuitized Wealth in Post-Retirement Behavior.' *American Economic Journal: Macroeconomics*, 10(3): 71–117.

Love, D. A., M. G. Palumbo, and P. A. Smith (2009). 'The Trajectory of Wealth in Retirement.' *Journal of Public Economics*, 93(1): 191–208.

Malmendier, U. and L. S. Shen (2024). 'Scarred Consumption.' *American Economic Journal: Macroeconomics*, 16(1): 322–355.

Mitchell, O. S. and A. Lusardi (2011). 'Financial Literacy and Planning: Implications for Retirement Wellbeing.' In O. S. Mitchell and A. Lusardi, eds., *Financial Literacy: Implications for Retirement Security and the Financial Marketplace.* Oxford: Oxford University Press, pp. 17–39.

Olafsson, A. and M. Pagel (2018). 'The Liquid Hand-to-Mouth: Evidence from Personal Finance Management Software.' *Review of Financial Studies*, 31(11): 4398–4446.

Pagel, M. (2017). 'Expectations-Based Reference-Dependent Life-Cycle Consumption.' *Review of Economic Studies*, 84(2): 885–934.

Pistaferri, L. (2015). 'Household Consumption: Research Questions, Measurement Issues, and Data Collection Strategies.' *Journal of Economic and Social Measurement*, 40(2015): 123–149.

Poterba, J., S. Venti, and D. Wise (2011a). 'The Composition and Draw-Down of Wealth in Retirement.' *Journal of Economic Perspectives*, 25: 95–117.

Poterba, J., S. Venti, and D. Wise (2011b). 'Family Status Transitions, Latent Health, and the Post-Retirement Evolution of Assets.' In D. A. Wise, ed., *Explorations in the Economics of Aging.* Chicago: University of Chicago Press, pp. 23–74.

Poterba, J., S. F. Venti, and D. A. Wise (2012). 'Were They Prepared for Retirement? Financial Status at Advanced Ages in the HRS and AHEAD Cohorts.' In D. A. Wise, ed., *Investigations in the Economics of Aging.* Chicago: University of Chicago Press, pp. 69–75.

Reis, R. (2006). 'Inattentive Consumers.' *Journal of Monetary Economics*, 53(8): 1761–1800.

Schwerdt, G. (2005). 'Why Does Consumption Fall at Retirement? Evidence from Germany.' *Economics Letters*, 89(3): 300–305.

Skinner, J. (2007). 'Are You Sure You're Saving Enough for Retirement?' *Journal of Economic Perspectives*, 21(3): 59–80.

Stephens Jr., M. and D. Toohey (2025). 'Changes in Nutrient Intake at Retirement.' *American Economic Journal: Applied Economics*, 17(1): 510–552.

Chapter 12

# Does 401(k) Loan Repayment Crowd Out Retirement Saving?

## Implications for Plan Design

*John Beshears, James J. Choi, Joel M. Dickson, Aaron Goodman, Fiona Greig, and David Laibson*

In the United States, 401(k) plans serve not only as vehicles for long-term retirement saving but also as sources of short-term liquidity. For instance, in 2023, among plans for which Vanguard was the recordkeeper, 10% of participants accessed their plan assets either via a loan or a hardship withdrawal.[1] Similarly, Beshears et al. (2012) and Lu et al. (2017) found that over 40% of 401(k) participants took at least one loan over a five- to seven-year period. Recent legislative changes under SECURE 2.0, including the emergency withdrawal provision allowing participants to take annual penalty-free distributions of up to $1,000, are likely to increase early withdrawals in coming years. As more participants use 401(k) assets to fund emergency spending needs, it is important to understand the tradeoffs between liquidity and long-run wealth accumulation.

This chapter examines the extent to which utilization of 401(k) liquidity features reduces ongoing 401(k) contributions. Answering this question requires a joint analysis of distribution and contribution behavior not found in prior empirical work in the 401(k) literature.[2] Leveraging administrative data covering Vanguard's recordkeeping population, we study participants taking loans and hardship withdrawals, and we establish a new empirical fact: elective contributions are remarkably stable after liquidity-based distributions. Participants accessing their assets during employment usually did not elect to reduce their contribution rates, with roughly three-quarters of loan and hardship withdrawal takers maintaining or increasing their contribution rates in the two years following the distribution. Relative to a control group of observably similar participants who did not take a loan, loan takers' average contribution rates fell by only 0.8 percentage points over a two-year

John Beshears et al., *Does 401(k) Loan Repayment Crowd Out Retirement Saving?*. In: *Retirement Saving, Investment, and Spending*. Edited by: Olivia S. Mitchell and Nikolai Roussanov, Oxford University Press. © Pension Research Council, The Wharton School, The University of Pennsylvania (2026). DOI: 10.1093/oso/9780197845752.003.0012

horizon. This contribution stability holds across the income and loan size distributions as well as for hardship withdrawal takers who were not subject to mandatory contribution suspensions.

Our results have implications for the implementation of the optional emergency withdrawal feature newly permitted under SECURE 2.0. Beginning in 2024, plan sponsors may allow participants to take penalty-free withdrawals of up to $1,000 per calendar year for 'unforeseeable or immediate financial needs relating to necessary personal or family emergency expenses.'[3] The lack of a 10% tax penalty—along with the self-certification of financial need[4]—makes the new emergency withdrawals a uniquely flexible liquidity option that could yield high participant usage rates at adopting employers. This additional liquidity is valuable to participants facing pressing spending needs, but the potential for increased withdrawal activity raises the risk of substantial retirement saving leakage (i.e., reductions in retirement savings account balances driven by participants' decisions to access their balances prior to retirement).

Our empirical findings point toward practical steps that plan sponsors could take to reduce unnecessary leakage arising from the new emergency withdrawals. One effective intervention would be an automatic repayment feature that encouraged or defaulted participants into repaying the withdrawals through payroll deferrals incremental to their elective contributions, essentially treating the withdrawal as if it were a loan.[5] The stability of elective contributions after loan issuance suggests that emergency withdrawal takers would also repay the withdrawn amount while maintaining their previous contribution rates.

We find that most participants could pay back a $1,000 withdrawal within a two-year period via a two-percentage point increase in their contributions. Automatic repayment, which could be implemented with designated repayment transactions or with a small increase in the elective contribution rate, would nudge participants to replenish their retirement accounts in a timely manner and ensure that the withdrawn funds resume earning market returns. Maintaining elective deferrals during the repayment period would prevent unnecessary saving reductions and ensure that participants do not miss out on valuable employer matching contributions.

Like other aspects of participant behavior, our results are probably partially driven by participants' passive adherence to plan defaults. In the absence of automatic contribution suspensions (which are rarely used for loans and prohibited for hardship withdrawals from 2020 onward), the default path for contribution rates is to continue on their pre-distribution trajectory. Indeed, about 40% of the loan and hardship withdrawal takers in our sample see their contribution rates automatically *escalated* during the two-year period following the distribution. Downward contribution adjustments require an active choice from participants, which in most cases is not forthcoming.

Because loan repayments are generally collected through mandatory payroll deferrals, the stability of elective contribution rates implies that loan takers experience large increases in their total deferral rates (contributions plus repayments) at the time of the loan issuance. This fact, along with participants' tendency toward default adherence, presents intriguing possibilities for the design of the plan loan feature itself. For example, plan sponsors could encourage or default participants who have successfully paid off a loan into an elective contribution increase, to maintain a portion of the increased total deferral rate that occurred during the loan repayment period. Successful repayment histories effectively reveal participants' ability to support higher deferral rates, and, given the substantial size of loan repayments (about 6% of income on average), policies that act on this information to raise ongoing contribution rates could achieve meaningful increases in retirement wealth accumulation. Successful repayment could provide particularly valuable information about savings capacity for less engaged participants whose pre-loan contribution rates were set by plan defaults rather than active choices.

An important limitation of our analysis is our lack of broader household financial data. Because we can only track participants' financial activity within the 401(k) plan, we cannot speak to adjustments that might occur in other parts of their household budgets. In particular, it is possible that loan takers finance a portion of their increased payroll deferral burden by cutting back on essential spending needs, leaving bills unpaid, or taking on credit card debt. The margins on which budgets adjust as a consequence of loan repayment affect the normative implications of the observed stable contribution activity. The consistency of our main empirical results across the income and loan size distributions partially addresses this concern: if loan repayment caused household financial stress, we might expect to see at least some of that stress appear for the lower-income participants and smaller loans in our sample. The design of an automatic repayment system also matters: making contribution increases for loan and emergency withdrawal takers the default, but not mandatory, gives participants experiencing household financial stress the freedom to opt out.

The remainder of the chapter is organized as follows. First, we describe the administrative 401(k) data and our event study approach to analyzing loan takers' contribution rates. Next, we present the main empirical results, followed by a discussion of our results. A final section concludes.

## Data and Methodology

### Vanguard Administrative Data

We use anonymized administrative 401(k) plan data from Vanguard. This database includes all information that Vanguard collects in the normal course of its recordkeeping responsibilities, including employee hire and separation dates, employee contribution rates, employee and employer contribution transactions, loan issuances and repayments, and hardship withdrawals and other distributions. Vanguard administers over 1,700 plans covering roughly 5 million participants. Because our primary empirical focus is on loan repayment, most of the analysis is restricted to a slightly smaller set of about 1,400 plans that offer loans. Since larger plans are more likely to offer loans, this subset contains over 90% of the participants in Vanguard plans.[6]

### Sample Time Frames

We track the contribution behavior of loan takers for two years following loan issuance. As a result, the most recent set of loan takers we track had loans issued in December 2021. The first sample is formed by extending the loan issuance time frame back through the beginning of the calendar year, and we consider all participants issued a plan loan in 2021. Taking December 2019 as the last month of pre-pandemic contribution activity, we define the pre-pandemic sample as participants with loans issued in 2017. Analyzing recent cohorts of loan takers requires us to use data from the COVID-19 pandemic period. To ensure that our findings are relevant outside of this period, we analyze both a recent sample of loans issued in 2021, and also a pre-pandemic sample of loans issued in 2017. As shown below, the empirical results are quite similar for the 2017 and 2021 samples; contribution crowd-out during loan repayment was in fact slightly smaller for the more recent 2021 sample. The similarity of our results across the two time periods suggests that participants' ability to maintain elective deferrals while repaying loans is a durable empirical pattern.

Though contribution behavior during loan repayment is our primary focus, contribution behavior after hardship withdrawals (which tend to be smaller than loan amounts and used for purposes similar to the new emergency withdrawals) is also informative. We supplement our analysis by studying the contribution activity of participants who took hardship withdrawals during the same 2017 and 2021 time frames.

## Summary Statistics

Table 12.1 gives summary statistics for the loan and hardship withdrawal takers in Vanguard plans. The median loan taker is just over 40 years old with a plan tenure of five years and an annual income around $60,000. The average loan amount is about $10,000 in 2017 and about $12,000 in 2021; given the skewness of the loan size distribution, the corresponding median loan amounts are substantially smaller ($6,000 in 2017 and roughly $7,000 in 2021). Small loans approximating the size of the new emergency withdrawals are relatively rare but still common enough to study empirically: the 10th percentile of the loan size distribution in both samples is just over $1,000.

TABLE 12.1 Summary Statistics for Loan and Hardship Withdrawal (HW) Samples

| | Loan issuances | | Hardship withdrawals | |
|---|---|---|---|---|
| | 2017 | 2021 | 2017 | 2021 |
| Median participant age | 43 | 42 | 42 | 41 |
| Median plan tenure (years) | 5 | 5 | 6 | 5 |
| Estimated annual income ($) | | | | |
| Mean | 65,669 | 72,050 | 52,748 | 59,999 |
| Percentiles | | | | |
| 10th | 23,159 | 26,320 | 15,736 | 22,120 |
| 25th | 35,870 | 40,229 | 28,699 | 34,992 |
| Median | 54,028 | 59,689 | 44,865 | 51,257 |
| 75th | 80,158 | 87,098 | 65,789 | 73,457 |
| 90th | 114,840 | 125,769 | 93,204 | 103,593 |
| Loan/HW amount ($) | | | | |
| Mean | 10,385 | 11,923 | 6,235 | 8,206 |
| Percentiles | | | | |
| 10th | 1,200 | 1,419 | 604 | 665 |
| 25th | 2,480 | 2,988 | 1,151 | 1,296 |
| Median | 6,000 | 7,021 | 2,525 | 2,985 |
| 75th | 15,000 | 17,000 | 5,965 | 7,000 |
| 90th | 26,035 | 30,000 | 13,475 | 17,627 |
| Number of participants | 334,406 | 253,300 | 56,405 | 72,118 |

*Notes:* If multiple loans were issued for a given participant during one of the sample years, only the first loan issuance for that sample year is considered. Similarly, if a participant took multiple hardship withdrawals during one of the sample years, only the first withdrawal for that sample year is considered. Annual participant income is estimated as (average monthly employee contributions in the six months before loan or hardship withdrawal)/(average elective contribution rate in the six months before loan or hardship withdrawal)*12.

*Source:* Authors' calculations.

Because hardship withdrawals are less common than plan loans, the hardship withdrawal samples are significantly smaller than the loan samples. Hardship withdrawals are also noticeably smaller in dollar terms: median withdrawal amounts are below $3,000 in both the 2017 and 2021 samples, and roughly 25% of withdrawals are smaller than the new $1,000 emergency withdrawal limit. Finally, hardship withdrawal takers had slightly lower incomes than loan takers, with median values about $8,000 less than the corresponding figures for the loan samples.

## Event Study of Loan Takers

For each loan taker in the 2017 and 2021 samples, we analyze contribution behavior—the participants' elected contribution rates[7]—for six months prior to and 24 months after loan issuance. We restrict the event study analysis to loan takers still employed at the same plan sponsor 24 months after issuance (thereby eliminating cases where contribution rates dropped to zero for separated employees). If a participant took multiple loans during either of our 2017 or 2021 sampling time frames, we index event time relative to the participant's first such loan.

Changes in loan takers' contribution rates over time may reflect a variety of factors, including macroeconomic shocks, changes in participant incomes, and plan-specific features such as annual automatic-escalation policies, among others. To focus on contribution rate changes that we can plausibly attribute to the effect of the loan issuance itself, we compare loan takers to a control group of participants who did not take loans during the specified time frames but who were otherwise similar in plan tenure, age, income, and initial contribution rate. Specifically, we match each loan taker to one control participant who:

- was in the same plan as the loan taker,
- was employed at the same plan sponsor 24 months after the relevant loan issuance,
- did not take any loans or hardship withdrawals in the six months before or during the month of the relevant loan issuance,
- had the same tenure (measured as whole years since plan entry) as the loan taker at the time of the relevant loan issuance,
- had an absolute age difference with the loan taker of five years or less,
- had an absolute income difference with the loan taker of 25% or less at the time of the relevant loan issuance,
- and had the same elected contribution rate as the loan taker six months before the relevant loan issuance.

If multiple potential control participants satisfy all these criteria, we chose one randomly; if no suitable control participants existed, we excluded the relevant loan taker from our event study analysis. Because we screen for loans and hardship withdrawals only in the six months before the relevant loan issuance, it is possible for a control participant to take a loan or hardship withdrawal after their matched loan taker's loan issuance (or outside of our 31-month time frame altogether).

The Online Appendix shows how our sample size is affected by each of the filtering steps taken when moving from the full 2017 and 2021 loan issuance samples to the subsamples analyzed in our event study. Restricting to loan takers who are still employed 24 months after issuance drops about 20% of participants. A small minority of plan sponsors do not report participants' elected contribution rates (our main outcome variable) to Vanguard; dropping participants from these plans causes another small reduction in sample size. After successfully matching about 60% of the remaining loan takers to suitable control participants, we were left with 137,698 loan takers in the 2017 sample, and 114,752 in the 2021 sample. We restrict attention to this smaller matched sample only in analyses that compare loan takers' contribution rates and those of the control group.

## Results

### Finding 1: Contribution Activity Is Remarkably Stable During and After Loan Origination and Hardship Withdrawals

Loan repayment patterns and voluntary contribution changes among our samples indicate that participants did maintain their previous contribution levels even after taking liquidity-based distributions. Those who took loans or hardship withdrawals rarely reduced their contribution rates after the distribution. Moreover, the vast majority of 401(k) loan takers who remained employed long enough to repay their loans through payroll deferrals did so successfully.

To illustrate these points, we first compute default rates for the 401(k) loans in our sample.[8] Because loan repayment periods can stretch up to five years, it is important to note that we only capture defaults occurring within our two-year post-issuance period. The default rate was 4% among participants still employed at the lending plan's sponsor two years after issuance. Among participants who separated within this two-year period, the default rate was 71%. The disparity in default rates between the two groups echoes similar findings from prior research using Vanguard recordkeeping data (Lu et al. 2017) and is likely attributable to employers' ability to require that the full amount of outstanding loan balances be repaid at the time of separation. In the case of the new emergency withdrawals under SECURE 2.0, the optional nature of repayment means there would be no requirement from the plan sponsor (or tax-penalty incentive for the participant) to accelerate repayment at the time of separation. The share of participants in the 2017 sample defaulting during employment was slightly higher, at 10%.

Changes in elective contribution rates after loan issuance provide additional information about participants' repayment capacity. In particular, voluntary decreases in contribution rates could indicate that loan repayment stressed participants' finances or otherwise interfered with their ability to save for retirement. Figure 12.1 demonstrates that voluntary decreases were not typical, as only 26% of loan takers and 24% of hardship withdrawal takers in the 2021 sample voluntarily decreased their contribution rate

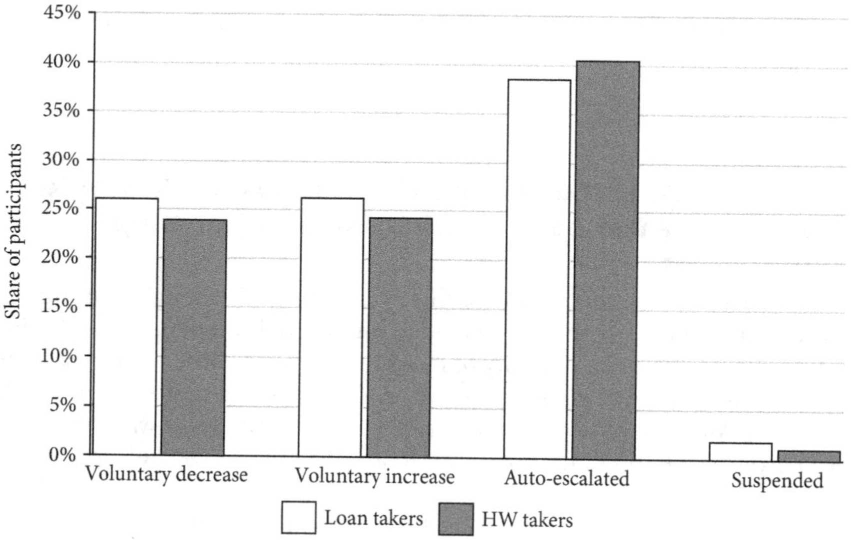


**Figure 12.1** Voluntary contribution decreases following loan issuances and hardship withdrawals (HW) are not typical

*Notes:* This plot summarizes contribution rate changes during the two-year period following loan or hardship withdrawal issuance. Voluntary decreases (made at the participant's request) and suspensions (automatic changes that force the contribution rate to zero and are implemented by the plan sponsor) are distinct events. The bars for a given sample may sum to more than 100% because a single participant may exhibit multiple types of contribution rate changes. Results are shown for the 2021 samples of loan and hardship withdrawal takers.
*Source:* Authors' calculations.

at any point in the two years following loan issuance. The share of participants who voluntarily *increased* their contribution at any point during the two-year post-issuance period was essentially the same, with 26% of loan takers and 24% of hardship withdrawal takers doing so. The most common type of contribution rate change (affecting 38% of loan takers and 41% of hardship withdrawal takers) was automatic escalation, a common feature of automatic enrollment plans that usually raises participant contribution rates by one or two percentage points on an annual basis.[9]

Contribution rate changes during the two-year post-issuance period for both the 2017 and 2021 samples are provided in the Online Appendix. Voluntary changes are similar across the two samples. The most important difference is the share of hardship withdrawal takers whose contributions were suspended in 2017 versus 2021. Suspensions are distinct from voluntary decreases and occur when a participant's contribution rate is automatically set to zero by the plan sponsor. Prevailing IRS rules in 2017 required many plan sponsors to suspend employee contributions for the six months following a hardship withdrawal. As a result, the suspension rate in our 2017 sample was 80%. This requirement was eliminated in 2019 and the suspension rate in our 2021 sample dropped to near zero. There was only a slight rise in voluntary decreases among the 2021 sample (in which 24% of participants had a voluntary decrease versus 21% in the 2017 sample), suggesting that the pre-2019 rules mostly did not suspend participants who otherwise would have chosen to lower their contribution rates. Participants thus appeared willing and able to continue their normal contribution activity even after hardship withdrawals that often occur during periods of significant household financial stress.

## Finding 2: 401(k) Loan Takers Are Able to Sustain Their Retirement Saving During Repayment, Regardless of Loan Size

Loan takers' contribution rates (beyond their loan repayment amounts) decreased by only a small amount relative to the control group, indicating that most participants could maintain their elective contribution activity even while repaying loans. Contribution rates were similarly stable for hardship withdrawal takers when they were not subject to mandatory contribution suspensions.

Figure 12.2 illustrates our central finding: elective contribution rates were remarkably stable around and after loan issuance. Focusing on loans for $1,000 or less in the 2021 sample, we show average contribution rates and loan repayment amounts as a percentage of monthly income over the course of our 31-month time frame. Repayment amounts rose from zero in the month of loan issuance to a peak of about 2.5% of income, then

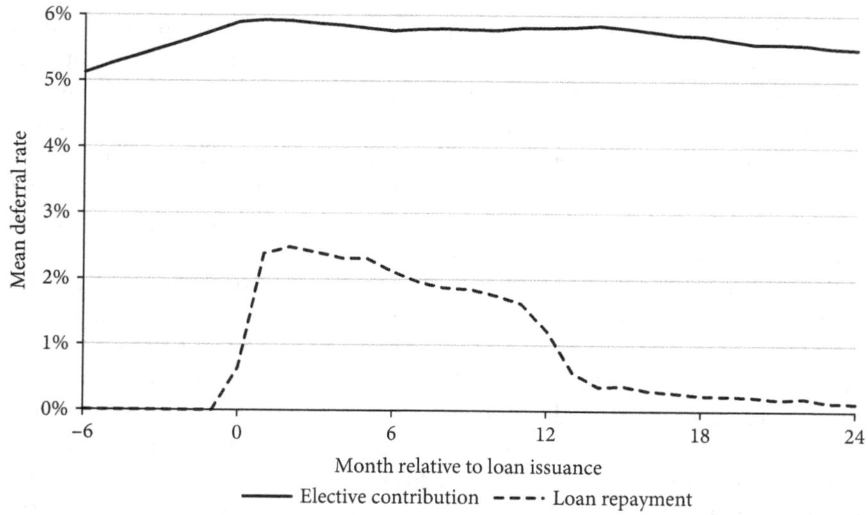


**Figure 12.2** Elective contribution rates are stable during repayment of small loans

*Notes:* We estimate loan repayment rates in the following way. First, we estimate participants' monthly income as (average monthly employee contributions between month −6 and month −1)/(average elective contribution rate between month −6 and month −1). We then divide monthly loan repayment amounts by the monthly income estimate. Loan repayment rates reflect only the loan issued in month 0. Results are shown for participants in the 2021 sample with loan issuances of $1,000 or less.

*Source:* Authors' calculations.

gradually decreased as participants with the shortest repayment schedules began to pay off their balances. Elective contribution rates showed little change during the repayment period. After increasing gradually during the pre-issuance period, the contribution rate peaked during the month of issuance, decreased slightly, then stabilized. Two years after loan issuance, contribution rates were roughly the same as a few months before issuance.

Figure 12.3 expands our analysis of post-issuance contribution behavior by considering all loans in the 2021 sample and comparing loan takers' elective contribution rates to those of their matched control participants. Because it makes a comparison to the control group, Figure 12.3 (along with Figure 12.4) restricts to the subset of loan takers who were successfully matched to a control participant. Once again, our main empirical finding is evident: loan takers' contribution rates decreased by a small amount relative to the control group. In the six months before issuance, loan takers and control participants followed the same upward trajectory (the result of annual automatic escalation policies and voluntary increases that generally caused contribution rates to trend upward over time). At the time of loan issuance, loan takers' contribution rates showed a slight decrease, then flattened out, and eventually stabilized just above their initial level. Control participants

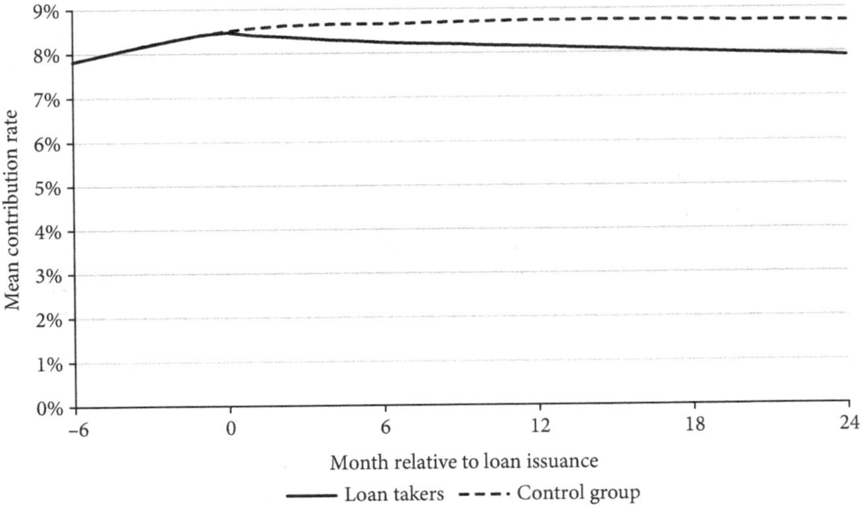


**Figure 12.3** Loan takers show little crowd-out of elective contributions relative to the control group

*Notes:* The control group is selected using the criteria discussed in the text. Results are shown for the 2021 sample of loan takers.
*Source:* Authors' calculations.

maintained their gradual contribution growth through the entire 31-month time frame. The net result at the end of the two-year post-issuance period was that loan takers' contribution rates fell by about 0.8 percentage points relative to the control group. As mean contribution rates began at roughly eight percentage points, this represents a proportional decrease of about 10%, but the decline was relatively small compared to the contemporaneous loan repayment amounts.

Figure 12.4 displays contribution crowd-out separately for four categories of loan size. It shows that the stability of loan takers' elective contributions was consistent across the loan size distribution. Contribution crowd-out evolved similarly for all four groups, and it was modestly increasing in loan size. At 24 months, participants taking loans for $1,000 or less fell 0.5 percentage points behind the control group, and those taking loans for $10,000 or more fell 1.0 percentage point behind. Since the loans in our sample most similar to the new emergency withdrawals were those for $1,000 or less, Figure 12.4 implies that the main empirical finding of limited crowd-out is just as relevant for likely emergency withdrawal takers as it is for the full participant population. The Online Appendix further splits the sample by participant income, and similarly it shows that contribution crowd-out was smaller for those with lower incomes.

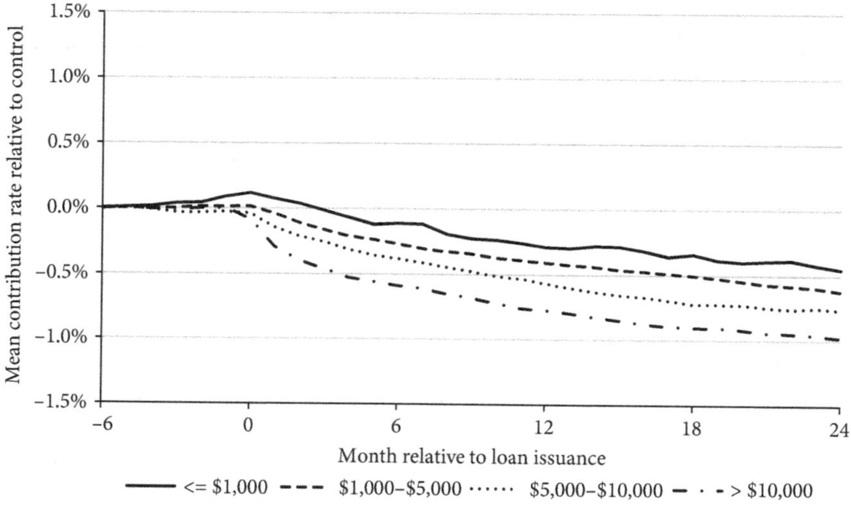


**Figure 12.4** Loan takers' contribution crowd-out is consistently small across the loan size distribution

*Notes:* This plot shows elective contribution rates for loan takers minus the elective contribution rate for their matched control participant. The results are disaggregated by the principal value of the loan issuance. Results are shown for the 2021 sample of loan takers.
*Source:* Authors' calculations.

Additional contribution and repayment results are provided in the Online Appendix. Our main crowd-out results were similar for the 2017 pre-pandemic sample. A regression analysis of the loan taker-control comparison demonstrates that the crowd-out estimates are precise (the standard error of the loan taker effect is about two basis points). The contribution crowd-out was generally larger (though still around one percentage point at 24 months) among loan takers whose initial contribution rate was strictly higher than their employer's matching contribution cap. Since participants above the cap did not lose employer matching contributions when making marginal decreases in their contribution rate, they may have had less of an incentive to maintain their elective contributions, and the slightly larger crowd-out for them is sensible. This relationship held for larger loans, but among the loans for $1,000 or less most comparable to the new emergency withdrawals, participants' placement relative to their employer's match cap did not appear to be a good predictor of contribution crowd-out.

Focusing on the extensive margin (i.e., the share of participants who made any voluntary decrease in their contribution rate), we also find that two years after issuance, the share of loan takers with at least one voluntary decrease was 12 percentage points higher than among control participants, indicating that only about half of the voluntary decreases documented in Figure 12.1 were incremental to the control group. Turning to participants' total deferral rates (elective contributions plus loan repayments), the stability of loan takers' elective contributions as loan repayment began caused their mean total deferral rate to rise by about four percentage points at the time of loan issuance, and it remained three percentage points above the control group after 24 months.

## Finding 3: Hardship Withdrawal Takers Maintained Their Retirement Savings and Benefited from Employer Matches When Their Elective Contributions Were Not Suspended

Next, we exploit a recent policy change concerning hardship withdrawals to better understand the sensitivity of contribution behavior to plan defaults. Prior to 2019, IRS rules required many plan sponsors to suspend employee contributions for the six months following a hardship withdrawal. Accordingly, 80% of participants who took a hardship withdrawal in the 2017 sample were subject to a mandatory six-month contribution suspension following the withdrawal, compared to almost no one in the 2021 sample.

Figure 12.5 shows how contribution rates evolved for participants in the 2017 and 2021 hardship withdrawal samples. The effect of the policy change is clearly visible. Mean employee contribution rates in the 2017 sample fell by 3.7 percentage points immediately after the withdrawal, then increased at the six-month mark, and eventually regained their pre-withdrawal level.

Figure 12.5 also illustrates a crucial additional cost arising from interruptions in employee contributions: foregone employer matching contributions. For participants in the 2017 sample, the total decrease in retirement saving during the six months following the withdrawal was 6.7 percentage points, after accounting for a drop in employer contributions of three percentage points.[10] By contrast, in the 2021 sample, which was not subject to mandatory suspensions, employee contribution rates were comparatively stable, decreasing slightly over the 18 months following the withdrawal before flattening out and remaining just below their initial level. The 2021 contribution path constitutes additional evidence that participants could maintain elective contributions after taking liquidity-based distributions, when plan rules allowed them to do so.

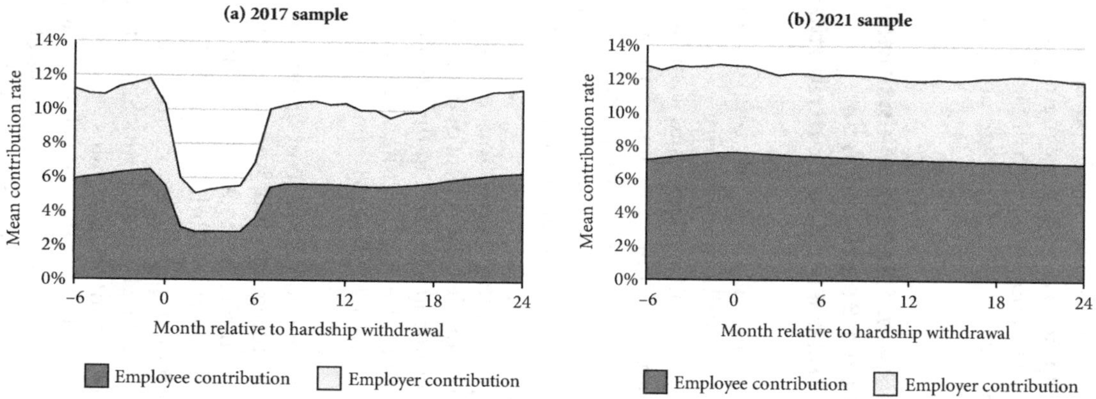


**Figure 12.5** Hardship withdrawal takers have stable contribution rates when they are not subject to mandatory suspensions

*Notes:* The employee contribution series in these plots reflect participants' elective contribution rates. The employer contribution series are computed in the following way. First, we estimate participants' monthly income as (average monthly employee contributions between month −6 and month −1)/(average elective contribution rate between month −6 and month −1). We then divide monthly employer contribution amounts by the monthly income estimate. Because the employer contribution series are derived from an income estimate and reflect monthly transaction totals (which can vary with the number of paychecks in a month, the timing of quarterly or annual employer contributions, and other factors), they are more volatile than the employee contribution series. An IRS rule requiring six-month contribution suspensions for many hardship withdrawal takers applied to the 2017 sample but not to the 2021 sample.

*Source:* Authors' calculations.

## Finding 4: Most Participants Can Repay a $1,000 Withdrawal Over the Course of Two Years Through a Two-Percentage Point Increase in Their Contributions

In light of the SECURE 2.0 provision allowing emergency withdrawals of up to $1,000, it is useful to examine potential automatic repayment time frames. Loans for $1,000 or less, which approximate the size of the new SECURE 2.0 emergency withdrawals and may be more likely to arise from short-term liquidity needs, were typically repaid within one to two years.

Observed repayment periods for 401(k) loans, often selected by the loan takers themselves, can be a useful guide to understand participants' repayment capacity. IRS rules generally require that loans be repaid within five years. As Figure 12.6 demonstrates, most of the smaller loans in our sample were repaid well in advance of this five-year limit. For loans of $1,000 or less, 50% were fully repaid within 12 months, 65% within 18 months, and 74% within 24 months. Among loans between $1,000 and $5,000, 42% were repaid within 18 months and 55% within 24 months. Most participants taking small and modest-sized loans thus appeared willing and able to repay over timelines of one to two years.

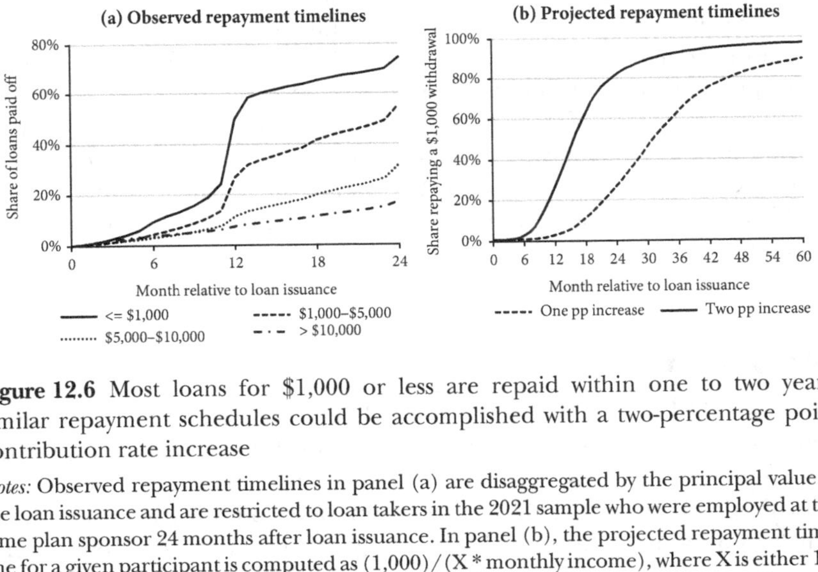


**Figure 12.6** Most loans for $1,000 or less are repaid within one to two years; similar repayment schedules could be accomplished with a two-percentage point contribution rate increase

*Notes:* Observed repayment timelines in panel (a) are disaggregated by the principal value of the loan issuance and are restricted to loan takers in the 2021 sample who were employed at the same plan sponsor 24 months after loan issuance. In panel (b), the projected repayment timeline for a given participant is computed as (1,000)/(X * monthly income), where X is either 1% or 2%. We estimate participants' monthly income as (average monthly employee contributions in the six months before loan issuance)/(average elective contribution rate in the six months before loan issuance). Projected repayment timelines are shown for the income distribution among participants in the 2021 sample with loan issuances of $1,000 or less (approximating the size of the new penalty-free emergency withdrawals, which are capped at $1,000).

*Source:* Authors' calculations.

The preceding contribution and repayment results suggest that most emergency withdrawal takers could repay the withdrawal while maintaining their previous elective contributions. Since most loans for $1,000 or less were repaid within one to two years, 18 months is a natural time period for emergency withdrawal repayment. One way to administer repayment would be to treat the emergency withdrawal in the same way that recordkeepers currently treat loans: that is, to specify a repayment length (e.g., 18 months), calculate the exact amount that must be deferred from each paycheck to repay over the specified timeline, and deduct that amount from future paychecks in addition to the participant's elective contributions. Another option, which might be easier for some recordkeepers to implement, is to increase participants' elective contribution rates by a small amount at the time of the withdrawal.[11] An integer increase in the elective contribution rate (i.e., one or two percentage points) would yield similar repayment profiles as an exact repayment schedule, but it would not require recordkeepers or participants to calculate the precise payroll deferral amount necessary to repay within a given time frame.[12]

Figure 12.6 additionally shows how an integer contribution rate increase would operate given the distribution of incomes in the 2021 loan taker sample. We limit our attention to the participants taking loans of $1,000 or less since this group tends to have lower incomes and may better represent future emergency withdrawal takers than the full loan taker sample. A two-percentage point increase appears to be a useful reference point as it would ensure that 63% of participants repaid a $1,000 withdrawal within 18 months and that 82% repaid within 24 months. A one-percentage point increase produces only an 11% repayment rate at 18 months, so this could therefore be more appropriate for participants with above-average incomes.

## Discussion

We study 401(k) participants taking loans and hardship withdrawals from their 401(k) plans because their contribution behavior provides policy-relevant insights for plan sponsors and recordkeepers. Elective contributions are remarkably stable around and following loans and hardship withdrawals, indicating that participants can maintain their normal retirement saving activity after tapping their 401(k) assets for liquidity purposes. In the case of plan loans, where elective contributions occur on top of mandatory repayments, stable contribution rates imply sharp increases in total deferral rates at the time of loan issuance. Even so, the vast majority of loan takers, who remain employed long enough to repay their loans through regular payroll deferrals, do so successfully.

For plan sponsors considering the introduction of penalty-free emergency withdrawals under SECURE 2.0, our findings suggest that most participants could repay these withdrawals while maintaining their previous elective contribution rates. Given that most of the smaller loans in our analysis were repaid within one to two years, we view repayment over 18 months as a natural starting point for an emergency withdrawal repayment schedule. A two-percentage point increase in the elective contribution rate, which could be easier for recordkeepers to implement than an exact dollar repayment schedule, would ensure that most participants repaid a $1,000 withdrawal within 18 months. Faster repayment schedules can ensure that withdrawn funds begin earning market returns sooner, but circumstances for individual participants may warrant different repayment timelines.

Important technical considerations would accompany the implementation of automatic repayments. First, as noted above, repayment could occur through explicit repayment transactions with an exact amortization schedule or via an increase in elective contribution rates. These two repayment methods have similar tax consequences for most participants,[13] and both methods reestablish participants' eligibility for future emergency withdrawals.[14] Because the two methods are largely equivalent from the participant's perspective, plan sponsors could implement repayment policies using whichever method they find easiest to adopt within their administrative and recordkeeping systems.

A major potential difference between the two repayment methods is that the employer match structure applied to explicitly designated repayments might differ from the match structure applied to elective contributions.[15] Nevertheless, plan sponsors are likely to find it easier to apply a single employer match structure to the sum of explicitly designated repayments and elective contributions. Since the two repayment methods are largely equivalent from participants' perspective, offering an employer match for one type of deferral but not the other could create an essentially dominated alternative and allow participants to make costly financial mistakes. Implementing repayment through incremental elective contributions (which always earn employer matches) would have the benefit of ensuring that participants were not presented with dominated choices.

The presence of employer matching contributions gives rise to another technical consideration for plan sponsors contemplating the introduction of emergency withdrawals: the risk of participant strategic gaming behavior. If repayments are match-eligible, then participants without actual liquidity needs could withdraw and quickly repay funds, earning additional employer matches without making net contributions to the plan (and without incurring taxes or penalties). Making explicit repayments match-ineligible would not prevent all such gaming behavior, as participants could also repay with match-eligible elective contributions. Plan sponsors must therefore determine whether the risk of undesirable gaming behavior outweigh the liquidity value their participants would derive from the new emergency withdrawals.[16]

Finally, for the substantial number of participants who take new loans each year, our empirical results may justify interventions aimed at increasing long-run retirement wealth accumulation. Plan sponsors generally have limited financial information about their participants: age and individual income are usually known, but household-level income, spending needs, total assets, and debt are almost always unknown. As a result, identifying the optimal contribution rate for any given participant is exceedingly difficult, and the default contribution rates embedded in automatic enrollment plans must be appropriate for a wide range of participants. Loan repayment provides a unique opportunity to bypass this missing information problem and directly observe whether participants are capable of increasing their deferral rates for sustained periods of time. Participants who successfully repay loans without decreasing their elective contributions demonstrate that they have this capability. By actively encouraging or defaulting these participants into elective contribution increases that make a portion of the additional repayment deferrals permanent, plan sponsors can nudge them toward higher savings rates that are demonstrably within their reach. Even a policy that maintained half of the average loan repayment amount in our sample (6% of income) would make a meaningful difference in retirement readiness.

## Conclusion

Using administrative data from Vanguard 401(k) plans, we show that participant contribution behavior is remarkably stable around and following loans and hardship withdrawals. This stability of contribution rates likely arises from participants' passive adherence to plan defaults and invites interventions from plan sponsors aimed at increasing long-run retirement saving. Among such interventions, we consider policies that automate the repayment of new penalty-free emergency withdrawals and raise contribution rates after successful loan repayment.

## Notes

1. This calculation is restricted to plans offering loans and is based on the Vanguard 401(k) administrative data described below.
2. Wenger and Weller (2014) and Mitchell et al. (2007) are notable because they studied whether the availability of plan loans increases participation and saving rates in 401(k) plans, but they did not analyze changes in contribution behavior after loan issuance.

3. Consolidated Appropriations Act of 2023, H.R. 2617, Section 114. In addition to emergency withdrawals, SECURE 2.0 also permitted employers to establish Pension Linked Emergency Savings Accounts (PLESAs) that enable employees to save for short-term needs through Roth payroll deferrals. We focus our policy discussion on the penalty-free emergency withdrawal feature because it is easier to implement than PLESAs and thus more likely to be taken up by employers in the near term.
4. As with the COVID-19 hardship withdrawals introduced in the CARES Act, employers may rely on participants' self-certification that they are experiencing the unforeseeable or immediate financial need that qualifies them for an emergency withdrawal.
5. Participants who take an emergency withdrawal are not eligible to take another emergency withdrawal until either the total amount of plan contributions they have made since the withdrawal is at least as large as the withdrawal or three years have elapsed. For example, a participant taking a $1,000 withdrawal reestablishes eligibility after making $1,000 in subsequent elective contributions. Our definition of 'repayment' is more stringent than the one used for eligibility purposes: we consider repayment to be an increase in the contribution rate that maintains participants' prior contribution activity and returns the withdrawn funds to the 401(k) account.
6. For more detailed statistics on the size and composition of Vanguard's recordkeeping population, see Clark and Young (2022) and Clark (2023).
7. Set either by default values in automatic enrollment plans or by participants' active choices, the elected contribution rate is the percentage that is multiplied by participants' earnings to determine the 401(k) contribution amounts deferred from each paycheck. Contribution rates can generally be set only in integer percentage increments (1%, 2%, 3%, etc.). To aggregate elected contribution rates to the monthly level, we take day-weighted averages (e.g., if a participant's contribution rate changes from 2% to 3% on the 15th day of the month, the corresponding monthly contribution rate is 2.5%). We sum deferral rates across all contribution types available to the participant (e.g., if a participant contributes 3% on a pre-tax basis and 3% on a Roth basis, we compute the elected contribution rate as 6%). To restrict focus to the payroll deferral burden borne by participants themselves, we consider only employee contributions and exclude all employer contributions.
8. 401(k) loan defaults occur when participants fail to make the required repayments on time. This can happen during employment if participants inform the employer that they no longer wish to have repayments deducted from their paychecks (or if repayments were collected through other means, like checks or electronic transfers, and participants unilaterally cease those transactions). Employers may also require that the full amount of any outstanding loan balances be repaid at the time of separation, and defaults can occur when separating participants are unable or unwilling to meet this accelerated repayment requirement. The outstanding balance at the time of default is treated as an early distribution on which participants must pay income taxes and a 10% penalty. See Lu et al. (2017).

9. Contribution suspensions tied to loan issuance are rare in our sample; most of the suspensions in Figure 12.2 occurred because the participant took a hardship withdrawal after loan issuance.
10. Employer contributions need not decrease by the same amount as employee contributions in Figure 12.5. This is because: (1) match schedules can award employer contributions in ratios other than 1:1 (e.g., 0.5:1 or 2:1); (2) participants already receiving the maximum employer match do not lose employer contributions until their contribution rate falls below the maximum-match threshold; and (3) some employer contributions are non-matching contributions that do not depend on the employee's contribution activity.
11. This increase in the elective contribution rate could be temporary (lasting for 18 months or some other time frame) or permanent. A temporary increase would ensure that the original withdrawal is repaid (or approximately repaid) within a specified time frame. A permanent increase could be used to encourage a sustained savings increase among participants who may be likely to take additional liquidity-based distributions in the future (since emergency withdrawals can be taken once per year and current withdrawal activity may predict future withdrawal activity).
12. Explicit repayment transactions and incremental elective contributions would have similar tax and eligibility consequences for most participants; see above.
13. Explicit repayments offset the taxable income generated by the original withdrawal. Incremental elective contributions do not erase the withdrawal's income tax liability, but if they are made on a pre-tax basis, then they reduce the participant's taxable income by the same amount and thus would have a similar effect on the participant's ultimate tax bill. One minor difference between the two methods could arise from repayment timing: if an explicit repayment is made in a different tax year than the original withdrawal, the participant may have to amend the prior tax return rather than reducing taxable income in the current tax year. If the participant's marginal tax rate differs between the two tax years, this could cause the tax consequences of an explicit repayment and elective contribution to differ.
14. In fact, participants are eligible for their next emergency withdrawal if the total amount of elective contributions they have made since the prior withdrawal is at least as large as the prior withdrawal. In other words, participants need not make incremental contributions to reestablish eligibility. As long as their initial contribution rate is sufficiently high, they will restore eligibility simply by maintaining their prior contribution activity. For example, participants who take a $1,000 emergency withdrawal and have a 4% contribution rate will reestablish eligibility within a year as long as their annual salary is at least $25,000. This means that most participants will reestablish eligibility in the normal course of their contribution activity, which makes eligibility considerations relatively unimportant from a plan-design perspective.
15. Another difference between the two methods is that elective contributions are constrained by the 402(g) limits on annual employee contributions whereas explicit repayments are not. Because emergency withdrawal usage is likely to be

relatively uncommon among participants contributing at the 402(g) limit, this distinction is unlikely to matter in practice.

16. One important factor to consider when making this determination is the share of participants who are currently contributing at or above the employer match cap (since these participants do not earn matches on marginal contributions and thus would not have gaming incentives).

## References

Beshears, J., J. Choi, D. Laibson, and B. Madrian. (2012). 'The Availability and Utilization of 401(k) Loans.' In D. A. Wise, ed., *Investigations in the Economics of Aging*. Chicago: University of Chicago Press, pp. 145–178.

Clark, J. W. (2023). *How Americans Can Save More for Retirement*. Malvern, PA: The Vanguard Group. institutional.vanguard.com/content/dam/inst/iig-transformation/insights/pdf/2023/how-americans-can-save-more-for-retirement.pdf

Clark, J. W. and J. A. Young (2022). 'The Vanguard Participant Saving Rate Index.' *Vanguard Research*, July. Malvern, PA: The Vanguard Group.

Lu, T., O. S. Mitchell, S. P. Utkus, and J. A. Young. (2017). 'Borrowing from the Future? 401(k) Plan Loans and Loan Defaults.' *National Tax Journal*, 70(1): 77–109.

Mitchell, O. S., S. P. Utkus, and S. Yang. (2007). 'Turning Workers into Savers? Incentives, Liquidity, and Choice in 401(k) Plan Design.' *National Tax Journal*, 60(3): 469–489.

Wenger, J. B. and C. E. Weller. (2014). 'Boon or Bane: 401(k) Loans and Employee Contributions.' *Research on Aging*, 36(5): 527–556.

Chapter 13

# Reforming the US Long-Term Care Insurance Market

*R. Anton Braun and Karen A. Kopecky*

One of the biggest financial risks Americans face late in life is the risk of needing formal long-term care (LTC) assistance. One in three 50-year-old Americans will experience a health event that results in a nursing home (NH) stay in excess of 100 days, and about one in 10 will incur out-of-pocket LTC expenses of $200,000 or more (Braun et al. 2019; Favreault and Dey 2022).

The baby boomers are now moving into retirement, and as they age, the overall number of LTC events and aggregate losses associated with these events will increase. This will stress government coffers and the personal finances of aging boomers. The Penn Wharton Budget Model predicts that expenditures on LTC by Medicaid, the main public insurer, will increase from 0.62% of GDP in 2022 to 1.25% of GDP by 2050 (He 2022). Medicaid expenditures account for about half of total aggregate expenditures on LTC services (Chidambaram and Burns 2022). Therefore, total US expenditures on LTC could rise from about 1.2% of GDP to as high as 2.5%.

Given the high probability of a costly LTC event, one might expect that the private market for long-term care insurance (LTCI) would be healthy and growing. Yet surprisingly, only 10% of Americans age 65+ own a private LTCI policy, and the number of individuals with such a policy has been falling steadily since 2021. The objectives of this chapter are to describe how Americans currently cope with LTC risk, provide an assessment of why the private LTCI market is so small, and consider alternative strategies for reforming the market.

## Demand For and Provision of Long-Term Care Services in the US

### What Is Long-Term Care?

People's demand for health care services can be categorized into three main types: acute care, hospice care, and LTC. Acute care consists of medical

R. Anton Braun and Karen A. Kopecky, *Reforming the US Long-Term Care Insurance Market.* In: *Retirement Saving, Investment, and Spending.* Edited by: Olivia S. Mitchell and Nikolai Roussanov, Oxford University Press.

DOI: 10.1093/oso/9780197845752.003.0013

and/or nursing interventions aimed at treating specific acute conditions, such as an infection, heart attack, or injury, with the goal of promoting recovery. Hospice care provides support to individuals who are disabled and nearing death. LTC services offer ongoing assistance with daily activities for individuals who are not in the terminal stage of life. The primary objectives of LTC are to enhance individuals' quality of life and promote functional independence.

The extent of need for LTC services is usually determined by counting the number of activities of daily living (ADLs) a person is unable to perform without assistance. The six ADLs consist of eating, bathing, dressing, transferring in and out of a chair or bed, toileting, and continence. An additional determinant of LTC service needs is cognitive decline, often measured by counting the number of instrumental activities of daily living (IADLs) a person is unable to perform without assistance. Examples of IADLs include an individual's ability to manage their own medication, shop for groceries, prepare meals, use a telephone, drive or use transportation, handle personal finances, do laundry, and housekeep. The Health Insurance Portability and Accountability Act of 1996 defines an LTC event as requiring assistance with two or more ADLs for an expected duration of 90 days or more or needing substantial supervision due to severe cognitive impairment. The IRS uses this definition to determine whether premiums paid for a private LTCI are tax deductible.

In the analysis that follows, we summarize the demand for LTC services using a frailty index that combines into a single measure an individual's difficulty with ADLs and IADLs, and other indicators of health status following Braun et al. (2019). A higher value of the index corresponds to a higher level of frailty.

## Who Needs Long-Term Care?

The likelihood of needing LTC services varies systematically with gender, marital status, education, and wealth. This is partly due to the fact that LTC needs are positively correlated with age. Women typically outlive men, and individuals with higher levels of education and wealth tend to have higher life expectancies than the less-educated and less-affluent. The intensity of LTC needs also varies by demographic characteristics. Females in a given age group tend to have higher rates of difficulties with ADLs and IADLs than males of the same age, and individuals who are single or unmarried tend to have poorer health as compared to married individuals.

Thus, the evidence shows that at age 65, the likelihood of experiencing a LTC event before death is 47% for men and 58% for women, 51% for married individuals, and 54% for unmarried individuals.[1] The average duration of care is currently 3.2 years for men and 4.4 years for women. Married individuals experience an average of 3.6 years of care whereas unmarried individuals use care for 4.3 years.

### Who Provides Long-Term Care Services?

About 69% of LTC services in the US are provided informally by a relative, 18% are provided by formal care providers at home, and 13% are provided in skilled NH facilities. The typical caregiver is a woman in her fifties or sixties who provides care for her mother. Informal care provided by the spouse is also common accounting for 32% of informal LTC services (Gruber and McGarry 2025).

Informal care is frequently provided either for free or at rates well below market prices. Yet many family members and spouses are inadequately equipped to provide LTC services to persons with multiple ADLs and/or IADLs. Consequently, approximately 45% of those age 65 are projected to experience an LTC event that necessitates the use of formal LTC services before their deaths. Of these, 53% will require less than one year of formal care, 37% will need two to four years of formal care, and 10% will require more than five years of formal LTC services (Favreault and Johnson 2021).

Formal care in the US is also quite expensive. The Genworth (2024) Cost of Care Survey reported that the median cost of one year of assisted living services in 2024 was $70,800, the median cost of formal home-provided health care was $70,720, and the median cost of a private room in a skilled nursing home facility was $111,325. Given the magnitude of these expenses combined with the fact that they tend to be concentrated near the end of life, one might expect that there would be a large and active private insurance market for LTC risks. Nevertheless, as we explain next, this is not the case.

## US Insurance Arrangements for Long-Term Care Risk

### Public Insurance

One reason we draw a distinction between acute health care and hospice care on the one hand and LTC on the other, is the structure of insurance markets in the US for these risks. Medicare offers near-universal public coverage for individuals age 65+, serving as the primary payer of acute health care expenses including formal care services during short-term hospital and/or nursing home stays lasting 20 to 90 days.[2] Medicare also covers hospice care for individuals certified as disabled and nearing the end of life. Yet Medicare does not provide insurance coverage for LTC events, such as nursing home stays exceeding 90 days.

A different government program, Medicaid, does provide coverage of long-term nursing home stays, but it is a secondary payer, and eligibility hinges on satisfying strict income and asset tests. For instance, the asset threshold in most states is set at less than $3,000. As a secondary payer, Medicaid only steps in once individuals have exhausted their private LTCI benefits, spent down most of their assets (equity in a home is exempt or deferred in some cases), and depleted Social Security and other retirement income. Moreover, Medicaid imposes strict guidelines regarding the nursing home amenities it covers (Kaiser Commission on Medicaid and the Uninsured 2010; MedicaidLongTermCare.org 2024).

## The Private LTCI Market

Despite the limited coverage of LTC risks provided by public insurance in the US, the private market for LTCI is small, and the market has been declining steadily since 2012—only about 10% of current retirees hold such a policy (Braun et al. 2019). For perspective, according to the National Association of Insurance Commissioners (2025), approximately 5.1 million individuals in the US owned an LTCI policy in 2022. In contrast, in 2021, over 55 million individuals (comprising 95% of those enrolled in both Medicare Part A and Part B) had Medicare Advantage or supplemental Medicare benefits managed by a private insurer.[3]

The US LTCI market has other noteworthy characteristics emphasized in previous literature (e.g., Braun et al. 2019; Brown and Finkelstein 2007; Gruber and McGarry 2025). Premiums for LTCI policies are higher than for life insurance products, representative LTCI policies offer incomplete coverage against expected losses, and denial rates of applicants by private insurers are high. Hendren (2013) attributed the last observation to adverse selection and Chade and Schlee (2020) showed that it is optimal for a monopolist that faces variable administrative costs to deny coverage to adversely selected risk groups.

## Why Don't Americans Purchase LTCI?

There is an urgent need to reform the US LTCI market. But to properly target policy reforms and build a consensus behind them, we require a better understanding of demand elasticities for private LTCI. In particular, it is necessary to understand how these elasticities vary across individuals due to differences in their exposures to LTC risk as well as their alternative insurance options. For instance, a wealthy individual may prefer to self-insure against LTC risk if private LTCI insurance is sufficiently expensive. We also need to understand why LTCI is so expensive and why some risk groups are denied coverage. Additionally, we need to understand how supply-side frictions influence the pricing and coverage of insurance contracts offered by private insurers. To this end, we now analyze how Medicaid, administrative costs, and adverse selection influence LTCI take-up, coverage levels, and pricing using a generalized version of the model of Braun et al. (2019).

## Medicaid, Administrative Costs, and Adverse Selection Drive Low LTCI Take-Up Rates

Braun et al. (2019) developed a quantitative structural model of the US private LTCI market, which we use in the analysis below. Individuals in the model differ by permanent earnings (PE) and frailty. They work when young and save for their retirement. Upon retiring, they receive private information about their likelihood of needing formal LTC in the future. The retirement period then proceeds in two stages. During the first stage, people experience a shock to their wealth as well as a mortality shock. Individuals who survive move to the second stage where they face a LTC shock.

In the model, people have three ways to ensure against the risk of becoming old, impoverished, and in need of LTC. First, they can self-insure by saving while working. Second, they can purchase private LTCI at the beginning of retirement. Third, they can receive assistance from public insurance provided by the government, modeled after the main features of Medicaid. Public LTC benefits are means-tested and public LTCI is a secondary payer, meaning government benefits are only provided to individuals after they exhaust any private LTCI benefits. Finally, the government guarantees a minimum consumption level for destitute individuals. Our model is designed to isolate LTC risk from other risks such as mortality, eliminating the need for additional insurance options.

Private LTCI contracts are offered to individuals by an insurer with monopoly power, who faces fixed as well as variable costs of insurance provision. The private insurer also contends with information constraints, since it only observes individuals' PE and frailty, both of which are noisy indicators of peoples' true health status. Using this imperfect information, the insurer sorts people into risk groups, where individuals in each risk group have private information about whether they are healthy and their risk of needing formal LTC will be low, or unhealthy and will have a high risk of needing such care. We do not explicitly model informal care, but it is worth keeping in mind that private information can encompass additional unobserved factors, such as the willingness and availability of family members to provide informal care services. Within a given risk group, unhealthy individuals have less elastic demand for private LTCI compared with healthy ones, while healthy individuals are less costly to insure. The insurer designs a menu of contracts for each risk group, which recognizes these distinctions between potential LTCI purchasers. Offering any amount of insurance to some risk groups may be unprofitable for the insurer, in which case, the insurer will deny coverage to that entire risk group. Coverage denials are more likely in risk groups where adverse selection problems are severe.

The specific timing of the model is illustrated in Figure 13.1. In period one, young individuals learn their PE and frailty status. At the same time, LTC insurers observe the population distributions of PE and frailty, and they design insurance contracts. Individuals then receive an initial endowment of earnings, and they make consumption and savings decisions. In period two, individuals receive a second endowment, representing their private and public pension income. They also discover their true private health type and decide whether to purchase a private LTCI contract if offered by the insurer. After this decision, they experience a consumption demand (wealth) shock and draw a realization from the survival distribution. The consumption demand shock is a parsimonious way to capture surprises requiring people to draw down wealth prior to the arrival of the nursing home shock. For instance, some people may experience large out-of-pocket medical expenses before entering a NH or may enter a NH later in life than others and have less residual wealth to provision for their care. Individuals who survive to period three make no new decisions, but they face the risk of requiring costly LTC. NH entrants who hold a private LTCI policy are indemnified by the insurer. After private insurance has paid, those with low remaining wealth receive public LTC benefits.

In the model, the demand for private LTCI varies with both permanent earnings and frailty status. For instance, those with low PE and low wealth are more likely to not purchase private insurance, due to the secondary payer provision of the public LTCI program. Conversely, high PE and high wealth individuals are more likely to decide to self-insure if the cost of private LTCI is too high.

Our ultimate objective is to assess the potential value of reforms to the LTCI market, so we made the following modifications to the model (see Braun and Kopecky 2024). First, we introduce a government budget constraint and assume that the public LTCI program is funded by a linear income tax on people's labor and asset income. Second, we close the economy by assuming the private LTC insurer is owned by people in the top 1% of the PE distribution and its profits are equally distributed among them. Third, we assume that like the private insurer, the public LTCI program faces costs of insurance provision.

The model is then parameterized to be consistent with many features of the US LTCI market. This is done by setting parameters either directly based on data or choosing them such that the model reproduces targeted data moments.[4] Table 13.1 highlights several of the empirical moments used in the calibration procedure together with their model counterparts. All dollar amounts are reported in 2024 US dollars.

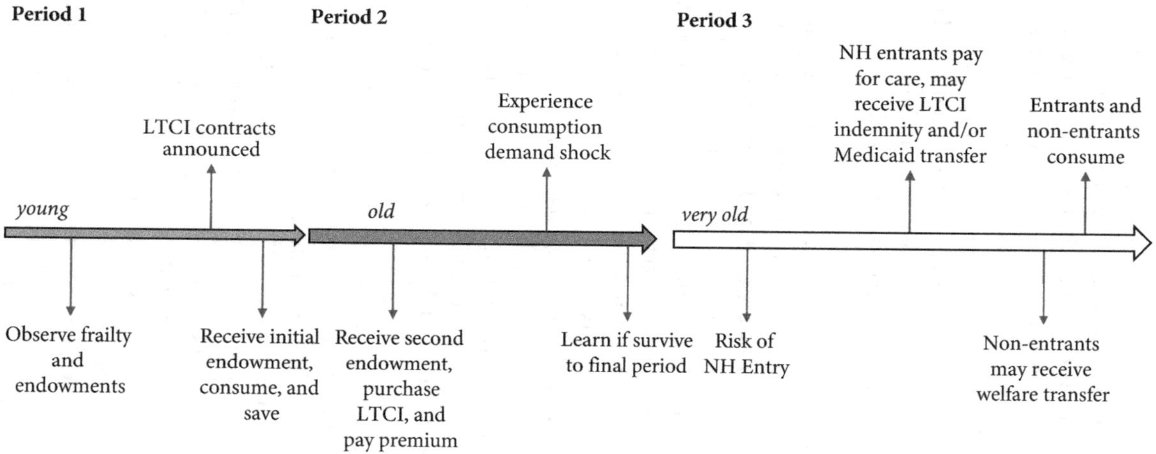


**Figure 13.1** Timeline of events in the model

*Source:* Authors' calculations.

TABLE 13.1 Data Facts That the Model Reproduces

| Data values set directly | |
|---|---|
| **Statistic** | **Data and Model** |
| permanent earnings (average, annualized) | $47,772 |
| replacement rate of retirement income (average) (%) | 57 |
| probability NH entry (average) | 0.30 |
| medical and nursing cost of LTC event | $117,974 |
| public insurance consumption floor | $11,916 |

| Data values targeted in calibration procedure | | |
|---|---|---|
| **Statistic** | **Data** | **Model** |
| wealth at NH entry/wealth ages 62–72 (average) | 0.62 | 0.65 |
| fraction of nursing home residents on Medicaid | 0.46 | 0.50 |
| private insurer's administrative costs (share of present value premium) | | |
| fixed cost (%) | 20 | 20 |
| variable cost (%) | 12.6 | 12.9 |

*Notes:* This table reports the fit of the model with statistics from US data that the model has been parameterized to reproduce.
*Source:* HRS and authors' calculations.

People in the model differ by PE and frailty, and these differences are correlated with their retirement income, wealth, survival, and nursing home entry risk. Average individuals in the model earn $47,772 a year and work for 40 years. Their retirement income replacement rate is 57%. Retirees face a 30% chance of surviving to the final period of life, entering a nursing home and incurring associated expenses of $177,974. Upon NH entry, their initial wealth will have declined by 32% on average. These statistics are taken from Braun et al. (2019) and details on the US data sources and construction can be found there. Here we highlight some key definitions. PE is computed as average annual earnings multiplied by 40 years and the replacement rate of retirement income is the ratio of Social Security and private pension income to labor earnings for Health and Retirement Study (HRS) respondents. Wealth at the age of NH entry relative to retirement and the probability of ultimately entering a nursing home for a long-term stay are also estimated using HRS data. Finally, NH expenses are given by the average costs of three years of care in a residential LTC facility in 2000. They consist of medical and nursing costs of residential LTC only. Room and board as well as other NH amenities are a consumption choice decision in the model.

To incorporate the scale of the public LTCI (Medicaid) program, we set the consumption floor of individuals in the final stage of life to $11,916 per year. The consumption floor derives from assuming a consumption allowance of $55 per month, and housing and food expenses of $938 per month. The $55 allowance aligns with Medicaid administrative rules, while $938 is the amount provided for a single elderly individual by the Supplemental Security Income system (Brown and Finkelstein 2007; Social Security Administration 2023). The fraction of NH residents on Medicaid in the model is 50%, in line with the Medicaid recipiency rate of NH residents in our HRS sample (Braun et al. 2019).

The fixed and variable costs of LTCI provision are set such that the private insurer in the model incurs administrative costs of insurance provision, which align with those in the industry. According to Eaton (2016), fixed administrative costs, which include underwriting costs and costs of paying claims, were 20% of present-value premium on average in 2000. Variable costs, including commissions and fees paid to agents and brokers, amounted to 12.6% of present-value premium. One potential benefit of public insurance provision is lower costs. That is, a public insurer does not conduct underwriting nor pay commissions to agents and brokers. To capture this difference between public and private insurance provision in a simple way, we assume that both insurers face the same variable administrative costs but that the fixed costs are only incurred by the private insurer.

Recall that the private insurer sorts individuals into risk groups based on their observed PE and frailty. Figure 13.2 illustrates that the model reproduces the variation in average NH entry across these groups. Higher PE in the model is associated with a slightly lower risk of NH entry, as in the data. Likewise, the model reproduces the slight decline in NH entry with frailty. The fact that NH entry declines with frailty in the data may be surprising, but the NH entry rates in Figure 13.2 are not conditional on survival. Highly frail individuals have a much lower probability of surviving to the final period of life when NH entry occurs.

Within each risk group, individuals differ in their true NH entry risk, which is private information. All else being equal, the larger the dispersion in private information within a risk group, the more severe the adverse selection problem within that group, and consequently, the higher the probability that the group will be denied coverage by the private insurer. Accordingly, we use the variation in LTCI take-up rates across PE and frailty quintiles to determine the unobserved differences in NH entry risk between healthy and unhealthy types. As Figure 13.2 shows, the model fits patterns of LTCI take-up with PE and frailty well. To further assess model fit, we compare the variation in private NH risk in the model to the variation in self-predicted NH entry probabilities of respondents in the HRS. These two probabilities are not exactly the same. HRS respondents are asked to report their self-assessed probability of NH entry in the next five years whereas the model values are lifetime NH entry probabilities. Still, the dispersion in these probabilities varies with PE and frailty similarly in the model and the data.

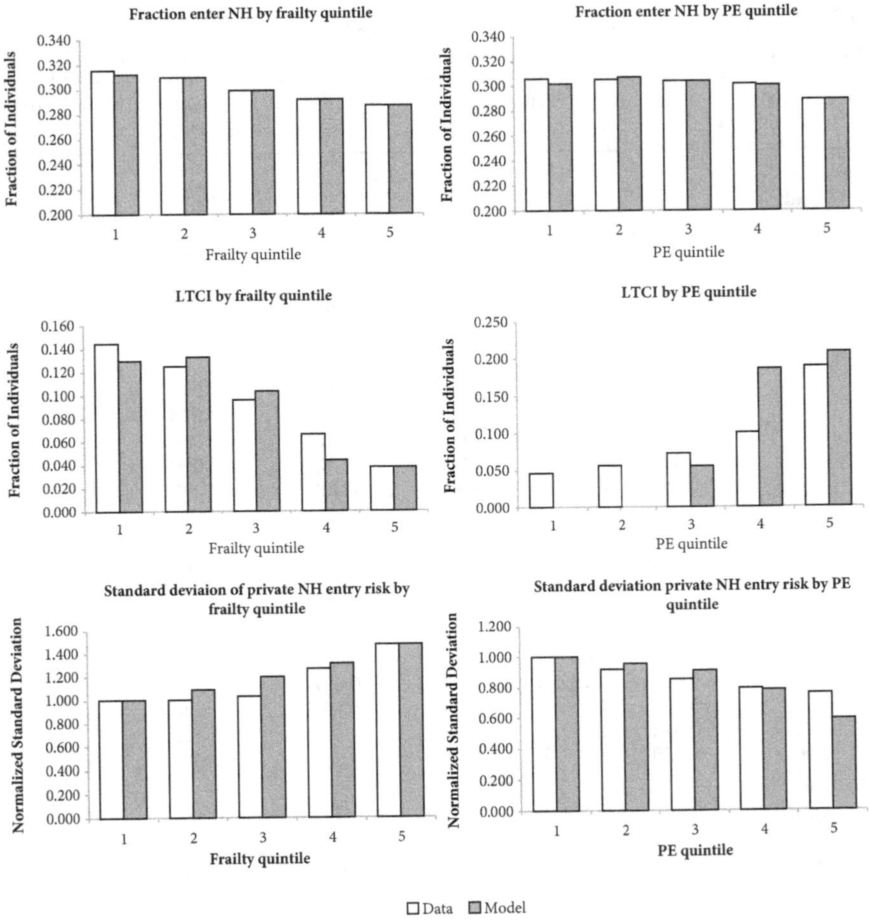


**Figure 13.2** NH entry rates, LTCI take-up rates, and the standard deviation of private NH entry risk by frailty and permanent earnings (PE) quintiles in the model and the data

*Notes:* NH entry rates are the estimated fraction of 65-year-olds who enter a NH for a stay of at least 90 days before the end of life. The standard deviations are of the self-reported probability of entering a NH within the next five years for HRS respondents ages 65 and older. The standard deviations are normalized such that the standard deviation in frailty (PE) quintile one is 1.

*Source:* HRS and authors' calculations.

Table 13.2 reports summary statistics about LTCI take-up rates, LTCI coverage levels, and pricing for our baseline specification, along with four counterfactuals. Turning first to the baseline results, we observe that it reproduces the empirical observation that LTCI take-up rates are low: only

TABLE 13.2 LTCI Take-Up, Coverage, and Loads in the Baseline, No Administrative Costs, No Medicaid, Full Information, and Public Partnership (PP) Economies

| Scenario | Baseline | No Admin. Costs | No Medicaid | Full Information | Public Partnership (PP) |
|---|---|---|---|---|---|
| Average LTCI take-up rate | 0.090 | 0.597 | 0.904 | 0.370 | 0.618 |
| Fraction of NH costs covered | 0.603 | 0.621 | 0.661 | 0.832 | 0.284 |
| Load | 0.406 | 0.330 | 0.557 | 0.480 | 0.662 |
| Take-up rates by PE Quintile | | | | | |
| 1 | 0.000 | 0.000 | 0.719 | 0.000 | 0.000 |
| 2 | 0.000 | 0.004 | 1.000 | 0.005 | 0.243 |
| 3 | 0.055 | 1.000 | 1.000 | 0.437 | 1.000 |
| 4 | 0.186 | 1.000 | 1.000 | 0.709 | 1.000 |
| 5 | 0.209 | 0.979 | 0.802 | 0.700 | 0.845 |
| High PE | | | | | |
| top 10 | 0.167 | 0.959 | 0.605 | 0.690 | 0.690 |
| top5 | 0.333 | 0.917 | 0.238 | 0.671 | 0.380 |
| top1 | 0.000 | 0.291 | 0.000 | 0.000 | 0.000 |
| Coverage rates by PE Quintile | | | | | |
| 1 | 0.000 | 0.000 | 0.934 | 0.000 | 0.000 |
| 2 | 0.000 | 0.426 | 0.731 | 0.692 | 0.153 |
| 3 | 0.577 | 0.500 | 0.598 | 0.767 | 0.226 |
| 4 | 0.572 | 0.609 | 0.561 | 0.824 | 0.313 |
| 5 | 0.638 | 0.756 | 0.533 | 0.880 | 0.356 |
| High PE | | | | | |
| top 10 | 0.601 | 0.714 | 0.496 | 0.838 | 0.340 |
| top5 | 0.601 | 0.622 | 0.487 | 0.799 | 0.344 |
| top1 | 0.000 | 1.000 | 0.000 | 0.000 | 0.000 |
| Loads by PE Quintile | | | | | |
| 1 | NA | NA | 0.646 | NA | NA |
| 2 | NA | 0.271 | 0.592 | 0.402 | 0.693 |
| 3 | 0.418 | 0.307 | 0.550 | 0.492 | 0.722 |
| 4 | 0.414 | 0.353 | 0.526 | 0.497 | 0.646 |
| 5 | 0.396 | 0.331 | 0.482 | 0.456 | 0.601 |
| High PE | | | | | |
| top 10 | 0.404 | 0.333 | 0.467 | 0.449 | 0.600 |
| top5 | 0.404 | 0.361 | 0.465 | 0.421 | 0.593 |
| top1 | NA | 0.118 | NA | NA | NA |

*Notes:* Results are reported by permanent earnings (PE) quintiles and for the top 10, 5, and 1 percentiles of the PE distribution.
*Source:* Authors' calculations.

9% of individuals purchase private LTCI. Our discussion above also noted that LTCI take-up rates are higher for higher PE quintiles in the data. An attractive feature of our model is that we can inspect LTCI take-up rates not only at PE quintiles but also among the highest PE groups. Table 13.2

indicates that the relationship between LTCI and PE is more subtle than our data suggest. LTCI take-up rates in the model are hump-shaped in PE. Demand for private LTCI insurance is zero for the lowest PE individuals because they qualify for free Medicaid LTC benefits. LTCI take-up rates are higher for middle-class individuals, but they are lower in the right tail of the PE distribution and fall to zero for the highest one percentile PE individuals. The most affluent individuals in our model prefer to self-insure against LTC risk.

The baseline specification also reproduces the empirical observations that LTCI policy coverage is incomplete and the price of LTCI insurance is high. On average, LTCI only covers 60% of expected LTC expenses in the model. To measure pricing distortions, we express premiums as loads—that is, as markups over the premium for actuarily fair insurance. The average load in our model is 41%. Table 13.2 also shows how coverage and loads vary with PE. Coverage rates rise with PE for most of the distribution because, as the likelihood of qualifying for Medicaid LTC benefits declines, individuals demand more coverage from the private insurer. Yet the highest PE individuals have the resources to self-insure most or even all of the costs of a LTC event, so the insurer responds by offering them less coverage and slightly lower loads.

The impact of Medicaid, administrative costs, and adverse selection on take-up rates and policies in the private LTCI market are apparent in Columns 2–4 of Table 13.2. LTCI products are more costly for insurers to administer than other insurance products. Screening of applicants is more thorough, and regulators require that insurers hold more reserves to provision for aggregate variation in interest rates and lapse rates. Insurers must often also pay benefits for multiple years, and hence they need to monitor recipients to ascertain whether LTC events are ongoing. These frictions are captured in the model with fixed and variable costs of writing LTCI policies. The 'no administrative costs' scenario sets these costs to zero. Removing administrative costs has a substantial impact on private LTCI rates, which increase from 9% to 60%. The poorest individuals still opt out, but all other PE groups purchase private LTCI. The increase in LTCI take-up is particularly pronounced among the highest PE individuals. LTCI coverage rates also increase but are still incomplete. Private LTCI now covers 62% of expected LTC expenses on average, as compared to 60% in the baseline, and loads fall both on average and across the PE distribution. Overall, removing administrative costs has the biggest impact on high PE individuals since without administrative costs, the insurer can now accommodate them with higher coverage and lower load contracts.

Next, we turn to the 'no Medicaid' economy. This scenario lowers the consumption floor provided by the public LTCI program to near zero.[5] As with administrative costs, removing Medicaid has a large impact on LTCI take-up rates, which rise from 9% to 90%. Coverage rates of LTCI policies also increase from 60% to 66%, but coverage remains incomplete. Removing Medicaid boosts the demand for private insurance significantly, and the insurer responds by charging higher premiums. On average, the load rises to 0.56 from 0.41 in the baseline. Removing Medicaid has the most pronounced impact on individuals with relatively low financial resources. They are the biggest beneficiaries of Medicaid, and without this program, they have relatively inelastic demand for private LTCI. Individuals in the lowest PE quintile receive nearly complete coverage in the event of a loss, but they also face the highest load. Coverage ratios and loads both fall monotonically with PE. Removing Medicaid has the smallest impact on the most affluent individuals, as they have adequate resources to self-insure against LTC risk and only a small fraction will qualify for Medicaid coverage in the baseline economy.

The fourth column of Table 13.2 documents how LTCI take-up rates and policies change when private information frictions are absent. In this scenario, the insurer directly observes each individual's risk exposure and price discriminates accordingly. A healthy (good risk) individual now faces lower premiums than an unhealthy (bad risk) individual in the same risk group. LTCI take-up rates rise to 37%, but this reflects greater take-ups by good risk types who are less costly to insure. Take-up rates of the bad risk types, in contrast, decline since they are not only more expensive to insure but the costs of their policies are also no longer subsidized by the healthier individuals in their risk group. As a result, their premiums are now higher than in the baseline. This full information scenario indicates that asymmetric information plays a central role in producing incomplete coverage. LTCI now covers 83% of the loss, as compared to 60% in the baseline specification. When the insurer directly observes each individual's private health type, it no longer needs to drive down coverage levels and raise premiums for good risk types to prevent bad risk types from preferring the good-type contract.

In summary, our structural model reveals the important and distinct effects of Medicaid, administrative costs and adverse selection on the private LTCI market. All three factors reduce LTCI take-up and coverage rates; however, administrative costs raise premium loads whereas Medicaid and adverse selection lower them. Additionally, the effects on take-up and coverage vary with PE. While all three factors are important for middle-income individuals, Medicaid matters most for the low take-up and coverage rates among poorer individuals, and administrative costs and adverse selection are most important for the low take-up and coverage of those with high PE.

## Reforming the US LTCI Market

Our discussion thus far documents that the risk of needing LTC is high for older individuals, and the market price of LTC services is substantial relative to their resources during the life stage where this risk is most pronounced. Even though retirees have a high likelihood of incurring a costly LTC event, the US private LTCI market suffers from low take-up rates, and few policies that provide complete coverage of LTC costs at actuarily fair premiums. As Americans age, a higher fraction of the US population will be exposed to LTC risk in the future. This will create fiscal stress because higher government outlays will be required to maintain current levels of public LTCI. Aging could also have negative macroeconomic consequences if a rising share of households consumes less and saves more to provide for LTC.

Results from our quantitative model indicate that Medicaid has a particularly large and negative impact on private LTCI take-up, especially for middle- and lower-income individuals. Nevertheless, private LTCI take-up rates are also low among those with high incomes who choose to self-insure LTC risk. In this section, we ask whether it makes more sense to reduce the scale of Medicaid to foster a larger private market or to instead increase the scale of Medicaid and offer universal coverage for LTC risk.

To answer this question, we assess the impact of reducing or increasing the scale of public LTCI using three criteria. The first is the fiscal cost of providing public LTC insurance, measured by the tax burden on individuals. The second focuses on how each reform influences the functioning of the private LTCI market. And the third evaluates how each measure affects aggregate and individual welfare.

In the ensuing discussion, it will be helpful to keep in mind that two general equilibrium effects operate in the model. First, Medicaid is financed by a linear income tax, and any changes in the scale of Medicaid are accompanied by corresponding changes in the income tax rate. Second, the private insurer's profits are distributed to individuals in the top 1% of PE. Thus, changes in the profitability of offering private LTCI affect the incomes of the most affluent individuals in the economy.

We start by analyzing the 'no Medicaid' economy introduced above, where the consumption floor guaranteed by the public LTCI program is close to zero (as in Braun and Kopecky 2024). The upper panel of Table 13.3 reports the aggregate effects of this policy reform. Scaling back Medicaid substantially produces large fiscal savings. The low guaranteed consumption floor implies that only the neediest NH entrants qualify for public LTCI benefits, and the fraction of individuals receiving Medicaid transfers falls from 50% to 6%. Consequently, Medicaid outlays decline by 88.4%, which induces a reduction in the tax rate because the government has smaller tax revenue needs.

TABLE 13.3 Welfare and Indicators of Private and Public LTCI in the Baseline, No Medicaid, Universal Medicaid, and Public Partnership (PP) Economies

| Scenario | Baseline | No Medicaid | Universal Medicaid | Public Partnership (PP) |
|---|---|---|---|---|
| Welfare (newborn) | −2.778 | −3.396 | −2.776 | −2.774 |
| Compensating variations (%) | | 22.23 | −0.071 | −0.129 |
| Average: | | | | |
| Medicaid outlays (% change from baseline) | | −88.44 | 173.9 | 8.758 |
| Govt tax revenue | 0.018 | 0.002 | 0.041 | 0.020 |
| NH entrants on Medicaid (%) | 49.94 | 5.564 | 100.0 | 56.00 |
| Profits/Premium revenue (%) | 0.101 | 31.39 | 0.000 | 31.68 |
| LTCI take-up rate | 0.090 | 0.904 | 0.000 | 0.618 |
| Fraction of NH costs covered | 0.603 | 0.661 | NA | 0.284 |
| Load | 0.406 | 0.557 | NA | 0.662 |
| Profits/Premium revenue (%) by PE Quintile | | | | |
| 1 | NA | 35.51 | NA | NA |
| 2 | NA | 37.40 | NA | 9.338 |
| 3 | 0.002 | 22.67 | NA | 39.56 |
| 4 | 0.033 | 16.84 | NA | 29.56 |
| 5 | 0.011 | 7.990 | NA | 19.83 |
| High PE | | | | |
| top 10 | 0.022 | 2.550 | NA | 14.36 |
| top5 | 0.045 | 0.718 | NA | 7.030 |
| top1 | NA | NA | NA | NA |
| Compensating variations (%) by PE Quintile | | | | |
| 1 | | 44.18 | 3.282 | 0.081 |
| 2 | | 11.76 | −2.299 | 0.094 |
| 3 | | 2.037 | −4.160 | −0.677 |
| 4 | | −0.434 | −2.547 | −0.559 |
| 5 | | −1.913 | −0.267 | −0.245 |
| High PE | | | | |
| top 10 | | −2.785 | 0.421 | −0.432 |
| top5 | | −4.274 | 1.024 | −0.959 |
| top1 | | −15.85 | 2.029 | −5.933 |

*Notes:* Results are reported by permanent earnings (PE) quintiles and for the top 10, 5, and 1 percentiles of the PE distribution.
*Source:* Authors' calculations.

Reducing the scale of Medicaid has a large impact on the demand for private LTCI, especially for lower- and middle-income individuals. Aggregate LTCI take-up rates increase by a factor of 10 rising from 9% to 90%, driven by a dramatic increase in demand among those in PE quintiles 1–4

(Table 13.2). Absent public insurance, the relatively inelastic private LTCI demand of individuals in lowest income groups is good for the insurer, who responds by charging higher loads. Profits increase from 0.1% to 31.4% of premium revenue, with a large share of this increase generated by low- and middle-class individuals (Table 13.3).

Given these outcomes, it is perhaps not surprising that aggregate welfare will decline if Medicaid were essentially removed. As shown in Table 13.3, newborn who do not yet know their initial PE and frailty levels will be worse off in the 'no Medicaid' scenario than in the baseline. Indeed, a newborn in the 'no Medicaid' scenario would need 22.2% more consumption to be indifferent between this scenario and the baseline economy. Welfare losses are particularly high among the low income: the compensating variation for individuals in the lowest PE quintile is 44.2%. High PE groups in contrast prefer the 'no Medicaid' economy, as they are less likely to qualify for Medicaid benefits in the baseline, and with Medicaid severely scaled back, their taxes decline. Thus, compensating variations in PE quintiles four and five are negative. Individuals in the top 1% of PE especially prefer the 'no Medicaid' economy since, as owners of the private insurer, they also benefit from the increase in its profits.

In the case with universal public insurance for LTC risk, or the 'universal Medicaid' scenario, government outlays for LTC rise by nearly 174%, reaching approximately 1.1% of GDP (equivalent to about 20% of US Social Security outlays in 2023). Ex ante, welfare increases moderately: a newborn would have to give up only 0.07% of consumption to make him indifferent between this scenario and the baseline. These welfare gains are driven by middle-class individuals who are the biggest beneficiaries of universal public LTCI. Compensating variations are negative for PE quintiles two–five and are particularly large for PE quintile three (−4.2%). Interestingly, PE quintile one and all three of the highest PE groups prefer the baseline. Public insurance of LTC risk is similar in both economies for those in PE quintile one, but their income taxes are lower without universal coverage. Most individuals in the highest PE groups have the resources to self-insure LTC risk and, like those in the lowest PE quintile, do not wish to pay higher income taxes to finance public benefits for the middle class. The top PE group experiences the largest welfare losses because of the lost profit income when the private LTCI market becomes dormant.

The two reforms we have considered so far have very different impacts on poor, middle-class, and wealthy people. We next show that a key element of the Long-Term Care Partnership Program (PP) preserves the safety net provided by public LTCI and at the same time creates a more sustainable private LTCI market. PP offers $1 of asset exemption from the Medicaid asset test for each $1 of benefits paid out by a qualifying private LTCI policy. Exempted assets are also protected from estate recovery upon the policyholder's death. The program dates to 1992 when California, Connecticut, Indiana, and New York were allowed to participate on an experimental basis. Expansion of the program was frozen in 1992 and then reopened to all states in 2005. As of 2023, the only nonparticipating states were Hawaii, Alaska, Utah, Mississippi, and Washington, DC (MedicaidLongTermCare.org 2023).

The specific requirements for an LTCI policy to qualify for PP vary by state, but the main provisions are as follows. First, under Medicaid, a recipient's primary residence (up to a cap on the equity value) is exempt from the asset test (MedicaidLongTermCare.org 2023).[6] The cap varies by state, ranging from about $680,000 to over $1,000,000. Asset exemptions for partnership policies are subject to the same caps. Second, Medicaid benefits are also subject to an income test and income spend-down provisions, and these eligibility restrictions also apply to holders of partnership policies. Third, a PP policy must be a qualified LTCI policy for Federal tax purposes. Fourth, partnership policies must include an inflation protection rider.[7] Fifth, states that participate in PP must also offer reciprocity—partnership LTCI policies purchased in one state must maintain the same Medicaid asset test exemption if the individual moves to another participating state. Finally, qualifying partnership policies must meet specific minimum coverage thresholds. In particular, a qualifying PP policy has to provide at least $32,850 in benefits (six months of benefits at $180/day).

The federal government's objective in offering states the option to participate in PP was to reduce Medicaid outlays for LTC. The expectation was that the asset exemption would increase private LTCI take-up, and, since Medicaid is a secondary payer, public outlays would decline. Nevertheless, this direct effect of offering PP policies is somewhat mitigated by PP's relaxation of the Medicaid asset test, which broadens the pool of individuals eligible for public LTC benefits.

Most prior research on PP has used empirical methods to assess its impact and concluded that the impact thus far has been small. Using HRS data, Lin and Prince (2013) found that the program induced a less than one percentage point increase in LTCI take-up rates, with the increase concentrated among affluent individuals. In particular, they estimated that LTCI take-up increased by about three percentage points for individuals with assets of $46,5000+, but they found no discernible response in take-up among less wealthy individuals. Bergquist et al. (2018) reached a similar conclusion using data from the National Association of Insurance Commissioners on LTCI policy applications and sales. They concluded that the introduction of partnership policies had a positive impact on LTCI applications, but take-ups did not increase. Goda (2011) analyzed PP policies and other state tax subsidies offered to purchasers of LTCI, and she concluded that these subsidies induced a 2.7 percentage point increase in private insurance take-up rates. She also found that the increase was concentrated among wealthier individuals who were less likely to qualify for Medicaid benefits. In a simulation analysis, she estimated that each dollar of lost tax revenue due to the subsidies resulted in a 84 cent reduction in Medicaid outlays.

Our structural model permits us to isolate the impact of the PP asset test exemption on the US LTCI market. By modeling both private and public LTC insurance provision, we can assess how this program impacts public LTC expenditures, private LTCI uptake, as well as insurer pricing and profits. Additionally, we can examine the nuanced trade-offs in the distribution of the net benefits of this reform across individuals. Finally, we shed light on why previous research has found a small impact of PP and explore potential strategies for refining the program.

We model the PP asset exemption by allowing individuals to exempt \$1 of assets from the Medicaid means-test for each \$1 of private LTCI coverage (Braun and Kopecky 2024). Column 5 in Table 13.2 and 4 in Table 13.3 report the results from this scenario. According to our model, PP increases public expenditures on LTC by 8.8%, and Medicaid outlays per recipient decrease by 3.0%, due to Medicaid's secondary payer status. Nevertheless, the dominant effect on Medicaid outlays is the rise in the fraction of NH entrants who qualify for Medicaid benefits which goes from 49.9% to 56.0% with the relaxation of the Medicaid asset test.

Previous research has concluded that the overall impact of PP on the private market is small and concentrated among more affluent households. Yet our results in Tables 13.2 and 13.3 indicate that the PP asset test exemption has a large and widespread effect in our model. Private LTCI take-up rates increase by 52.8 percentage points, and insurers push through large increases in premiums as indicated by the average load which rises from 0.406 to 0.662. The average load in the PP scenario is even higher than the average load in the 'no Medicaid' scenario, and at 31.7%, profits as a share of premium revenue are also higher. The distribution of profits is also very different in the PP scenario compared to the 'no Medicaid' case. When Medicaid is virtually non-existent, loads and profits are very regressive. With PP, in contrast, loads and profits are hump-shaped across the PE distribution. Profit ratios are highest in the third PE quintile, but they are also large in the top two PE quintiles and are sizable even within the top 10 and top 5 percentiles of the distribution.

We also compute welfare effects, and we find that a newborn prefers PP over both the baseline and the 'universal Medicaid' economies. Compared to universal Medicaid, the welfare impacts of the program are also much more equally spread across the PE distribution. Individuals in the lower two PE quintiles continue to favor the baseline scenario, because the PP program does not influence their Medicaid eligibility, and, consequently, the primary effect of PP on their circumstances is to increase their income taxes. Because the rise in Medicaid expenditures is less pronounced under PP compared to universal Medicaid, however, the welfare costs of this tax hike are relatively small for these groups. The compensating variations for individuals in all other PE groups are negative, indicating that they prefer the PP economy to the baseline. The largest welfare benefits are concentrated in the top PE percentile, which benefits from the large increase in private insurer profits.

On net, the PP asset test exemption looks like a good arrangement, yet we still must reconcile the empirical findings of low impact with our results. Our model abstracts from other important provisions of the PP program. First, we do not model the cap on the equity held in one's primary residence exempted from the asset test. Such a cap eliminates the benefits of purchasing a partnership policy for more affluent individuals in our model. Second, recall that to qualify for Medicaid benefits in practice under PP, individuals still must satisfy the Medicaid income test. In our model, eligibility for Medicaid LTC benefits relies on a single means-test that does not differentiate between assets and income. Third, recall that PP imposes minimum coverage ratios. Coverage ratios are not restricted in our model and many model contracts fail to meet current PP requirements.

To understand the potential impact of adding the first two provisions on aggregate LTCI take-up in the model, we can assume that in the presence of these provisions, individuals in the top PE quintile no longer increase their take-up rate relative to the baseline. Under this assumption, the aggregate increase in private LTCI take-up under PP falls from 52.8 to 40.0 percentage points. If we assume that take-up rates do not change in either of the top two PE quintile then the overall increase in LTCI take-up with PP is only 23.8 percentage points.

Adding a minimum coverage ratio to the model, in line with the third provision, would depress LTCI take-up even further. In the model, the average private LTCI policy under PP covers only 28.4% of the loss. This figure is notably lower than the 60.3% coverage ratio in the baseline specification, and it falls short of the minimum coverage ratio under current PP requirements. Given our model's nursing home costs and the coverage ratio thresholds of the PP program, coverage should be at least 34% of the loss. Model coverage ratios are particularly low in PE quintiles two and three at 15.3 and 22.6%, respectively. Implementing a required minimum coverage ratio would reduce take-up in these two groups.

Overall, our results raise the possibility that PP could have a much larger impact on the US private LTCI market if current Medicaid provisions were relaxed, including the cap on the exemption of equity in the primary residence, income restrictions, and minimum coverage ratios on qualifying PP policies. These reforms would increase the take-up of private LTCI by both affluent and middle-class individuals.

## Conclusions

The US private LTCI market currently suffers from a variety of ailments: the market is small, coverage provided by policies is incomplete, and premiums are relatively high compared to other insurance products. Results from our structural model indicate that Medicaid, administrative costs, and adverse selection all contribute to low take-up rates and incomplete coverage. Additionally, administrative costs drive up premium loads.

Our work shows that exposure to LTC risk and ability to pay varies importantly across the income distribution and that this leads to important conclusions. Affluent individuals prefer a smaller public LTCI program combined with a large private LTCI market. In contrast, low- and middle-income individuals prefer universal public LTCI provision. One policy reform we explore involves exempting asset holdings from the Medicaid asset test on a dollar-for-dollar basis with private LTCI coverage. Surprisingly, this emerges as the most favorable policy reform as it boosts social welfare by encouraging private LTCI uptake while maintaining Medicaid as a safety net for low-income individuals.

Our results also illustrate how a quantitative model can be a useful tool for analyzing reforms of the US LTCI; in Braun and Kopecky (2024), we analyzed an even broader range of policy reforms including LTCI mandates. Government mandates to obtain private insurance can facilitate pooling and reduce administrative costs by lower marketing costs and fees paid to brokers. Our model can also be used to analyze newer and more complex LTCI products. For instance, households with high life expectancy also face elevated long-term care risk and have incentives to purchase hybrid products that bundle longevity and LTC risk coverage. There is also considerable diversity in LTC care needs based on gender and marital status, and the implications of these factors for the LTCI market should be explored in future research.

## Acknowledgments

The authors appreciate helpful comments from Sudipto Banerjee and the editors.

## Notes

1. These statistics use the Health Insurance Portability and Accountability Act definition of a long-term care event (Favreault and Dey 2022).
2. The ensuing discussion assumes that individuals are covered by Medicare if they are enrolled in Medicare part A and B (Social Security Administration 2024).

3. The Kaiser Family Foundation estimates that 27.6 million individuals had Medicare plans and that another 22.2 million had Medigap or employer-provided supplemental insurance (Ochieng et al 2023).
4. Note that we do not recalibrate the modified version of the model. Despite this, it still matches targeted data moments well.
5. The new consumption floor is set to the same positive level as in Braun et al. (2019) and ensures that consumption remains positive in the final stage of life for all individuals in the economy.
6. In contrast to assets protected by PP, the home is not exempt from Medicaid estate recovery.
7. Individuals over the age of 80 at the time they purchased the policy are exempt from this requirement.

## References


Bergquist, S., J. Costa-Font, and K. Swartz (2018). 'Long-Term Care Partnerships: Are They Fit to Purpose?' *Journal of the Economics of Ageing*, 12: 151–158.

Braun, R. A. and K. Kopecky (2024). 'Reforming the US Long-Term Care Insurance Market.' Federal Reserve Bank of Cleveland Working Paper No. 24-17.

Braun, R. A., K. Kopecky, and T. Koreshkova (2019). 'Old, Frail, and Uninsured: Accounting for Features of the US Long-Term Care Insurance Market.' *Econometrica*, 87(3): 981–1019.

Brown, J. R. and A. Finkelstein (2007). 'Why is the Market for Long-Term Care Insurance So Small?' *Journal of Public Economics*, 91(10): 1967–1991.

Chade, H. and E. Schlee (2020). 'Insurance as a Lemons Market: Coverage Denials and Pooling.' *Journal of Economic Theory*, 189: 105085.

Chidambaram, P. and A. Burns (2022). '10 Things About Long-Term Services and Supports.' *Kaiser Family Foundation*. www.kff.org/medicaid/issue-brief/10-things-about-long-term-services-and-supports-ltss/

Eaton, R. (2016). *Long-Term Care Insurance: The SOA Pricing Project*. Society of Actuaries Report No. 2652.

Favreault, M. M. and J. Dey (2022). *Long-Term Services and Supports for Older Americans: Risks and Financing*. Washington, DC: Department of Health and Human Services, Office of the Assistant Secretary for Planning and Evaluation.

Favreault, M. M. and R. W. Johnson (2021). *Projections of Risk of Needing Long-Term Services and Supports at Ages 65 and Older*. Washington, DC: Department of Health and Human Services, Office of the Assistant Secretary for Planning and Evaluation.

Genworth (2024). *Genworth Cost of Care Survey*. Genworth Report 131168-030425. Richmond, VA: Genworth Financial, Inc.

Goda, G. S. (2011). 'The Impact of State Tax Subsidies for Private Long-Term Care Insurance on Coverage and Medicaid Expenditures.' *Journal of Public Economics*, 95(7): 744–757.

Gruber, J. and K. M. McGarry (2025). 'Long-Term Care in the United States.' In J. Gruber and K. McGarry, *Long Term Care Around the World*. Chicago: University of Chicago Press, pp. 353–388.

He, Y. (2022). Projecting Medicaid's Long Term Care Expenditures. *Penn Wharton Budget Model.* budgetmodel.wharton.upenn.edu/issues/2022/3/9/projecting-medicaids-long-term-care-expenditures

Health Insurance Portability and Accountability Act. 42 USC § 201 (1996).

Hendren, N. (2013). 'Private Information and Insurance Rejections.' *Econometrica,* 81(5): 1713–1762.

Kaiser Commission on Medicaid and the Uninsured (2010). *Medicaid Financial Eligibility: Primary Pathways for the Elderly and People with Disabilities.*' Kaiser Commission Publication No. 8048. San Francisco: Kaiser Commission.

Lin, H. and J. Prince (2013). 'The Impact of the Partnership Long-Term Care Insurance Program on Private Coverage.' *Journal of Health Economics,* 32(6): 1205–1213.

MedicaidLongTermCare.org (2023). 'Which States Have Long-Term Care Partnership Programs?' www.medicaidlongtermcare.org/protection/long-term-care-partnership-program/#states

MedicaidLongTermCare.org (2024). 'Medicaid Benefits in Nursing Homes: What Is and Is Not Covered.' www.medicaidlongtermcare.org/benefits/medicaid-coverage-nursing-homes/

National Association of Insurance Commissioners (2025). *Long-Term Care Insurance Experience Reports for 2023.* Washington, DC: NAIC.

Ochieng, N., G. Clerveau, J. Cubanski, and T. Neuman (2023). 'A Snapshot of Sources of Coverage Among Medicare Beneficiaries.' *Kaiser Family Foundation.* www.kff.org/medicare/issue-brief/a-snapshot-of-sources-of-coverage-among-medicare-beneficiaries/

Social Security Administration (2023). *Annual Report of the Supplemental Security Income Program.* SSA Report No. SSI23. Baltimore, MD: Social Security Administration.

Social Security Administration (2024). 'Review the Parts of Medicare.' www.ssa.gov/medicare/plan/medicare-parts

## The Pension Research Council

The Pension Research Council is a research center at the Wharton School of the University of Pennsylvania committed to generating knowledge and debate on key policy issues affecting pensions and other employee benefits. For 70 years, the Council has sponsored high-level analysis of private and public retirement security and related benefit plans around the world. Research projects are motivated by the need to address the long-term issues that underlie contemporary concerns about retirement system structures and resiliency. Members seek to broaden understanding of the complex economic, financial, social, actuarial, and legal foundations for and impacts of privately and publicly provided benefits. The Pension Research Council is a non-profit organization, and contributions to it are tax-deductible. For more information about the Pension Research Council please visit http://www.pensionresearchcouncil.org.

## The Boettner Center for Pensions and Retirement Research

Founded at the Wharton School to support scholarly research, teaching, and outreach on global aging, retirement, and public and private pensions, the Center is named after Joseph E. Boettner. Funding to the University of Pennsylvania was provided through the generosity of the Boettner family, whose intent was to spur financial well-being at older ages through work on how aging influences financial security and life satisfaction. The Center disseminates research and evaluation on challenges and opportunities associated with global aging and retirement, how to strengthen retirement income systems, saving and investment behavior of the young and the old, interactions between physical and mental health, and successful retirement. For more information see http://www.pensionresearchcouncil.org/boettner/.

## Executive Director

Olivia S. Mitchell, International Foundation of Employee Benefit Plans Professor, Professor of Business Economics/Public Policy and Insurance/Risk Management, The Wharton School, University of Pennsylvania.

## Advisory Board

## Members of the Pension Research Council



## Recent Pension Research Council Publications

*Reducing Retirement Inequality*. Olivia S. Mitchell and Nikolai Roussanov, eds. 2025. (ISBN 978-0-19-893903-0.)

*Real-World Shocks and Retirement System Resiliency*. Olivia S. Mitchell, John Sabelhaus, and Stephen P. Utkus, eds. 2024. (ISBN 978-0-19-889413-1.)

*Pension Funds and Sustainable Investment: Challenges and Opportunities.* P. Brett Hammond, Raimond Maurer, and Olivia S. Mitchell, eds. 2023. (ISBN 978-0-19-288919-5.)

*New Models for Managing Longevity Risk: Public-Private Partnerships.* Olivia S. Mitchell, ed. 2022. (ISBN 978-0-19-285980-8.)

*Remaking Retirement: Debt in an Aging Economy.* Olivia S. Mitchell and Annamaria Lusardi, eds. 2020. (ISBN 978-0-19-886752-4.)

*The Disruptive Impact of FinTech on Retirement Systems.* Julie Agnew and Olivia S. Mitchell, eds. 2019. (ISBN 978-0-19-884555-9.)

*How Persistent Low Returns Will Shape Saving and Retirement.* Olivia S. Mitchell, Robert Clark, and Raimond Maurer, eds. 2018. (ISBN 978-0-19-882744-3.)

*Financial Decision Making and Retirement Security in an Aging World.* Olivia S. Mitchell, P. Brett Hammond, and Stephen Utkus, eds. 2017. (ISBN 978-0-19-880803-9.)

*Retirement System Risk Management: Implications of the New Regulatory Order.* Olivia S. Mitchell, Raimond Maurer, and J. Michael Orszag, eds. 2016. (ISBN 978-0-19-878737-2.)

*Reimagining Pensions: The Next 40 Years.* Olivia S. Mitchell and Richard C. Shea, eds. 2016. (ISBN 978-0-19-875544-9.)

*Recreating Sustainable Retirement.* Olivia S. Mitchell, Raimond Maurer, and P. Brett Hammond, eds. 2014. (ISBN 0-19-871924-3.)

*The Market for Retirement Financial Advice.* Olivia S. Mitchell and Kent Smetters, eds. 2013. (ISBN 0-19-968377-2.)

*Reshaping Retirement Security: Lessons from the Global Financial Crisis.* Raimond Maurer, Olivia S. Mitchell, and Mark Warshawsky, eds. 2012. (ISBN 0-19-966069-7.)

*Financial Literacy.* Olivia S. Mitchell and Annamaria Lusardi, eds. 2011. (ISBN 0-19-969681-9.)

*Securing Lifelong Retirement Income.* Olivia S. Mitchell, John Piggott, and Noriyuki Takayama, eds. 2011. (ISBN 0-19-959484-9.)

*Reorienting Retirement Risk Management.* Robert L. Clark and Olivia S. Mitchell, eds. 2010. (ISBN 0-19-959260-9.)

*Fundamentals of Private Pensions.* Dan M. McGill, Kyle N. Brown, John J. Haley, Sylvester Schieber, and Mark J. Warshawsky. 9th Ed. 2010. (ISBN 0-19-954451-6.)

*The Future of Public Employees Retirement Systems.* Olivia S. Mitchell and Gary Anderson, eds. 2009. (ISBN 0-19-957334-9.)

*Recalibrating Retirement Spending and Saving.* John Ameriks and Olivia S. Mitchell, eds. 2008. (ISBN 0-19-954910-8.)

*Lessons from Pension Reform in the Americas.* Stephen J. Kay and Tapen Sinha, eds. 2008. (ISBN 0-19-922680-6.)

*Redefining Retirement: How Will Boomers Fare?* Brigitte Madrian, Olivia S. Mitchell, and Beth J. Soldo, eds. 2007. (ISBN 0-19-923077-3.)

*Restructuring Retirement Risks.* David Blitzstein, Olivia S. Mitchell, and Steven P. Utkus, eds. 2006. (ISBN 0-19-920465-9.)

Available on the Pension Research Council website: www.pensionresearchcouncil.org/

# Index

*For the benefit of digital users, indexed terms that span two pages (e.g., 52–53) may, on occasion, appear on only one of those pages.*

Tables and figures are indicated by an italic *t* and *f* following the paragraph number.